THE ELEMENTS OF LOGIC

The Elements of Logic

Stephen F. Barker, Department of Philosophy

The Johns Hopkins University

McGraw-Hill Book Company

New York   St. Louis   San Francisco   Toronto   London

Preface

This book is intended both for the individual reader who wishes to become acquainted with logic and for use as a textbook in courses in elementary logic at the undergraduate level. It aims to combine practical ideas useful for the criticism of reasoning, technical ideas of modern symbolic logic, and philosophical notions relevant to logic.

When people asked me what I was working on, I would answer that, among other things, I was writing a textbook on elementary logic. "What! Another textbook on logic?" they would reply. "Aren't there more than enough of those already?" This response is not soothing to an author's feelings, but it does have its point. There are already in print many elementary books on logic, and some of them are of very good quality. Since this book is not novel in its range of topics or radical in its approach to them, one may well ask whether it deserves to have been written. Insofar as I can reply to this, my answer is that of the fox rather than of the hedgehog; there is no one big innovation in the book, but there are many small ones.

v

My hope is to have succeeded in expressing many small points of logical doctrine in slightly better ways: for instance, the notion of distribution in traditional logic, the notion of the material conditional in the logic of truth functions, the technique of natural deduction in the logic of quantification, the classification of fallacies, and the nature of reasoning by analogy in inductive logic. In connection with these notions and many others, I hope to have expressed matters more clearly than previous textbooks have done. I have tried to write concisely throughout and have almost completely resisted the temptation, to which some textbook authors succumb, of coining new technical terminology. I have tried to ensure both that the exercises have intrinsic interest of their own and that they actually illustrate what they are supposed to illustrate. Also, I have given somewhat more attention than is usual to the connections between philosophy and logic, for many students of logic will go on to study more philosophy.

The book contains somewhat more material than can conveniently be covered in a one-term course. However, the chapters are largely independent of one another, and a teacher can omit one or more of them without appreciable loss of continuity. Chapter 2 can be omitted by those who feel that the traditional logic of the syllogism is too outdated to deserve attention; Chapter 4, which is perhaps somewhat more difficult than the other chapters, can be omitted by those who want a comparatively relaxing course; and Chapter 8 should be omitted by those instructors who feel that my philosophical views are too shallow even to serve as a basis for useful discussion. (Perhaps they will wish to substitute their own profounder insights.)

Some able professors of logic nowadays feel that an elementary course attempting to include such traditional topics as the theory of the syllogism, fallacies, and induction must become a rather disreputable 'grab bag' of topics. They prefer a more highly unified approach that omits these traditional topics in favor of an abstract exposition of deduction, mathematical in its rigor and style, with up-to-date emphasis upon the nature of formalized systems. I certainly recognize that a first course in logic conceived in this more systematic and abstract spirit can be a very good course. However, the advocates of such an approach seem to me to overlook the real intellectual benefits that the more customary 'grab bag' affords: It has a much greater chance of giving useful guidance to students in their actual thinking (although I do not say that it has a great chance), and it has a much closer connection with philosophical terminology and with familiar philosophical problems. In my view, this more customary style of course is likely to be of greater intellectual benefit to most students than is a more highly unified and abstract approach. This is a question of pedagogy that each teacher must decide for himself, however. I have no wish to win over to my view any reluctant converts, as I feel that almost any teacher teaches best when he is teaching whatever he thinks is best.

My opinions about a number of the philosophical aspects of logic have been influenced by views that I heard Prof. John Wisdom express some years ago, and I believe there are things in this book that reflect his influence. Readers must not suppose, however, that anything I say concerning philosophical aspects of logic does justice to his views, nor should they assume that he is in any way responsible for the obscurities and mistakes that may occur in my presentation. In the second section of Chapter 8, I have taken the liberty of using an example imitated from one of his. I must also acknowledge that in Chapter 2 I have used two mnemonic devices adopted from Swinburne's *Picture Logic,* a too little known classic of Victorian pedagogy.

I am greatly indebted to the publisher's several anonymous reviewers, each of whom made detailed and valuable criticisms of the manuscript; they have enabled me to make this book far less defective than it would otherwise have been. My best thanks

are due to Profs. Arnold Levison and George Tovey for their kind-
ness in making helpful comments. Above all, I am indebted to
my wife, Dr. Evelyn Masi Barker. Because she was one of those
who used this material in their own teaching, she was able to
make practical as well as doctrinal suggestions for improvement;
she has assisted with the manuscript; and she has been a constant source of encouragement.

S. F. BARKER

Contents

ix

THE ELEMENTS OF LOGIC

1. *Introduction*

LOGIC AND PHILOSOPHY

Most courses in the curriculum of a university today are relatively new ones and were not taught in the universities of a few generations ago. Logic is an exception, for courses in logic have been offered to students ever since the first universities came into existence some eight or nine hundred years ago. Why is this? What is there about logic that for so many centuries has made men regard it as deserving to be a part of higher education? The reasons are at least twofold, because logic—the critical study of reasoning—is a subject having both theoretical interest and practical utility.

On the one hand, the study of logic can be intellectually rewarding as knowledge for its own sake, on account of the clear and systematic character of many of its principles and its close relations with basic philosophical questions and nowadays with the foundations of mathematics. On the other hand, to study logic is also of practical value, because a mastery of its principles can

1

help us to become more effective in recognizing and avoiding mistakes in reasoning—both in the reasoning that others use in trying to convince us and in our own reasoning. A person who can recognize and avoid logical mistakes in reasoning will be able to think more clearly and correctly, more soundly and surely, whatever may be the subjects about which he is going to think. This book will deal both with theoretical aspects of logic and with practical aspects, but, because this is an elementary book, the practical side will be emphasized more than in advanced books.

Logic is a study with a long history. Like so much of our intellectual heritage, it goes back to the ancient Greeks, among whom the formal study of logic began with Aristotle in the fourth century B.C. Aristotle's most important contribution to logic was his theory of the syllogism. (The nature of the syllogism will be discussed in Chapter 2.) Later, Stoic philosophers worked out some of the principles of truth-functional logic. (Truth functions will be explained in Chapter 3.)

During medieval times, Aristotle's writings on logic were read and admired far more than anyone else's, and so thinkers in the medieval tradition came to regard the theory of the syllogism as the central and most important part of logic. This view persisted into modern times, and as late as the eighteenth century the German philosopher Kant reflected the opinion of most thinkers at that time when he declared that this aristotelian system of logic was a completed science: a subject whose essentials were fully understood and in which no new principles remained to be discovered.

This opinion proved to be mistaken, however. During the nineteenth century the Irish logician Boole showed that the field of truth functions was far richer than had previously been realized, and he devised powerful new methods for treating problems in that branch of logic. Also, the German mathematician Frege originated the theory of quantification, a profoundly important new departure in logic. (Quantification will be discussed in Chapter 4.) The new developments in logic were systematized by Whitehead and Russell in their famous work *Principia Mathematica*, written early in the twentieth century. In that work they not only undertook to develop the new logic in a systematic manner but also tried to establish the thesis that the laws of pure mathematics can be derived from those of logic alone.

This modern logic, when properly understood, does not in any way contradict the traditional aristotelian logic, when that is properly understood. However, modern logic differs from traditional aristotelian logic in two important ways. It is much more general, dealing with a far wider variety of forms of reasoning, and it employs more symbolism and in its style and method is more akin to mathematics. In what follows, we shall be concerned both with the main ideas of traditional aristotelian logic and with some of the simpler ideas of modern symbolic logic.

The more advanced logical studies nowadays have taken on a character like that of pure mathematics, while elementary parts of logic have their especial interest on account of their practical value in helping to detect mistakes in reasoning. Thus it perhaps seems as though logic does not have much relation to philosophy. Yet logic has always been regarded as a branch of philosophy, and there are some good reasons for this. Let us briefly consider what some of the various branches of philosophy are and what they have in common.

Moral Philosophy

Moral philosophy, or ethics, is that branch of philosophy which investigates the notions of good and evil, right and wrong, duty and obligation, and the like. It tries to explain the nature of these notions in order to clarify general questions such as these:

Is there a difference between good and evil?

Can we tell the difference between them?

What general kinds of things are good?

What connections are there among goodness, rightness, and duty?

In treating such questions, moral philosophy seeks to analyze the critical standards used in making moral judgments.

Metaphysics

Metaphysics is that branch of philosophy which tries to understand the nature of the real universe, considered in its most general aspect. It seeks to analyze the standards employed in judging whether things really exist. It treats such questions as these:

Is the universe fundamentally physical, or is it spiritual in nature?

Is everything real located in space and time?

What are space and time?

Does everything that happens have a cause?

Does the universe have a cause?

Questions of these sorts fall under the heading of metaphysics. Sometimes metaphysical philosophers have asked their questions in ways that were not very clear, and sometimes the answers they have offered have not been free of confusion. Nevertheless, these are intellectual problems of great importance to all thinking people.

The Theory of Knowledge

The theory of knowledge, or epistemology, is that branch of philosophy which investigates the nature and scope of knowledge. It seeks to analyze the standards employed in judging the genuineness of claims to the possession of knowledge. It asks such questions as these:

What is it really to know something?

Can we have knowledge of things that are outside our minds?

How can we know what happened in the past or what is going to happen in the future, when we cannot now observe the past or future?

Can we ever really know what is in the mind of another person?

How does mathematical knowledge differ from the knowledge that experimental science yields?

The theory of knowledge tries to deal with questions such as these.

Aesthetics

Aesthetics is the branch of philosophy that deals with the notions of beauty and ugliness and with other general notions related to the value of works of art. It tries to examine the critical standards used in judgments about the beauty and ugliness of things. It asks questions such as these:

What is the nature of beauty?

Is there an objective standard of beauty, or is beauty entirely a matter of individual taste?

Can we ever prove that a thing is beautiful?

Does art provide us with some kind of insight into the nature of reality?

These questions, and others connected with them, belong to the field of aesthetics.

Logic as Philosophy

These are four of the main branches of philosophy, and they are akin to one another in important ways. They all deal with extremely general problems:

Is the universe basically physical or spiritual?

Is it possible to have knowledge?

What is the difference between good and evil?

Moreover, these all are problems unlike those with which science normally deals. Scientific problems usually must be settled by means of observations and experiments, as when an engineer answers the question of how much weight a bridge can bear by testing it, or similar structures, until it breaks. Philosophical problems, however, cannot be solved through observations and experiments; such procedures cannot settle philosophical questions, for they cannot provide the kind of information that is needed. These philosophical questions are ones with which we can make headway only through reflecting upon our own standards of various kinds (our moral standards, our standards of what counts as reality, our standards of what counts as knowledge, etc.). By obtaining a clearer view of these standards, we may be able to make progress toward unraveling philosophical questions: toward answering them in some cases and in other cases toward clarifying the misconceptions that have given rise to the questions.

Although the study of logic differs in some ways from the pursuit of other branches of philosophy, it is no accident that logic always has been classified as a branch of philosophy. This is because logic has a basic kinship with these other branches. Like them, it deals with some very general questions: questions about what good reasoning is and about the difference between correct and incorrect steps in thinking. Moreover, like other branches of philosophy, logic is a reflective study; experiments are not necessary, and no laboratory work is appropriate for verifying its principles.

To be sure, someone might make observations and conduct experiments in order to find out how people reason and to find the causes that make them reason as they do. Such an investigation would belong to psychology, however, not to logic, for such questions are questions about human psychology. There is a difference between studying how people reason (a matter of psychology) and studying the nature of correct reasoning (a matter of logic). Logic does not undertake to describe or explain how people think; it has the different aim of analyzing what correct reasoning is, irrespective of whether people do, in fact, reason correctly.

ARGUMENTS

In elementary logic the main task is that of studying the difference between good reasoning and bad. But just what is reasoning? How is it recognized? For the moment we shall not worry about the difference between good and bad reasoning; we shall first consider what reasoning itself is.

When a person is reasoning, he starts from certain statements that he assumes to be true; then, in his thinking, he moves on to a consequence that he thinks follows from them. When he does this, he is making an *inference;* he is constructing an *argument;* he is trying to give a *proof*. What one starts with are called *premises,* and what one reaches is called the *conclusion*. An argument may have just one premise, or there may be two or more; but each argument has just one conclusion, for where several conclusions are drawn, there are several separate arguments.

For the purposes of logic, we shall use the words "argument" and "inference" rather differently from the way they are used in ordinary language. In ordinary discourse, the word "argument" means almost any sort of quarrel, disagreement, or debate; the word "inference" ordinarily means reasoning whose conclusion is quite speculative and doubtful. Thus when a detective guesses that someone is guilty of a crime, the accused person may object, "But that's a mere inference; you don't have any positive evidence against me". For the purposes of logic, however, we shall use these words in a more technical sense.

What we shall mean by an argument (or reasoning, or an inference, or a proof) involves two essential features. In the first place, the person who presents the argument must be claiming that, if certain things (the premises) are true, then something else (the conclusion) should be true also. In the second place, he must be claiming that the premises are indeed true. In making both these claims together, he aims to give a reason for accepting the conclusion as true. We shall say that there is an argument (or reasoning, or inference, or proof) when and only when both these claims are present.

The words "argument", "reasoning", "inference", and "proof" are not exact synonyms. *Inference* is the mental act of reaching a conclusion from one's premises, the achievement of coming to believe the conclusion because one comes to see, or thinks one sees, that it follows logically from premises already accepted as true. *Reasoning* is the mental activity of marshaling one's premises, reflecting upon their weight, and making inferences. An *argument* is a formulation, in words or other symbols, of premises and of a conclusion that is inferred from them. A *proof,* in the more ordinary sense of that term, is an argument that succeeds in establishing the truth of its conclusion. However, mathematicians and logicians sometimes use the word "proof" also in a weaker sense: A demonstration that a certain conclusion would strictly follow from certain premises is sometimes called a proof, even though there may be no reason to accept the premises and no reason to accept the conclusion.

In ordinary conversation, arguments can be expressed in many ways. Sometimes the premises are stated first; sometimes the conclusion is stated first. For example, the following are arguments:

Hugo is not in class, and he would not be absent unless he had a good excuse. Therefore, Hugo must have a good excuse.
Smulski has been disqualified, and so the Bison are bound to lose the game.
This liquid is acid, since it turns blue litmus paper red.
Platinum is more valuable than gold, and gold is more valuable than silver; it follows that platinum is more valuable than silver.
There must not be any life on Venus, since the atmosphere there is unsuitable and the temperature too extreme.

Words like "therefore", "since", and "it follows" are often signs of inference. "Therefore" and "it follows" are used to introduce the conclusion of an argument, while "since", "for", and "because" are used to introduce premises. Words like "must", "should", and "ought" in a sentence often serve to show that the sentence is a conclusion being derived from premises. However, none of these words is an infallible sign of inference, and in order to tell whether a statement is an argument we need to reflect with care about its intended meaning.

To scotch one kind of misunderstanding, consider the two remarks:

If today is Tuesday, tomorrow will be Wednesday.   (1)
Since today is Tuesday, tomorrow will be Wednesday.   (2)

Example (1) is not an argument in our sense. There is no inference here, for no claim is made that today is Tuesday; no premise is asserted and no conclusion is drawn. All that is claimed in (1) is that, if today were Tuesday, then tomorrow would be Wednesday; this is just a single sentence, not an argument. Example (2) is an argument, however; in (2) it is claimed that today is Tuesday (the premise) and from this it is inferred that tomorrow will be Wednesday (the conclusion). Here one thing is presented as an actual, not just a hypothetical, reason for believing another.

To scotch another sort of misunderstanding, consider the examples:

Hugo insulted me, and so I punched him on the nose.   (3)
Hugo is not at home; therefore he must have gone to town.   (4)

If one looks carelessly at these two examples, one might consider both of them arguments. But if one thinks carefully about the circumstances under which these remarks are likely to be made, one sees that they differ. Example (3) is most unlikely to be an argument, for the person who makes this remark would not be trying to prove that he punched Hugo on the nose. He would be trying to indicate the cause or motive which led him to such action. The remark as a whole is an assertion about the cause or motive; it is not an inference in which one thing is presented as a reason for believing another. Example (4) is different; there the word "therefore" functions to introduce the conclusion of an argument, a conclusion which the speaker wants to prove and for which he is giving evidence.

So far, we have considered only very simple examples. Let us now look at one example of more intricate reasoning, an example that has the flavor of real-life reasoning. In this piece of discourse, the French philosopher Descartes is discussing the question whether animals (brutes) can think.[1]

Although the brutes do nothing which can convince us that they think, nevertheless, because their bodily organs are not very different from ours, we might conjecture that there was some faculty of thought joined to these organs, as we experience in ourselves, although theirs be much less perfect, to which I have nothing to reply, except that, if they could think as we do, they would have an immortal soul as well as we, which is not likely, because there is no reason for believing it of some animals without believing it of all, and there are many of them too imperfect to make it possible to believe it of them, such as oysters, sponges, etc.

Let us separate the main ideas in this passage. Then we can consider what is being inferred from what. The main ideas are:

The bodily organs of brutes are not very different from ours.	(1)
Brutes have some faculty of thought less perfect than ours.	(2)
If brutes could think, they would have immortal souls.	(3)
If some animals have immortal souls, all animals do.	(4)
Many animals, such as oysters and sponges, are very imperfect.	(5)
Many animals do not have immortal souls.	(6)

In analyzing this passage, our problem is to tell what inferences are being made. Descartes starts by considering a possible inference, the inference of (2) from (1); he does not himself make

[1] Descartes, *Letter to the Marquis of Newcastle.*

this inference, although he seems to grant that (1) constitutes evidence tending to support (2). Descartes then goes on to argue that (2) is untrue, and he presents his argument in a backward manner that is common in informal reasoning. Statements (3), (4), and (6) constitute the premises from which Descartes infers that (2) is untrue. But (6) itself is the conclusion of another piece of reasoning, for it is inferred from (5). We can describe the whole thing as two steps of reasoning: from (5), (6) is inferred; and from (6), (4), and (3) together it is inferred that (2) is untrue. Here then is a case in which we can work out the structure of the reasoning. However, there are no hard-and-fast rules that enable us automatically to recognize arguments or to analyze their structure in cases like this; there is no substitute for a sensitive understanding of the language we speak.

Now, if we look for arguments in the books we read and in the conversations we hear, we find that most writers and speakers are seriously presenting arguments only a small fraction of the time. The larger portion of most discourse consists merely of assertions made one after another, without any of them being put forward as reasons for believing others. And this is perfectly justified where the matters discussed are not dubious or controversial. But whenever we are concerned with assertions that are doubtful or that have been challenged, there arguments are needed. Thoughtless people can make up their minds whether to accept doubtful beliefs without even considering arguments pro and con, but when a reasonable person is confronted with a questionable assertion, he will demand arguments before he makes up his mind, for that is part of what it is to be reasonable.

Exercise 1

In the preceding section we have been discussing arguments and the distinction between talk that contains arguments and talk that does not. This distinction, like many further distinctions that we shall meet later on, we want to be able to put to use. It does not do much good to be able to define an argument, unless we can also apply our definition and recognize actual examples of arguments. All through the study of logic, exercises form a very important part of the work, because they provide practice in applying the distinctions about which we are learning. In this first exercise, our task will be to distinguish between examples that contain arguments and ones that do not; where there is an argument, we should identify its premises and its conclusion. To illustrate the procedure, let us look at the first example; then we shall discuss how it is to be handled.

1 You admit then that I believe in divinities. Now if these divinities are a species of gods, then there is my proof that . . . I do believe in gods. If, on the other hand, these divinities are sons of gods, their natural sons, as it were, by nymphs or some other mortal mothers, as rumor makes them, why, then, let me ask you, is there any one in the world who could suppose that there are sons of gods and at the same time that there are no gods?   PLATO, *Apology*

In this example Socrates is speaking, and he is presenting an argument. The conclusion that he is trying to establish is that he, the speaker, believes in gods. (Socrates is on trial, and one of the charges against him is that he is an atheist.) His premises are, first, that he believes in divinities; second, the unstated assumption that divinities either are gods or are offspring of gods; third, the premise (expressed in a question) that one could not believe divinities to be offspring of gods without believing in the existence of gods. Socrates uses these three premises in trying to prove his conclusion.

> *For each of the following examples, decide whether the author is advancing an argument. If he is doing so, explain what the conclusion is and what the premises are.*

2 The medieval university was . . . "built of men." Such a
university had no board of trustees and published no cata-
logue; it had no student societies—except so far as the university itself was fundamentally a society of students—no
college journalism, no dramatics, no athletics, none of those
"outside activities" which are the chief excuse for inside in-
activity in the American college.

C. H. HASKINS, *The Rise of Universities*

3 The peculiar evil of silencing the expression of an opinion is,
that it is robbing the human race; posterity as well as the
existing generation; those who dissent from the opinion, still
more than those who hold it. If the opinion is right, they are
deprived of the opportunity of exchanging error for truth:
if wrong, they lose, what is almost as great a benefit, the
clearer perception and livelier impression of truth, produced
by its collision with error.

JOHN STUART MILL, *On Liberty*

4 O sinner! Consider the fearful danger you are in: it is a
great furnace of wrath, a wide and bottomless pit, full of the
fire of wrath, that you are held over in the hand of that God,
whose wrath is provoked and incensed as much against you,
as against many of the damned in hell. You hang by a slender
thread, with the flames of divine wrath flashing about it, and
ready every moment to singe it, and burn it asunder; and you
have . . . nothing to lay hold of to save yourself, nothing to
keep off the flames of wrath, nothing of your own, nothing
that you ever have done, nothing that you can do, to induce
God to spare you one moment.

JONATHAN EDWARDS, "Sinners in the Hands of an Angry God"

5 Civilization has made man if not more bloodthirsty, certainly
more vilely, more loathsomely bloodthirsty. In former days
he saw justice in bloodshed and with his conscience at peace
exterminated those he thought proper to kill. Now we do

think bloodshed abominable and yet we engage in this abomination, and with more energy than ever. Which is worse?

DOSTOEVSKY, "Notes from the Underground"

6 As Gregor Samsa awoke one morning from uneasy dreams he found himself transformed in his bed into a gigantic insect. He was lying on his hard, as it were armor-plated, back and when he lifted his head a little he could see his dome-like brown belly divided into stiff arched segments on top of which the bed quilt could hardly keep in position and was about to slide off completely. His numerous legs, which were pitifully thin compared to the rest of his bulk, waved helplessly before his eyes.   KAFKA, "The Metamorphosis"

7 When, in ordinary life, we speak of *the* colour of the table, we only mean the sort of colour which it will seem to have to a normal spectator from an ordinary point of view under usual conditions of light. But the other colours which appear under other conditions have just as good a right to be considered real; and therefore, to avoid favouritism, we are compelled to deny that, in itself, the table has any one particular colour.   BERTRAND RUSSELL, *The Problems of Philosophy*

8 Of the many impulses that rule man with demoniacal power, that nourish, preserve, and propagate him, without his knowledge or supervision, of these impulses of which the middle ages present such great pathological excesses, only the smallest part is accessible to scientific analysis and conceptual knowledge. The fundamental character of all these instincts is the feeling of our oneness and sameness with nature; a feeling that at times can be silenced but never eradicated by absorbing intellectual occupations, and which certainly has a *sound basis,* no matter to what religious absurdities it may have given rise.   ERNST MACH, *The Science of Mechanics*

9 Nothing, Pizarro well knew, was so trying to the soldier as prolonged suspense in a critical situation like the present, and he feared lest his ardor might evaporate, and be succeeded by that nervous feeling natural to the bravest soul at such a crisis, and which, if not fear, is near akin to it. He returned an answer, therefore, to Atahuallpa, deprecating his change of purpose, and adding that he had provided everything for his entertainment, and expected him that night to sup with him.   PRESCOTT, *The Conquest of Peru*

10 Plato, I suppose, and after him Aristotle, fastened this confusion upon us [viz., the confused notion that succumbing to temptation is a matter of losing control of oneself], as bad in its day and way as the later, grotesque, confusion of moral weakness with weakness of will. I am very partial to ice cream, and a bombe is served divided into segments corresponding one to one with the persons at High Table: I am tempted to help myself to two segments and do so, thus succumbing to temptation. . . . But do I lose control of myself? Do I raven, do I snatch the morsels from the dish and wolf them down, impervious to the consternation of my colleagues? Not a bit of it. We often succumb to temptation with calm and even with finesse.

J. L. AUSTIN, "A Plea for Excuses"

DEDUCTIVE AND INDUCTIVE ARGUMENTS

"Divide and conquer" is a fine old maxim, as valuable in the intellectual sphere as in the political. Thus if we are to gain mastery over arguments, we must divide them into different types which can be considered separately. We shall begin by distinguishing between what are called deductive and what are called inductive arguments. There are good and bad arguments belonging to both types.

First let us consider arguments like these:

Jones belongs to the CIO. All members of the CIO pay union dues. Therefore Jones pays union dues.   (1)
This man is a bachelor. Hence, he has no wife.   (2)

Here we have arguments that are *conclusive*. Each argument has premises whose truth would ensure that necessarily the conclusion must be true also; the premises give us absolutely sufficient reason for believing the conclusion. Thus a contradiction would be involved in accepting the premises but denying the conclusion.

Arguments of this kind belong to the type called deductive arguments. An argument that succeeds in being conclusive is a good deductive argument, but we also want to allow for the possibility of bad deductive arguments. We shall therefore say that, if the premises are put forward with the claim that they conclusively establish the conclusion, the argument is deductive, even if this claim is mistaken. For example, suppose someone argues:

**Jones is an atheist. All Communists are atheists. Therefore Jones
must be a Communist.** (3)

If the speaker is claiming that his premises provide conclusive proof of the conclusion, we shall classify his argument as deductive, although it is a bad deductive argument, for the premises are not sufficient to establish the conclusion. The essential feature of a *deductive* argument is that it establishes its conclusion absolutely conclusively, or at any rate that the speaker claims it does so.

Now let us look at some contrasting examples of a different sort:

**Kelly belongs to the CIO. Most members of the CIO vote Democratic.
Therefore, probably Kelly votes Democratic.** (4)
**I bought a pair of socks of this brand and style once before and they
lasted a long time. If I buy another pair, most likely they will last a
long time too.** (5)

We shall regard these arguments as having the sentences "Kelly will vote Democratic" and "If I buy another pair, they will last a long time" as their respective conclusions; we interpret the words "probably" and "most likely" not as parts of the conclusions but as indications of the degree of connection claimed to hold between premises and conclusions.

An important feature of these two arguments is that in each case the conclusion makes some prediction or expresses some conjecture which goes beyond what the premises say but about which we can find out by further observations. (We can wait until the election to see how Kelly votes; we can test the socks over a period of time to discover how long they wear.) Arguments that are not deductive and that possess this feature are called *inductive* arguments; that is, inductive arguments are nondeductive arguments whose conclusions express conjectures that go beyond what their premises say and yet can be tested by further observations.[2]

To say that the conclusion of an argument 'goes beyond' the assertion in the premises means that there would be no contradiction involved in accepting the premises but rejecting the conclusion. Thus, the truth of the premises cannot provide absolutely conclusive reason for believing the conclusion. The premises of such an argument may give good reason for accepting the conclusion. They may render the conclusion highly probable. But always it remains logically possible that the premises are true and the conclusion nevertheless is false.

Deductive and inductive arguments are the only types of argument that are much studied by logicians; indeed, logicians have studied deduction much more fully than induction, because deductive reasoning admits of being described more readily in terms of definite general rules. Whether there is any genuine reasoning that is neither deductive nor inductive is a question to which we shall return later (in Chapter 7).

Exercise 2

In this exercise our task is to apply the distinction between deductive and inductive arguments. Examine each example

---

[2] There is no unanimity among logic writers about the definition of induction; the definition adopted here is not the simplest in current use, but it is perhaps the least likely to be misleading in the long run.

and decide whether it contains an argument. If it does, de-
termine the conclusion and the premises. Then decide whether
the argument is deductive or inductive.

1   Messer Bernardo replied, "I do say that in their pleasantries
and practical jokes women may sting men for their faults more
freely than men may sting them. And this is because we ourselves have set a rule that a dissolute life in us is not a vice, or
fault, or disgrace, while in women it means such utter oppro-
brium and shame that any woman of whom ill is once spoken
is disgraced forever, whether what is said be calumny or not.
Therefore, since even to speak of women's honor runs the risk
of doing them grave offence, I say that we ought to refrain
from this and sting them in some other way; because to deal
too hard a thrust with our pleasantries or practical jokes is to
exceed the bounds proper to a gentleman."

CASTIGLIONE, *The Courtier*

2   "How, in the name of good fortune, did you know all that, Mr.
Holmes?" he asked. "How did you know, for example, that
I did manual labor? It's true as gospel, for I began as a ship's
carpenter."

"Your hands, my dear sir. Your right hand is quite a
size larger than your left. You have worked with it and the
muscles are more developed."

A. CONAN DOYLE, "The Red-headed League"

3   A struggle for existence inevitably follows from the high rate
at which all organic beings tend to increase. Every being,
which during its natural lifetime produces several eggs or
seeds, must suffer destruction during some period of its life,
and during some season or occasional year, otherwise, on the
principle of geometrical increase, its numbers would quickly
become so inordinately great that no country could support the
product. Hence, as more individuals are produced than can
possibly survive, there must in every case be a struggle for

existence, either one individual with another of the same species, or with the individuals of distinct species, or with the physical conditions of life.   DARWIN, *The Origin of Species*

4 It is necessary that the land and the surrounding waters have the figure which the shadow of the earth casts, for at the time of an eclipse it projects on the moon the circumference of a perfect circle. Therefore the earth is not a plane, as Empedocles and Anaximenes opined . . . or again a cylinder, as Anaximander . . . but it is perfectly round. . . .
     COPERNICUS, *On the Revolutions of the Celestial Spheres*

5 A prudent ruler ought not to keep faith when by doing so it would be against his interest, and when the reasons which made him bind himself no longer exist. If men were all good, this precept would not be a good one; but as they are bad, and would not observe their faith with you, so you are not bound to keep faith with them.   MACHIAVELLI, *The Prince*

6   . . . You are wise;
Or else you love not; for to be wise and love
Exceeds man's might; that dwells with gods above.
     SHAKESPEARE, *Troilus and Cressida*

7 It is a very common event for a dream to give evidence of knowledge and memories which the waking subject is unaware of possessing. One of my patients dreamt . . . that he had ordered a 'Kontuszówka' while he was in a cafe. After telling me this, he asked me what a 'Kontuszówka' was, as if he had never heard the name. I was able to tell him in reply that it was a Polish liqueur, and that he could not have invented the name as it had long been familiar to me from advertisements on the billboards. At first he would not believe me; but some days later, after making his dream come true in a cafe, he noticed the name on a billboard at a street corner which he must have gone past at least twice a day for several months.
     FREUD, *The Interpretation of Dreams*

8 My reason for believing that there is one absolute World-Self, who embraces and is all reality, whose consciousness includes and infinitely transcends our own, in whose unity all the laws of nature and all the mysteries of experience must have their solution and their very being,—is simply that the profoundest agnosticism which you can possibly state in any coherent fashion, the deepest doubt which you can any way formulate about the world or the things that are therein, already presupposes, implies, demands, asserts, the existence of such a World-Self. . . . There is no escape from the infinite Self except by self-contradiction. . . . This truth is, I assure you, simply a product of dry Logic.

JOSIAH ROYCE, *The Spirit of Modern Philosophy*

TRUTH AND VALIDITY

In this section we shall consider the notion of truth, which relates to the premises and conclusions of arguments, and the notion of validity, which relates to arguments themselves. We must distinguish between the notions of truth and validity; however, we shall see that they are connected in an important way.

Premises and Conclusions

What are the premises and conclusions of arguments? We shall speak of them as being kinds of sentences. Sentences are *expressions*—series of words or symbols. A *sentence* may roughly be defined as a series of words that form a complete utterance, according to the rules of language. The sentences that serve as premises and conclusions of arguments ordinarily are what grammarians call declarative sentences, and they differ from other kinds of sentences in that they have the distinctive feature of being *true or false*. Other kinds of sentences, such as questions and exclamations, ordinarily would not be appropriate as parts of an argument, for they do not usually possess truth or falsity. (In the first example of Exercise 1 a question serves as a premise, but it is a rhetorical question, one that does not call for an answer but serves instead to make a statement.)

To say that the premises and conclusions of arguments are sentences is a serviceable but crude way of speaking. It is serviceable in enabling us to talk about parts of arguments without our having to speak in tedious circumlocutions. It is crude, however, because it glosses over the distinction between a declarative sentence and the statement, or assertion, that a speaker makes by uttering the sentence on a particular occasion. Saying that the premises and conclusion of an argument are sentences suggests that sentences as such are true or false and that we can analyze the logic of an argument merely by studying the sentences (the series of words) that occur in it. But we cannot do that. Suppose a speaker argued:

If Jones is mad, he needs psychiatric treatment. Jones is mad. Therefore, Jones needs psychiatric treatment.

Whether this argument is logical depends, for one thing, upon whether the word "mad" is used in the same sense in both premises. If, in uttering the first sentence, the speaker was asserting that if Jones is insane then he needs treatment, while in uttering the second the speaker was asserting that Jones is angry, then the argument is not good logic. Merely by inspecting the words themselves one cannot determine how the speaker is using them, and one cannot determine whether the argument is good or bad logic. To determine those things one must consider the *context* in which these sentences are uttered. Perhaps one must take account of what the speaker said before or afterward, what he saw and knew, perhaps his gestures and tone of voice.

A less crude way of stating this would be to say that the premises and conclusions of arguments are not the sentences that speakers utter but rather are the assertions that they make by uttering these sentences. The difficulty is that this way of speaking would be very cumbersome later on, when we come to discuss the logical forms of arguments. In the rest of this book, whenever a remark is made about some logical aspect of a sentence, the meticulous reader should understand this as short for a more cumbrous remark about some aspect of the assertion that a speaker would be likely to make by uttering that sentence.

Writers on logic have used various terms for referring to the premises and conclusions of arguments. Some have spoken of *propositions,* some of *judgments,* some of *statements.*

Naturally, a sentence that is a premise in one argument may be a conclusion in some other argument. Suppose I am trying to prove a conclusion, and in doing so I advance an argument that uses another sentence as its premise. My opponent, even if he grants that my conclusion follows from my premise, may question whether my premise is true; he may say that he will not accept my conclusion until I prove my premise. If he challenges my premise in this way, it becomes my duty to try to construct a new argument to establish that premise, that is, a new argument that will have a new premise (or premises) and that will have as its conclusion the premise of the first argument. I would hope to be able to choose for my new argument a new premise that my opponent will not challenge; but if he challenges this new premise also, then I must try to prove it too. This illustrates how the same sentence can be treated sometimes as a premise and sometimes as a conclusion.

Two Kinds of Mistakes in Reasoning

We noted earlier that an argument has two essential features: The speaker who presents the argument is claiming that his premises are true, and he is also claiming that, if these premises are true, the conclusion should also be true. Every argument, whether good or bad, must have these two features if it is to be an argument in our sense of the term. We can see from this that there are at least two ways in which a person can err when he advances an argument. On the one hand, the person presenting the argument may make a mistake in claiming that his premises are true. In this case he is making a *factual* error. (Here we suppose that his premises are false but not logically self-contradictory.) His mistake is that his facts are wrong, and he has reasoned from assumptions that are untrue.

On the other hand, the second kind of mistake might be the

mistake of claiming that, if the premises are true, the conclusion should be true too, when this is not so. This would be a *logical* error, resulting from misunderstanding the logical relation between premises and conclusion. Logic, insofar as it is concerned with errors, is primarily concerned with errors of the second sort. It is not the business of logic to tell us what premises to start with in our thinking (except that we should start with premises that are logically consistent), but it is the business of logic to help us see how conclusions ought to be related to their premises.

The first kind of mistake is the mistake of using false sentences as premises. Sentences can be true or false, but whole arguments are not spoken of as being true or false. When the premises of an argument are related to the conclusion in such a way that, if the premises are true, the conclusion should be true too, the argument is called *valid*.[3] An argument is *invalid* if its premises are not related to its conclusion in this way. Thus, the second kind of mistake is the mistake of employing an invalid type of argument.

To see clearly the difference between truth and validity, let us think about deductive arguments. (For inductive arguments, truth and validity are related in a different way, which will be discussed in Chapter 6.) A deductive argument is valid provided that, if its premises are true, its conclusion must necessarily be true also. However we must note that, even when a deductive argument is valid, its conclusion may not be true. For example, the argument "All creatures that fly have wings; all pigs fly; therefore all pigs have wings" is an argument that is deductively valid; that is, if the premises are all true, the conclusion necessarily will be true also. But the conclusion is false, and that is possible because the premises are not all true.

We should note also that a conclusion invalidly reached may

---

[3] Some writers restrict the term "valid" to good deductive arguments. They do not choose to call an inductive argument valid, no matter how good it is. We shall not follow that usage, however.

happen to be true. For example, the argument "All birds have wings and all chickens have wings; therefore all chickens are birds" is an argument whose conclusion happens to be true even though the argument is invalid.[4] The one thing that cannot happen is for a false conclusion to be validly deduced from premises all of which are true; this cannot happen in virtue of what we mean when we call a deductive argument valid.

One further bit of terminology: In ordinary language the word "imply" means "hint" or "suggest", but in logic this word is used in a different and stronger sense. When we say that the premises of an argument *imply* the conclusion, we mean that the argument is a valid deductive argument. More generally, to say that one sentence or group of sentences implies another sentence means that, if the former are true, the latter must necessarily be true also.[5] We do not say that the premises infer the conclusion in a valid deductive argument, as that is not good English. Implication is a logical relation that can hold between sentences; inference is an act that people perform when they derive one sentence from another.

Exercise 3

In each case, is the argument valid? Are its premises all true? Is its conclusion true? Notice how each example differs from every other.

1 All birds have feathers, and all crows have feathers. Therefore, all crows are birds.

[4] If someone does not see that this example is invalid, a good way to show him is to make use of an *analogy*. We say to him, "If you say that this is valid, then you might as well say that 'All birds have legs and all pigs have legs, and so all pigs are birds' is a valid argument".

[5] This is the only notion of implication that we shall employ. However, many modern logic writers follow the somewhat confusing precedent set by Russell, who used the word "implication" as a name for the truth-functional conditional (which we shall discuss in Chapter 3).

2 All birds have feathers, and all crows are birds. Therefore, all crows have feathers.

3 All birds are quadrupeds, and all crows are birds. Therefore, all crows are quadrupeds.

4 All birds are quadrupeds, and all crows are quadrupeds. Therefore, all crows are birds.

5 All birds are quadrupeds, and all crows are quadrupeds. Therefore, all birds are crows.

6 All birds are quadrupeds, and all dogs are birds. Therefore, all dogs are quadrupeds.

7 All birds have feathers, and all crows have feathers. Therefore, all birds are crows.

EMPIRICAL AND NECESSARY SENTENCES

We have called the premises and conclusions of arguments sentences. Let us now note a distinction between two basically different types of true-or-false sentences. Discussing this distinction may help indirectly to clarify the sense in which we have spoken of the conclusion of a valid deductive argument as following necessarily from its premises.

Most of the sentences encountered in ordinary discourse are *empirical* (or *a posteriori*) sentences. To see what this means, let us consider a few examples.

Arsenic is poisonous.
Some pigs can fly.
Caesar conquered Gaul.
Ted's age plus Jim's age equals thirty-two.

The term "empirical" means "based on experience", and each of these sample sentences is based on experience in the following sense. To know whether one of these sentences is true, a person must possess evidence drawn from experience, that is, sensory evidence regarding what has been seen or heard or felt or smelled or tasted. A person could believe that arsenic is poisonous even though he did not have evidence for this; but belief, even when it is true belief, is not knowledge in such a case unless it is based upon good reasons. The kinds of reasons needed to enable anyone to know whether these sentences are true are reasons based on sensory observation. If I do not have any sort of observational evidence relative to arsenic, then my claim to know that it is poisonous is a false claim. Similarly, if I claim to know it to be false that some pigs fly, then my claim, if it is justified, must rest upon observations of pigs (and perhaps also of birds and blimps), observations made by me or by other observers with whose findings I am acquainted. It would be a contradiction in terms to suppose that one could know this kind of thing without knowing it on the basis of sense experience.

Putting the point in a more general way, we shall define an empirical sentence as a sentence such that merely understanding its meaning never is sufficient to enable a person to know whether it is true; in addition to understanding the sentence a person must have appropriate experience if he is to know whether the sentence is true. There is nothing about the meaning of an empirical sentence to make it necessarily true or necessarily false; consequently, we may say that an empirical sentence is a sentence that, if true, might conceivably have been false or that, if false, might conceivably have been true. (For this reason, empirical sentences are also called *contingent* sentences.) Putting it another way, we may say that to utter an empirical sentence is to make a claim about how the world actually happens to be, although the world might have been otherwise; the empirical sentence expresses information about our actual world by contrasting this world with other conceivable worlds.

However, there are other sentences that, if true, are necessarily true and could not have been false or that, if false, are necessarily false and could not have been true. Examples are:

Snow is white or it is not.
All dogs are animals.
Caesar conquered Gaul but it is not the case that he did.
Fifteen plus seventeen equals thirty-two.

Sentences like these, when understood straightforwardly in their likeliest senses, do not convey information about the world by contrasting this particular world which actually exists with other conceivable worlds. These are sentences that, if true, would be true in any possible world and, if false, would be false in any possible world. In discovering their truth or falsity, we do not have to make observations; we can simply reflect upon what they mean in order to see whether they are true. These *necessary* sentences are called *a priori* sentences (because one can know whether they are true before one observes the objects of which they speak). A person who understands the sentence, say, "All dogs are animals", and understands it straightforwardly, does not need in addition some sense experience to tell him that the sentence is true. He can know this by reflecting on the meanings of the words involved. No experience whatever, beyond that involved in learning the meanings of the words, is essential in order to enable him to know whether the sentence is true.

In logic we are interested in learning to tell the difference between arguments that are valid and arguments that are invalid. But to understand that the argument "No gentlemen are tactless; all baboons are tactless; therefore no baboons are gentlemen" is a valid deductive argument amounts to the same thing as to understand that the sentence "If no gentlemen are tactless and if all baboons are tactless, then no baboons are gentlemen" is a necessarily true sentence. The argument differs from the sentence in that it is an argument rather than a single sentence. (It consists of a series of sentences: premises that are asserted and a conclusion derived from them.) But to recognize the deductive validity of the argument is to recognize that the premises imply the conclusion. To say that the premises imply the conclusion amounts to saying that this "if-then" sentence is necessarily true.

Thus logic is very much concerned with necessary sentences. It is especially concerned with sentences that are necessarily true in virtue of their *logical form*. The logical form "If no ### are *** and if all /// are ***, then no /// are ###" is such that, with whatever three words or phrases we consistently fill the gaps, provided we make sense, we always get an overall "if-then" sentence that is true. Regardless of its subject matter, any sentence of this form is bound to be true. Thus we say that this particular sentence about gentlemen and baboons is true in virtue of its logical form, and the corresponding argument is valid in virtue of its logical form.

We should notice in passing, however, that not all valid arguments are valid in virtue of their logical forms. For instance, the argument "This glass is red; therefore this glass is colored" is a valid piece of deductive reasoning. (The truth of the premise would be absolutely sufficient to guarantee the truth of the conclusion.) But we cannot usefully analyze the logical form of the argument except as ". . . is ***, therefore . . . is ///". Since many arguments having this form are invalid, we cannot say that this argument is valid because of its logical form. Instead, its validity results from the special connection in meaning between the words "red" and "colored". In logic we are mainly interested in considering arguments whose validity depends upon their logical forms, that is, on the ways in which certain logical words such as "all", "some", "not", and "or" are arranged in them.

Returning to our distinction between empirical and necessary sentences, we must recognize that this is not an absolutely precise distinction; there are borderline cases of sentences that do not clearly belong in one category rather than the other. For example, consider the sentence "All spiders have eight legs". When straightforwardly understood, is this a necessary truth or is it an empirical truth? Is there or is there not a contradiction involved in supposing that there might be a species of spiders that did not have eight legs? Is having eight legs part of what the word "spider" means, or not? There are no answers to these questions, because the word "spider" as ordinarily used is somewhat indefinite in its meaning. Because the ordinary meaning of the word "spider" has this indefiniteness, there is no answer to the question whether the sentence as ordinarily understood is necessary or empirical. We could decide to change or sharpen the meaning attached to the word "spider"; then the sentence could become either definitely empirical or definitely necessary, but that does not alter what has just been said.

Thus some sentences cannot be definitely classified as necessary or as empirical. However, the distinction between necessary and empirical sentences still is a valuable distinction, in spite of such borderline cases, for the majority of sentences with which we ordinarily are concerned fit definitely into these categories. And the distinction between necessary and empirical sentences is of especial interest in two ways: first, in a theoretical way, and second, in a practical way.

First, the distinction between necessary and empirical sentences helps us to understand a fundamental difference between two types of knowledge: the a priori knowledge involved in logic and mathematics, on the one hand, and the empirical knowledge involved in the experimental sciences, on the other hand. The sentences in which are expressed the laws of physics, chemistry, and other experimental sciences typically are empirical sentences. They tell us about what actually is so, although it might have been otherwise. Scientists must make observations and conduct experiments in order to know whether the sentences in which they are interested are true.

In pure mathematics, however, and in logic, we do not have to employ observations or experiments; the sentences in which laws of mathematics and logic are expressed are necessary sentences. The principles of mathematics and logic give us no specific information about this particular world that happens to exist but apply equally to all conceivable worlds. Such of these principles as we attain knowledge of, we can know by means of reflection without appeal to sense experience.

Second, a practical reason why the distinction between necessary and empirical sentences is worth noticing is that it can help us to evaluate sentences met in ordinary discourse. Sometimes a person wishes to assert an informative, empirical thought but, without realizing the difference, he asserts something necessarily true but trivial instead. His hearers give the wrong weight to what he said and may ask for the wrong kind of reasons in its support if they are not aware of this distinction. Also, speakers sometimes utter necessarily false sentences without realizing that they are doing so; here too their hearers will give the wrong weight to what is said and may try in the wrong way to refute it if they are not aware of the distinction.

Exercise 4

State whether each sentence when straightforwardly understood is necessarily true, necessarily false, or empirical.

1 Some roses are red.

2 A rose is a rose.

3 A rose is a flower.

4 Few Buddhists live in Ohio.

5   Anyone who is a spinster is a woman.

6   There are spinsters who are not women.

7   Every cube has twelve edges.

8   Whatever will be will be.

9   Either Egbert is my friend or Egbert is my enemy.

10   Either Egbert is my friend or Egbert is not my friend.

11   If no first-year men are on the team, then nobody on the team is a first-year man.

12   If some Methodists are Hindus, then some Hindus are not non-Methodists.

13   The bride-to-be, Miss Mathilda Peebles, is just twenty years old; and she was only seven when she moved here to Pomona-ville with her late father, who was then commencing his two decades of service as our city's sanitary engineer.

14   If you eat an adequate, well-balanced diet, you will get all the vitamins your body normally needs.

15   No thinker can get outside his own world of thought.

16   An attitude of undue morbidity is not healthful.

17   The future lies before us.

18   If the present economic upward trend continues, there will be increased prosperity; however, if business conditions should worsen, the general state of the economy may not continue to improve and may even decline.

19   The Demopublican party will decrease government expenditures so that taxes can be cut; you may rest assured, however, that they will not allocate less funds to the various tasks, all of them essential, which our government performs.

20   An ideal man would always say far more than he means, and would always mean far more than he says.

OSCAR WILDE

In each case, if your answer is "yes", give an example to estab-
lish your answer. If your answer is "no", explain why there
can be no example.

1 Can there be a valid deductive argument consisting entirely of
empirical sentences?

2 Can there be a valid deductive argument consisting entirely of
necessary sentences?

3 Consider a valid deductive argument all of whose premises are
necessarily true. Can its conclusion be an empirical sentence?

4 Consider a valid deductive argument all of whose premises are
true empirical sentences. Can its conclusion be a necessary
sentence?

5 Consider a valid deductive argument all of whose premises are
false empirical sentences. Can its conclusion be a necessary
sentence?

In logic it is important to distinguish between what necessar-
ily follows from a remark and what is merely suggested by it.
In each of the following cases, suppose that someone says
(a). Then is (b) something that follows deductively from
what he has said, or something that is merely suggested by
what he has said, or something neither following from, nor
suggested by, what he has said?

1 (**a**) Only citizens who pay real estate taxes will vote on the
proposed bond issue.
(**b**) All citizens who pay real estate taxes will vote on the
proposed bond issue.

2 (**a**) Mr. Wilkinson is his uncle.
(**b**) He is Mr. Wilkinson's nephew.

3 (**a**) College students are as intelligent as they are industrious.
(**b**) College students are intelligent and industrious.

4 (**a**) I won't go if you do.
(**b**) I will go if you don't.

5 (a) Wilbur is taller than Hubert.

    (b) Hubert is shorter than Wilbur.

6 (a) Some students in this class are not lazy.

    (b) Some students in this class are lazy.

7 (a) I'll buy you a mink coat or a Cadillac.

    (b) I won't buy you both a mink coat and a Cadillac.

8 (a) Hilda has acquired a dog.

    (b) Hilda has acquired an animal.

9 (a) Not all television programs are intellectually stimulating.

    (b) Some television programs are not intellectually stimulating.

10 (a) I only know that I love you.

    (b) I know that only I love you.

11 (a) Carelessly he anchored in the target area.

    (b) He anchored carelessly in the target area.

12 (a) I'm very glad you asked me about this proposed 'Right to Work' law, which would prohibit the closed shop. This is a big issue in the present election, and I want to take this opportunity to state very frankly and candidly that, although some special interests will be offended by what I'm saying, I do indeed heartily favor any legislation that will effectively protect the legitimate interests of all the working men in this great nation of ours.

    (b) I am in favor of the 'Right to Work' law.

2. *The Traditional Logic of Categorical Sentences*

In this chapter we shall consider the traditional logic of categorical sentences, a part of logic that stems from Aristotle. This part of logic deals with arguments whose premises and conclusions all can be expressed as sentences of the kind called categorical. This was the aspect of logic mainly studied by logicians of medieval and early modern times, and they came to regard it as the principal part, perhaps even as the whole, of logic. Nowadays it can be seen that such a view is far too narrow; there are many valuable forms of argument not comprehended within this traditional part of logic, and the limited range of arguments that it treats is not of great theoretical importance. Nevertheless, this traditional part of logic still deserves attention, for arguments that can be analyzed in this traditional style occur very frequently in ordinary discourse.

CATEGORICAL SENTENCES

Let us focus our attention upon four specific forms of sentence, forms important enough so that they were long ago given the special names "**A**", "**E**", "**I**", and "**O**". These four forms of sentence are:

A: All so-and-so's are such-and-such's.
E: No so-and-so's are such-and-such's.
I: Some so-and-so's are such-and-such's.
O: Some so-and-so's are not such-and-such's.

Sentences of these four forms, and only these, we shall call *categorical* sentences.[1] Thus, for example, the sentence "All unicorns are animals" is a categorical sentence of **A** form; the sentence "No natural satellites of the earth are self-luminous bodies" is a categorical sentence of **E** form; and the sentence "Some birds are not dodoes" is a categorical sentence of **O** form.

To be in categorical form, a sentence must start with a *quantifier* (the word "all", "no", or "some"), followed by the word or phrase called the *subject* of the sentence, then the *copula* ("are" or "are not"), and finally the word or phrase called the *predicate*. The words or phrases that serve as subjects and predicates in categorical sentences are called *terms*.

The **A** and **E** sentences are said to be *universal,* because sentences of these forms sweepingly speak of the whole of the class

---

[1] The term "categorical" traditionally has been used because of its connection with the term "category", which comes from the Greek word for predicate. Thus, categorical sentences are sentences in which a predicate is connected with a subject. In Aristotle's philosophy, predicates were classified into some twelve basic types, such as substance (e.g., "man"), quantity (e.g., "two feet long"), quality (e.g., "white"), and others. These types of predicates, also regarded as corresponding to types of real entity in the universe, came to be called the categories. It was thought that in every categorical sentence the predicate had to belong to one of these categories.

of things to which the subject term applies. The **I** and **O** forms are said to be *particular,* because sentences of these forms give definite information only about part of the class of things to which the subject term applies. This is called *quantity.* **A** and **E** are said to be universal in quantity, and **I** and **O** are said to be particular in quantity.

The **A** and **I** forms say something *affirmative,* while **E** and **O** say something *negative.* This is called *quality.* **A** and **I** are said to be affirmative in quality, while **E** and **O** are said to be negative in quality. [The four letters used as names of these forms come from the vowels in the Latin words *"affirmo"* ("I affirm") and *"nego"* ("I deny"); in medieval and early modern times, logic, like all university subjects, was studied only in Latin.] We can use a little diagram to sum up these facts about quantity and quality (Figure 1).

Our consideration of categorical sentences will be smoother and clearer if we adhere to this comparatively strict and narrow point of view concerning the form of categorical sentences. (This will facilitate our discussion of immediate inference, later on.) Accordingly, let us insist that in a sentence in strictly categorical form the copula must be plural and the terms must be plural substantive general terms. Thus, the sentence "All gold is valuable" is not regarded as strictly in categorical form,

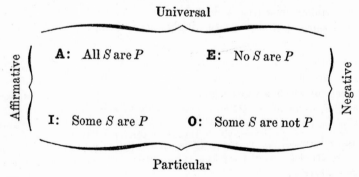

Figure 1

because its copula is "is" rather than "are" and because its predicate is
an adjective rather than a substantive (that is, nounlike) expression.
However, if we reword it as "All pieces of gold are valuable things",
then we have a sentence that is strictly categorical, for now the copula
is plural and both terms are plural forms of substantive general terms.

As another example, the sentence "All America is beautiful" falls
even further short of being a categorical sentence, for not only is
the predicate adjectival and the copula not plural, but the subject,
"America", is not even a general term.

The distinction between general terms and singular terms is of
some interest for logic; let us consider it briefly. A *general term* is a
word or phrase used in such a way that it can apply to many individual
things, to just one, or to none. Thus, the general term "dog" applies
to millions of individual dogs, the general term "natural satellite of
the earth" applies just to the moon, and the general term "unicorn"
applies to nothing. A speaker can use a general term (e.g., "dodo")
in saying many things that he knows to be true (e.g., in saying
"No dogs are dodoes", "Some birds are not dodoes", etc.) irrespective
of whether there is anything to which the term applies. In contrast,
a *singular term* is a word or phrase that, as used on a particular occasion,
purports to refer to exactly one thing. A speaker can use a singular
term (e.g., the proper name "Bruno") in saying a variety of things
that he knows to be true (e.g., in saying "Bruno is an intelligent
dog", "Bruno is not a cat", etc.) only if the term as he is using it refers
to just one individual thing. If he had made a mistake and there were
no such dog as the one he was calling "Bruno", then he would not have
said anything either true or false by uttering those sentences.

In categorical sentences we never allow a singular term just by
itself to serve as subject or as predicate. In the sentence "All America
is beautiful", the word "America" functions as a singular term, for whoever utters this sentence is thereby referring to one specific country, the
existence of which is a precondition of the truth or falsity of his remark.
However, we obtain a categorical sentence if we reword it as "All parts
of America are beautiful places". Now the phrase "parts of America"
is the subject of the sentence, and this phrase is a general term.

One further distinction, which it is useful to notice here, is the distinction between compound sentences and atomic sentences. Sentences
are said to be *compound* if they contain other simpler sentences with-

in themselves; sentences are said to be *atomic* if they do not contain other simpler sentences. Thus, the sentences "Clovis is coming and we shall have a party", "If Clovis is coming, then we shall have a party", and "We shall have a party because Clovis is coming" are examples of compound sentences, for each contains within itself the simpler sentences "Clovis is coming" and "We shall have a party". Such sentences as "It is not the case that Clovis is coming", "I believe that Clovis is coming", and "It is impossible that Clovis is coming" also may conveniently be considered compound sentences, for each contains within itself the one simpler sentence "Clovis is coming". This simpler sentence, however, presumably would be classified as atomic, that is, noncompound, since it does not have any other still simpler sentence as a part of itself.

Categorical sentences are not compound, as such. That is, a categorical sentence does not need to contain other simpler sentences as components of itself, and most ordinary examples of categorical sentences do not. However, it would be incorrect to say that all categorical sentences are atomic, for some categorical sentences contain other simpler sentences. For example, the sentence "All persons who believed that Evans was innocent are persons who believed that Christie was guilty" is a compound categorical sentence containing the simpler sentences "Evans was innocent" and "Christie was guilty". The best way to describe the situation is to say that categorical sentences need not be compound, although they need not be atomic either.

Before we can discuss the logical relationships among the four forms of categorical sentences, we must get clearly in mind what each form is to mean. With regard to the meaning of "some", two difficulties may cause misunderstanding. First, the word "some" is vague as it is used in ordinary conversation. By "some" we mean "a few"; but how many are a few? If a person says that some chairs are in the next room, is he claiming that there is at least one chair in the next room, that there are at least two, or perhaps that there are at least three? Such questions have no answer, for the word "some" is vague as it is ordinarily used. Vagueness of this kind is inconvenient for our present purposes. It will be best for us to decide more definitely what meaning we shall assign to the word "some". The most convenient way to do this is to assign it the minimum meaning: We shall take "Some so-and-so's are such-and-such's" to mean that there is *at least one* so-and-so that is a such-and-such.

A second difficulty is that the word "some" can give rise to ambiguity as it is ordinarily used. Vagueness and ambiguity are different. A word is *vague* if there is no way of telling just where correct use of the word begins and where it leaves off, as things vary in degree. For instance, the word "bald" is vague, for baldness is a matter of degree, and we cannot say just how many hairs must be missing before it is correct to describe a man as bald. A word is *ambiguous* if it has two quite different meanings. The word "heavy" in the sentence "This is a heavy book" is ambiguous, for it may have either of two quite different meanings, "hard to read" or "hard to lift".

The ambiguity involved with "some" comes to light if we consider a man who says that some women are boring. Is he thereby claiming that some women are *not* boring? In ordinary discourse this occasionally may be part of what his remark means, although more often it is not. For example, a student who says in an acid tone, *"Some* members of the faculty are worth listening to" is strongly suggesting that some are not, and perhaps we should regard his remark as asserting that some are and some are not worth listening to. But usually to say that some so-and-so's are such-and-such's is not to say that some are not.

For the purposes of logic, it is best to choose the minimum meaning of "some". We shall interpret the sentence "Some so-and-so's are such-and-such's" as meaning merely that there is at least one so-and-so that is a such-and-such. (This leaves it an open question whether there is any so-and-so that is not a such-and-such.) Similarly, we shall interpret the **O** sentence as meaning merely that at least one so-and-so is not a such-and-such. This leaves it an open question whether any is.

Another ambiguity connected with categorical sentences is concerned not with alternative possible meanings of the four categorical forms but with the viewpoint from which their interrelations are discussed. The **A** form "All so-and-so's are such-and-such's" certainly means that, if there are any so-and-so's, they are such-and-such's; in other words, there are not any so-and-so's that fail to be such-and-such's. The **E** form "No so-and-so's are such-and-such's" certainly means that, if anything is a so-and-so, it is not a such-and-such; in other words, there do not exist any so-and-so's that are such-and-such's. The **I** form asserts the existence of at least one so-and-so that is a such-and-such, and the **O** form asserts the existence of at least one so-and-so that is not a such-and-such.

But the ambiguity is this: When we discuss the relations among the **A, E, I,** and **O** forms, are we prepared to allow for the possibility that no so-and-so's exist, or are we presupposing that at least one so-and-so exists? In ordinary discourse, a speaker who utters one or more categorical sentences should in some cases be understood as taking for granted that so-and-so's exist, while in other cases he should be understood as leaving it an open question whether they exist or not. Thus, when a landowner states that all trespassers will be prosecuted or that no trespassers will be prosecuted, neither of these remarks need be construed as having the underlying presupposition that there will be trespassers. But if a lady says that all her jewels are diamonds or that no jewels of hers are rubies, these remarks normally should be understood as having the presupposition that there are jewels of hers.

These two different viewpoints for interpreting categorical sentences are important enough to deserve attention in logic. If we consider the categorical sentences from the viewpoint that presupposes that there exist things to which the subject term applies, we are adopting the *existential viewpoint*. If we consider categorical sentences in the minimum way as not taking for granted that such things exist, then we are adopting the *hypotheti-*

cal viewpoint. Traditional aristotelian logic considered categorical sentences only from the existential viewpoint. Modern symbolic logic usually treats categorical sentences according to the hypothetical viewpoint.

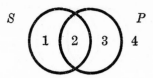

Figure 2

The meanings of the four forms of categorical sentences can be brought out especially clearly if we illustrate them by means of Venn diagrams. These diagrams were devised by the nineteenth-century English logician John Venn. Another type of diagram invented by the eighteenth-century mathematician Euler also can be used to represent categorical sentences; Venn diagrams are preferable, however, as with them it is always possible to illustrate exactly what the categorical sentence says, no less and no more, whereas Euler diagrams must sometimes appear to express more information than is contained in the sentences being diagrammed.

Let us draw two overlapping circles (Figure 2) and consider two classes of individuals, Swedes and Protestants. We shall now imagine that all the Swedes in existence are herded inside the left-hand circle; no one else and nothing else is allowed within that circle. Into the right-hand circle all Protestants are herded; no one else and nothing else may enter. In region 1 of this diagram we now shall find Swedes who are not Protestants, if there are any. In region 2 we shall find Swedes who are Protestants. In region 3 of the diagram we shall find Protestants who are not Swedes. And in region 4 will be all persons and things that are neither Swedes nor Protestants.

We now consider the I sentence "Some Swedes are Protestants". To illustrate what it says, we put an asterisk in region 2 to indicate that this region is not empty (Figure 3). This picture indicates that region 2 is

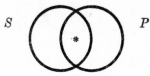

I: Some *S* are *P*

Figure 3

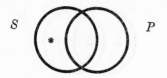

O: Some S are not P

Figure 4

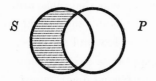

A: All S are P

Hypothetical viewpoint

Figure 5

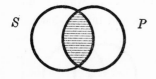

E: No S are P

Hypothetical viewpoint

Figure 6

occupied by at least one thing, and so it exhibits exactly the information conveyed by the **I** sentence, no less and no more. All other regions are blank in the diagram, indicating that the **I** sentence tells us nothing about whether they are vacant or occupied. Note that this one diagram serves to represent the **I** sentence, whether we are considering it from the existential or from the hypothetical viewpoint.

Using the same method, we can illustrate what the **O** sentence says (Figure 4). Here the asterisk in region 1 means that there is at least one thing that is an S but not a P. This diagram serves for both the hypothetical and the existential viewpoint.

Diagrams also can be drawn for the universal sentences. Here we shade a region to indicate that it is empty. The **A** sentence says that there are no S's that fail to be P's; from the hypothetical viewpoint, we leave it an open question whether S's exist (Figure 5). The **E** sentence says that there does not exist any S that is a P; from the hypothetical viewpoint we leave it an open question whether there exist any S's (Figure 6). But from the existential viewpoint, we take it for granted that there does exist at least one S (Figure 7).

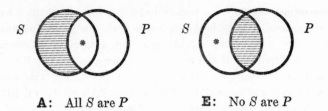

A: All S are P **E:** No S are P

Existential viewpoint

Figure 7

DISTRIBUTION OF TERMS

The notion of distribution of terms in categorical sentences is a bit of medieval logical lore which will be useful to us later on. Traditional definitions of this notion were rather unsatisfactory, but we may redefine it as follows: A term S occurring as the subject of a categorical sentence is said to be distributed in that sentence if and only if the sentence, in virtue of its form, says something about *every kind of S*. Similarly, a term P occurring as the predicate of a categorical sentence is said to be distributed in that sentence if and only if the sentence, in virtue of its form, says something about *every kind of P*.

A more rigorous formulation of the definition of distribution is as follows: Suppose that T is a term which occurs as subject or predicate in a categorical sentence s. Where T' is any other term, let s' be the sentence that is exactly like s except for containing the compound term $T' \& T$, where s contains T. Now, T is said to be distributed in s if and only if, for every term T', s logically implies s'.

To see the meaning of this definition, consider an example. Suppose that T were the term "prohibitionists" and s were the sentence "Some seamen are not prohibitionists". Then if T' were the term "rich", s' would be the sentence "Some seamen are not rich prohibitionists". To say that T is distributed in s is to say that every sentence of the form

"Some seamen are not . . . prohibitionists" is logically implied by *s*.

Old-fashioned logic books do not explain the notion of distribution in this way. They usually say that a term in a categorical sentence is distributed if and only if the sentence 'refers to' all members of the class of things to which the term applies. But this explanation is obscure and misleading. The sentence "All equilateral triangles are equiangular triangles" 'refers to' all equilateral triangles, and since necessarily these and only these are equiangular triangles, the sentence would appear to 'refer to' all equiangular triangles also. Thus, according to the old-fashioned account, it would seem that the predicate ought to count as distributed in this **A** sentence. The predicate is not considered to be distributed, however, and this illustrates one unsatisfactory aspect of the old-fashioned explanation of distribution.

Another unsatisfactory aspect of the old-fashioned account is that it is unclear in its treatment of the predicate of the **O** form. To claim that the sentence "Some seamen are not prohibitionists" 'refers to' all prohibitionists is to make an obscure and unsatisfactory claim. The notion of 'reference' employed in this old-fashioned account is too hazy to be respectable.

Consider the sentence "All Slavs are promiscuous persons". This sentence says something about every kind of Slav: young Slavs, old Slavs, male Slavs, female Slavs, blond Slavs, dark Slavs, and so on. Thus the subject term "Slavs" is said to be distributed in it. However, the sentence does not say anything about every kind of promiscuous person; it speaks only of Slavish ones and tells us nothing about non-Slavish kinds of promiscuous persons. Thus the predicate term is undistributed. In this **A** sentence the subject is distributed and the predicate is undistributed.

Consider next the sentence "No Slavs are promiscuous persons". Here again our sentence says something about every kind of Slav; it says that large ones, small ones, fat ones, slim ones are none of them promiscuous. And this sentence, though more indirectly, says something about all kinds of promiscuous persons; concerning promiscuous persons, whether gay or sad, wise or foolish, it says that none of them are Slavs. Thus both the subject and the predicate of this **E** sentence are distributed.

Now consider the sentence "Some Slavs are promiscuous persons". This sentence does not say anything about every kind of Slav; it speaks only about such of them as are promiscuous. Neither does it say anything about every kind of promiscuous person; it speaks only about such of them as are Slavs. Thus in this **I** sentence neither the subject nor the predicate is distributed.

Finally, consider the sentence "Some Slavs are not promiscuous persons". Here again nothing is said about every kind of Slav. However, in a roundabout way, a claim is made about every kind of promiscuous person. For this **O** sentence says that whatever kind of promiscuous persons we consider, sane ones, mad ones, tall ones, short ones, each of these kinds of promiscuous individuals is such as not to include all Slavs. That is, our sentence implies that some Slavs are not sane promiscuous persons, that some Slavs are not mad promiscuous persons, and so on. Thus in this **O** sentence the subject is undistributed but the predicate is distributed.

What has been said about these sample sentences clearly holds true in general. In any **A** sentence the subject is distributed and the predicate is undistributed; in any **E** sentence both subject and predicate are distributed; in any **I** sentence neither subject nor predicate is distributed; and in any **O** sentence the subject is not distributed but the predicate is. Whether we interpret sentences according to the existential or the hypothetical viewpoint makes no difference so far as distribution is concerned.

One way of remembering these facts is to remember that in any universal sentence the subject is distributed, while in any negative sentence the predicate is distributed. Another way of remembering them is to remember the mnemonic word

"AsEbInOp", which means that in **A** the subject is distributed, in **E** both subject and predicate, in **I** neither, and in **O** the predicate.

THE SQUARE OF OPPOSITION

Suppose that we have categorical sentences of different forms but with the same subject and the same predicate. What logical relations will hold among them? Let us take, for example, the four sentences "All Samoans are pantheists", "No Samoans are pantheists", "Some Samoans are pantheists", and "Some Samoans are not pantheists". We want to consider how these sentences are related.

First, let us see how these sentences are related to one another when we take for granted that there are Samoans (the existential viewpoint). If it is true that all Samoans are pantheists, then (since we take for granted that at least one Samoan exists) it must follow that some Samoans are pantheists. Thus the **A** sentence implies the **I**. On the other hand, that some Samoans are pantheists does not guarantee that all of them are (since some might be and some not). Thus we can fully describe the relation between **A** and **I** by saying that **A** implies **I** but **I** does not imply **A**.

Similarly, if it is true that no Samoans are pantheists then (since we take for granted that there are Samoans) it must follow that some Samoans are not pantheists. Thus the **E** sentence implies the **O**. However, that some Samoans are not pantheists does not guarantee that no Samoans are (for perhaps some of them are and some are not). Thus we can describe the relation between **E** and **O** by saying that **E** implies **O** but **O** does not imply **E**.

As for **A** and **E**, neither implies the other. But if we take for granted that there are Samoans, it cannot be true both that all Samoans are pantheists and that no Samoans are pantheists; that is, **A** and **E** cannot both be true. Might **A** and **E** both be false?

Surely, for if some Samoans are pantheists and some are not, then neither **A** nor **E** is true. Thus the relation between **A** and **E** may be described by saying that they cannot both be true but they may both be false. The traditional way of referring to this relationship was to call **A** and **E** *contrary* sentences.

The relationship between **I** and **O** is different but analogous. Neither implies the other. Both may be true. But if we take for granted that Samoans exist, then **I** and **O** cannot both be false; if there are Samoans, then either some of them are pantheists or some of them are not pantheists (or perhaps both). Thus **I** and **O** are related in such a way that they cannot both be false, although they may both be true. The traditional way of referring to this relationship was to call **I** and **O** *subcontraries.*

Now consider the relationship between **A** and **O**. If it is true that all Samoans are pantheists, it must be false that some of them are not pantheists. And if it is false that all Samoans are pantheists, then it must be true that some of them are not. Conversely, if it is true that some Samoans are not pantheists, it must be false that all Samoans are; and if it is false that some Samoans are not pantheists, then it must be true that all of them are. Thus **A** and **O** cannot both be true and they cannot both be false; they are opposite as regards truth and falsity. They are called *contradictories,* or *negations,* of each other.

Similarly, **E** and **I** are related in such a way that, if **E** is true, **I** must be false and, if **E** is false, then **I** must be true. **E** and **I** are always opposite as regards their truth and falsity, and so they too are contradictories of each other.

The facts about these relationships can be arranged in traditional pattern, which is called the square of opposition (Figure 8).

Some of the words used to describe the relationships of this traditional square of opposition are used *loosely;* this is a point that old-fashioned logic books often do not make clear.

In the strict sense, to say that one sentence *implies* another is to say

Square of Opposition

Existential viewpoint: We presuppose that at least one S exists.

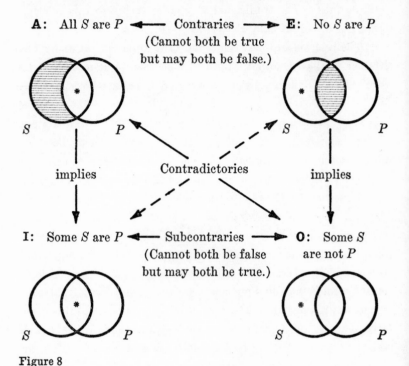

Figure 8

that, if the first is true, that alone is sufficient to guarantee that the second must necessarily be true also. **A** does not imply **I** nor does **E** imply **O** in this strict sense. These pairs of sentences involve implication only in the looser sense that, if the existential presupposition is true, then if **A** is true **I** must be true; and if the existential presupposition is true, then if **E** is true **O** must be true.

Similarly, to say that two sentences are *contraries* in the strict sense is to say that it is logically impossible for them both to be true. **A** and **E** are not contraries in this strict sense. They are contraries only in the looser sense that, if the existential presupposition is true, then **A** and **E** cannot both be true. Also, **I** and **O** are subcontraries only in a corresponding loose sense.

To say that two sentences are contradictories in the strict sense is to say that one asserts just what the other denies, no more and no less. As we have been understanding them, **A** and **O** are contradictories in this strict sense, as are **E** and **I**.

If we had regarded the existential assumption, that at least one *S* exists, not as a presupposition but as part of the meaning of each categorical sentence, the situation would have been different. Then **A** would have been understood as meaning "If anything is an *S*, it is a *P*, and there is at least one *S*", and **E** would have been understood as meaning "Nothing is both an *S* and a *P*, and there is at least one *S*"; **I** and **O** would have remained unchanged in meaning. Under these circumstances, **A** would not have been the contradictory of **O**, for **A** would have asserted more than what **O** denies, since **A** would contain the assertion that there exists an *S*, an assertion not denied by **O**, for **O** merely denies that there exists an *S* that is not a *P*. Also, **I** and **O** would not have been subcontraries, for it would have been possible for them both to be false, as would happen if nothing is an *S*. Because these consequences are inconvenient, we shall regard the existential claim not as part of the meaning of categorical sentences but rather as a presupposition that underlies our discussion of their interrelations.

So far, we have considered the square of opposition arranged on the presupposition that the things we speak about do exist. It is important to consider also how the four categorical forms are related to one another if we do not presuppose the existence of anything. Let us consider the relations among the sentences "All succubi are poltergeists", "No succubi are poltergeists", "Some succubi are poltergeists", and "Some succubi are not poltergeists". Here we do not wish to exclude the possibility that succubi may not exist.

Under these circumstances, **A** and **O** still are opposite as regards their truth and falsity; **A** says exactly what **O** denies, and so they are contradictories. **E** and **I** are contradictories also, for what **E** says is again exactly what **I** denies, no less and no more.

But **A** is not related to **I** nor is **E** related to **O** in the way they were before. Now **A** does not imply **I**, for it is possible that **A** might be true and **I** false. If S's do not exist, then there are no S that fail to be P, and so **A** is true but **I** is false. There is now no logical connection between **A** and **I**; knowledge of the truth or falsity of one of these sentences does not enable us to know whether the other is true or false. Similarly, **E** does not imply **O**, for **E** could be true but **O** false; this would happen if S's do not exist, for in that case it is true that no S are P but false that some S are not P. There is no logical connection between **E** and **O**.

Also, **A** and **E** no longer are contraries. No longer is it impossible for them both to be true, for these sentences are both true if there are no S at all. When nothing is an S, there certainly

Square of Opposition

Hypothetical viewpoint: We do not presuppose that any S exists.

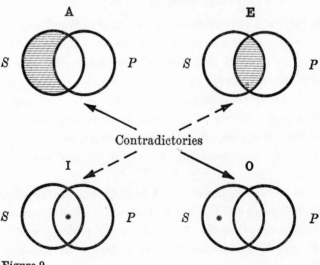

Figure 9

are no S that fail to be P and there are no S that are P; thus both the **A** and **E** sentences are true, from this hypothetical viewpoint. There is no logical connection now between **A** and **E**; knowing the truth or falsity of one of them does not enable us to tell the truth or falsity of the other. Similarly, **I** and **O** may both be false, and so they no longer are subcontraries. **I** says that there is at least one S that is P, while **O** says that there is at least one S that is not P; both these sentences are false if there are no S at all. Thus there is no logical connection between **I** and **O** either.

The result is that from the hypothetical viewpoint the square of opposition looks very different (Figure 9). Only the diagonal relationships are left in the diagram; the others do not hold.

Exercise 5

In each case, (a) suppose you know that the first sentence is true. Can you then infer that the second is true or that the second is false, or can you infer nothing about the second? (b) Suppose you know that the first sentence is false. What can you infer regarding the second? (c) Suppose you know that the second is true. What can you infer regarding the first? (d) Suppose you know that the second is false. What can you infer regarding the first? Are there any places where it makes a difference whether you adopt the existential rather than the hypothetical viewpoint in this exercise?

1   No reptiles are amphibians.   Some reptiles are not amphibians.

2.   Some sculptures by the Della Robbias are in terra cotta. All sculptures by the Della Robbias are in terra cotta.

3   Some plays that Shakespeare wrote are not comedies.   All plays that Shakespeare wrote are comedies.

4   No natives of Ceylon are Tamils.   Some natives of Ceylon are Tamils.

5 Some motor cars are not air-cooled.   Some motor cars are air-cooled.

6 All bishops are priests.   No bishops are priests.

IMMEDIATE INFERENCE

Next we shall consider some important relationships between pairs of categorical sentences that do not have exactly the same subjects and predicates.   The operations involved here have traditionally been called immediate inferences, because they correspond to simple, immediate types of argument in which only one premise yields the conclusion.

Conversion

A simple way to alter a categorical sentence is to make the subject and predicate trade places.   This is *conversion,* and the new sentence obtained by this operation is called the *converse* of the original sentence.   (It is sometimes called the *simple converse,* to contrast it with the converse by limitation which will be discussed presently.)   Let us consider how the meanings of the various forms of categorical sentence are affected by conversion.

Suppose we start with the **E** sentence "No syllogisms are perplexing things".   When subject and predicate trade places, we get the converse "No perplexing things are syllogisms".   A pair of Venn diagrams may help us to see how the original and its converse are related (Figure 10; in the diagram we adopt the

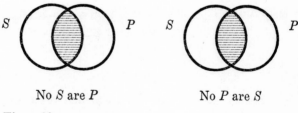

No *S* are *P*   No *P* are *S*

Figure 10

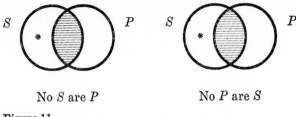

No S are P No P are S

Figure 11

hypothetical viewpoint). Two sentences are said to be *equivalent* if they are necessarily alike as regards truth or falsity. Here the diagrams are just the same, showing that the **E** sentence and its converse are equivalent.

A different diagram is needed for the existential viewpoint (Figure 11) but, according to this diagram too, the **E** sentence is equivalent to its converse. However, we must be careful to keep our existential presuppositions constant throughout a discussion, for if, in using the first sentence, we presupposed that S exist but did not presuppose that P exist, while in using the second sentence we presupposed only that P exist, then the two diagrams would not be alike.

The **I** sentence "Some syllogisms are perplexing things" has as its converse the sentence "Some perplexing things are syllogisms". Here again it is clear that conversion has not changed the meaning of the sentence: the **I** and its converse are equivalent, as the diagrams (Figure 12) show, whether considered from the hypothetical or from the existential viewpoint.

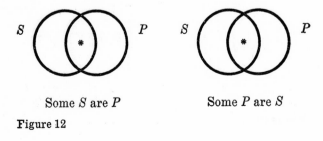

Some S are P Some P are S

Figure 12

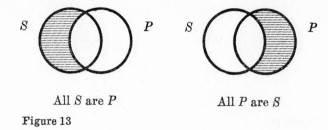

All S are P All P are S

Figure 13

Next let us consider the **A** sentence "All syllogisms are perplexing things". When subject and predicate trade places, we obtain the converse "All perplexing things are syllogisms". Has conversion altered the meaning of the sentence? From the diagram (Figure 13) it is clear that conversion has completely changed the meaning of the **A** sentence; the converse is an independent sentence that says something entirely different from what the original sentence said. In this pair of diagrams the hypothetical viewpoint has been adopted, but we get the same answer if we use a constant existential viewpoint.

Finally, if we convert the **O** sentence "Some syllogisms are not perplexing things", we obtain "Some perplexing things are not syllogisms". Here too it is clear from the diagram (Figure 14) that the original sentence and its converse are not equivalent, whether we picture them from the hypothetical or from the existential viewpoint.

What holds good in this example holds good in general. We can sum up by saying that any **E** or **I** sentence is equivalent

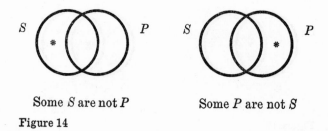

Some S are not P Some P are not S

Figure 14

to its converse, whereas no **A** or **O** sentence is equivalent to its converse. Another way of describing the matter is to say that when subject and predicate in the original sentence are alike as regards distribution (either both distributed or both undistributed) then the converse will be equivalent to the original sentence, but when the subject and predicate in the original sentence differ as regards distribution then the converse will not be equivalent to the original sentence.

Conversion by Limitation

Although an **A** sentence is not equivalent to its simple converse, we can validly derive from the **A** sentence another sentence in which subject and predicate have changed places; this is a feeble substitute for a converse, and it is called the *converse by limitation* (or the converse *per accidens*). This new sentence will be an **I**. From "All syllogisms are perplexing things" we may validly derive "Some perplexing things are syllogisms" (Figure 15). This process is legitimate only from the existential viewpoint. Moreover, the converse by limitation is not equivalent to the original sentence but is merely implied by it.

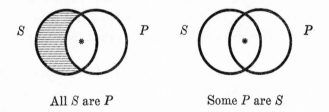

All *S* are *P*   Some *P* are *S*

Existential viewpoint

Figure 15

Obversion

The operation of conversion has the disadvantage that we cannot always convert a categorical sentence without changing its

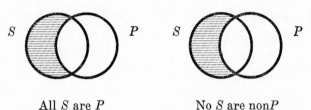

All S are P No S are non$P$
                                    (There are no S outside P circle.)

Figure 16

meaning.   Obversion is an operation free from this disadvantage.
However, it involves a slightly more complicated alteration.   To
form the *obverse* of a categorical sentence we do two things: We
change the quality of the sentence, and we negate the predicate.

Suppose we start with the **A** sentence "All saints are puritans".   This is a universal affirmative sentence, and so to change its
quality we must make it into a negative sentence.   We leave the
quantity unaltered, thus obtaining a universal negative sentence,
that is, a sentence of the **E** form.   Also we negate the predicate,
replacing it by its contradictory "nonpuritans".   The subject we
leave unaltered.   Thus we obtain the new sentence "No saints are
nonpuritans", which is the obverse of our original sentence.   Here
we can see (Figure 16) that the **A** sentence and its obverse are
equivalent.   This is so whether we picture them from the hypothetical or from the existential viewpoint.

If we start with the **E** sentence "No saints are puritans", we
form its obverse by changing the quality from negative to
affirmative and by negating the predicate.   Thus we obtain the
obverse "All saints are nonpuritans".   Here again we can see from
the diagram (Figure 17) how the original sentence and its obverse
are equivalent; we see this whether we picture them from the
hypothetical or from the existential viewpoint.

If we start with the **I** sentence "Some saints are puritans", we
form its obverse by changing it from particular affirmative to
particular negative and negating the predicate.   We obtain "Some

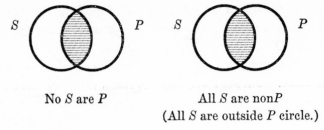

No *S* are *P*   All *S* are non*P*
(All *S* are outside *P* circle.)

Figure 17

saints are not nonpuritans". It is clear (Figure 18) that this is equivalent to our original sentence.

Finally, if we begin with the **O** sentence "Some saints are not puritans", we change from particular negative to particular affirmative and negate the predicate, thus obtaining the obverse "Some saints are nonpuritans". In this case the obverse is so very similar to the original sentence that it almost looks as though no change had taken place. But a change has taken place, for we consider the obverse to be in **I** form and to have the negation as part of its predicate, while the original sentence is in **O** form and has the negation as part of its copula. When we write such sentences, it will help to avoid confusion if "non" is always used to express negation that belongs to the predicate or subject and "not" is reserved to express negation that is part of the copula.

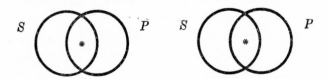

Some *S* are *P*   Some *S* are not non*P*
(Some *S* are not outside *P* circle.)

Figure 18

Contraposition

Suppose we start with an **A** sentence "All *S* are *P*" and obvert it into "No *S* are non*P*", then convert that into "No non*P* are *S*", and finally obvert that into "All non*P* are non*S*". These steps are performed in such a way that each new sentence is equivalent to the previous one. The final result is equivalent to the original, and it is related to the original in a way interesting enough to have a special name. "All non*P* are non*S*" is called the *contrapositive* of "All *S* are *P*". A briefer way of describing how the contrapositive is obtained is to say that the subject and predicate of the original sentence trade places and each is negated. As we see, with the **A** form, the contrapositive is equivalent to the original.

With the **E** form, this process of obverting, converting, then obverting again cannot be carried out without changing the meaning; the second step would involve converting an **A** sentence, and an **A** is not equivalent to its converse. If the original **E** sentence were "No *S* are *P*", its contrapositive would be "No non*P* are non*S*"; this is not equivalent to the original.

If we start with an **I** sentence, obvert it, then convert it, and obvert again, we would likewise find that the meaning is changed. In this case the second step would involve converting an **O** sentence, and the **O** is not equivalent to its converse. Thus the **I** sentence "Some *S* are *P*" is not equivalent to its contrapositive "Some non*P* are non*S*". However, if we start with an **O** sentence, we can obvert, convert, and obvert again without altering the meaning. The **O** sentence "Some *S* are not *P*" is equivalent to its contrapositive "Some non*P* are not non*S*".

Thus we see that, while conversion preserves the meanings of **E** and **I** but not of **A** and **O**, contraposition preserves the meanings of **A** and **O** but not of **E** and **I**.

Symmetry of These Relations

It is worth noticing that the relation between any categorical sentence and its converse is a symmetrical relation: If sentence *r* is the converse of sentence *q*, then sentence *q* is the converse of sentence *r*. That is to say, if we obtain *r* by transposing the subject and predicate of q, then were we to start with r and transpose its subject and predicate the result would be q.

Similarly, the relation between any categorical sentence and its obverse is a symmetrical relation. If r is the obverse of q, then q must be the obverse of r. For example, if q is "All S are P", its obverse r is "No S are non$P$". What is the obverse of r? If we change the quality and negate the predicate of r, we get "All S are non-non$P$", and, letting the double negation in the predicate cancel out, we have "All S are P", which is q. (This sort of double negation cancels out, but we must beware of supposing that two negatives of different types always cancel one another. For example, "No non$S$ are P" is not equivalent to "All S are P".)

Also, the relation between a sentence and its contrapositive is symmetrical. If r is the contrapositive of q, then q is the contrapositive of r. For instance, if q is "All S are P", then r, its contrapositive, is "All non$S$ are non$P$". But what is the contrapositive of r? If we transpose the subject and predicate of r and negate each of them, we obtain "All non-non$S$ are non-non$P$"; letting the double negations within the terms cancel out, we have "All S are P", which is exactly q.

The relation between an **A** sentence and its converse by limitation is not a symmetrical relation, however. Instead it is asymmetrical. If r is the converse by limitation of q, then q never is the converse by limitation of r.

Exercise 6

State in each case how the conclusion is related to the premise (converse, obverse, etc.), and indicate whether the argument is valid, making clear any existential presuppositions that may be required.

1   All birds are flyers. Therefore, all flyers are birds.

2   No pigs are swimmers. Hence all pigs are nonswimmers.

3 No baboons are members of the Senate. Therefore no members of the Senate are baboons.

4 Some hyenas are not courteous creatures. Therefore some courteous creatures are not hyenas.

5 Some snails are not speedy. Therefore some snails are non-speedy.

6 No elephants are unintelligent. Therefore, all elephants are intelligent.

7 Some uninteresting things are not unimportant. Therefore some important things are not interesting.

8 All illiterates are uninformed. Hence, all who are informed are literate.

9 All tricks are fair in love and war. Hence some things fair in love and war are tricks.

By means of what operation or sequence of operations can (**b**) *be derived from* (**a**)? *Make clear any existential assumptions.*

1 (a) No teenagers are registered voters.
(b) All registered voters are nonteenagers.

2 (a) Some stars are enormously hot bodies.
(b) Some enormously hot bodies are not nonstars.

3 (a) No Greek epics are poems on the subject of courtly love.
(b) Some poems on the subject of courtly love are not Greek epics.

4 (a) All things valuable are difficult as they are rare.
(b) Some things that are not valuable are less difficult than they are rare.

5 (a) All insects are nonquadrupeds.
(b) All quadrupeds are noninsects.

6   (a) No animals indigenous to Australia are mammals.

    (b) Some animals indigenous to Australia are nonmammals.

THE SYLLOGISM

The categorical syllogism is a particularly familiar form of reasoning, valuable because arguments encountered in ordinary discourse can very frequently be analyzed in terms of it. An argument is a *categorical syllogism* (or *syllogism,* for short) if and only if it consists of three categorical sentences containing three terms in all, each term appearing in two different sentences. The argument "All Pakistanis are Mohammedans; no Sinhalese are Mohammedans; therefore no Sinhalese are Pakistanis" is an example of a syllogism; it consists of three categorical sentences that contain three different terms, each term appearing in two different sentences.

The term appearing as the predicate of the conclusion (in this case "Pakistanis") is called the *major term* of the syllogism; the term appearing as subject of the conclusion (in this case "Sinhalese") is called the *minor term* of the syllogism; and the term appearing in the premises but not in the conclusion (in this case "Mohammedans") is called the *middle term.* The premise containing the major term is called the *major premise,* and the premise containing the minor term is called the *minor premise.* For the sake of having a standard procedure, let us always put the major premise first, then the minor premise, and last the conclusion.

In order to describe fully the logical form of a syllogism, we need to specify the forms of the categorical sentences in it, and we need to specify how the terms are arranged in these sentences. The example just given is a syllogism whose logical form may be exhibited as follows:

All P **are** M
No S **are** M

$\therefore$ **no** S **are** P

To give the *mood* of a syllogism is to state the categorical forms of its sentences. We mention these in the standard order: major premise, minor premise, conclusion. In our example of a syllogism, its major premise is an **A** sentence, its minor premise is an **E,** and its conclusion is an **E**; therefore this particular syllogism is in the mood **AEE.**

But there is more to say about its form, for other different syllogisms can share with it this mood **AEE.** For instance, a syllogism also is in the mood **AEE** if it has the structure

All *M* **are** *P*
No *S* **are** *M*

∴ **no** *S* **are** *P*

But this sort of syllogism differs from the previous example in an important way because of the different arrangement of its terms; one syllogism is valid, the other invalid. To specify fully the structure of a syllogism, we must say how its terms are arranged within the sentences in which they occur. This is called giving the *figure* of the syllogism.

There are four possible arrangements, four different figures, of syllogisms. We can represent these four figures as follows:

1		2		3		4	
M	*P*	*P*	*M*	*M*	*P*	*P*	*M*
S	*M*	*S*	*M*	*M*	*S*	*M*	*S*
S	*P*	*S*	*P*	*S*	*P*	*S*	*P*

It is easy to remember which figure is which if we think of the positions of the middle term as outlining the front of a shirt collar (Figure 19). The first form of syllogism we considered was **AEE**

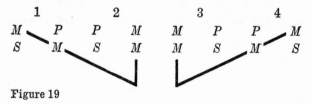

Figure 19

in the second figure; the second form was **AEE** in the first figure.

How many different kinds of syllogisms are possible? There are four possibilities as regards the form of the major premise (**A, E, I, O**), four possibilities as regards the form of the minor premise, four possibilities as regards the form of the conclusion, and four possibilities as regards the figure of the syllogism. This means that there are $4 \times 4 \times 4 \times 4$, or 256, possible forms in all.

How can we tell whether a given form of syllogism is valid? Venn diagrams provide the most straightforward method. The method is this: We draw a diagram showing exactly what the two premises of the syllogism say; then, by looking at it, we can see whether or not the conclusion necessarily follows from those premises.

The syllogism "All Pakistanis are Mohammedans; no Sinhalese are Mohammedans; therefore no Sinhalese are Pakistanis" is in the mood **AEE** and in the second figure, as we saw. To test its validity, we form a diagram showing exactly what the premises say. Since the premises contain three terms, the diagram must show relations among three classes of beings, Pakistanis, Sinhalese, and Mohammedans (Figure 20).

We now imagine that all Mohammedans are herded inside the M circle, no one else and nothing else being allowed inside it; all Pakistanis are placed inside the P circle, no one and nothing else being allowed there; and all Sinhalese are herded inside the S circle, no one and nothing else being allowed there. We must be sure to begin the diagram by drawing three circles that overlap in such a way as to allow for all possible subclasses formed by these three given

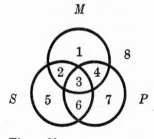

Figure 20

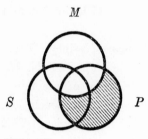

Figure 21

classes. The circles must overlap so as to yield eight distinct regions on the diagram, for there are eight distinct subclasses which we must be able to represent.

Region 1 of the diagram is the location of Mohammedans who are not Sinhalese and not Pakistanis. Region 2 would contain Mohammedans who are Sinhalese but who are not Pakistanis. In region 3 Mohammedans who are Sinhalese and also Pakistanis would be found. Region 4 would contain Mohammedans who are Pakistanis but not Sinhalese. Region 5 is the location of Sinhalese who are neither Mohammedans nor Pakistanis. Region 6 is for Sinhalese who are Pakistanis but not Mohammedans. Region 7 is the place for Pakistanis who are neither Sinhalese nor Mohammedans. And region 8 is occupied by those who are neither Mohammedans nor Sinhalese nor Pakistanis.

The major premise of our syllogism declares that all Pakistanis are Mohammedans. This means that all who are inside the *P* circle are inside the *M* circle, that is, that the part of the *P* circle outside the *M* circle is unoccupied. We indicate this on the drawing by crossing out regions 6 and 7 (Figure 21). The minor premise of the syllogism declares that no Sinhalese are Mohammedans. This means that all who are inside the *S* circle are outside the *M* circle; that is, that part of the *S* circle that is inside the *M* circle is unoccupied. We indicate this by crossing out regions 2 and 3 (Figure 22). We now have a diagram that shows exactly what the premises say, no more and no less.[2]

[2] The premises here have been considered from the hypothetical viewpoint rather than from the existential viewpoint. If one is in doubt about which viewpoint is more appropriate in a given case, it is better to choose the hypothetical, as one then can be confident that one is not reading too much into the argument.

We now inspect the diagram to see whether or not the conclusion validly follows from the premises. According to the diagram, all that part of the S circle which overlaps the P circle is unoccupied; that is, there are no Sinhalese who are Pakistanis. This means that the conclusion validly follows from the premises;

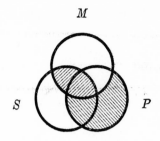

M

S   *P*

Figure 22

if the premises are true, the conclusion must necessarily be true also.

Next let us consider the syllogism "All Moslems are polygamous persons; no Samoans are Moslems; therefore no Samoans are polygamous persons". This syllogism is in the mood **AEE** and in the first figure. To test its validity, we again draw a diagram that will show exactly what the premises say. The major premise tells us that whatever is inside the M circle is inside the P circle, that is, that the part of the M circle outside the P circle is unoccupied. Accordingly we cross out regions 1 and 2 (Figure 23). The minor premise tells us that nothing inside the S circle is inside the M circle, that is, that the part of the S circle overlapping the M circle is unoccupied, and so we add to our diagram by crossing out regions 2 and 3 (Figure 24). Here the completed diagram shows that the syllogism is invalid, for according to the diagram there may or may not be no Samoans who are polygamous persons.

Using the same method, we can deal with the syllogism "No primates are marsupials; some salamanders are marsupials; therefore some salamanders are not primates". This syllogism is in the mood **EIO** and in the

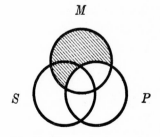

M

S   *P*

Figure 23

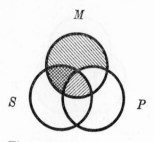

Figure 24

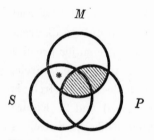

Figure 25

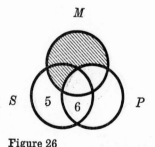

Figure 26

second figure. When we draw its diagram (Figure 25) we find that the diagram shows the syllogism to be valid.

In dealing with the syllogism "All martinets are pusillanimous individuals; some sergeants are not martinets; therefore some sergeants are not pusillanimous individuals", special care must be taken in drawing the diagram. To indicate the major premise is easy (Figure 26). But the minor premise gives trouble, for we wish to indicate on the diagram exactly the information expressed, no less and no more. The minor premise is a particular sentence, and it declares that a certain space on the diagram is occupied. But what space? To put an asterisk in region 5 would be to claim that the premise tells us there are sergeants who are neither pusillanimous nor martinets; this is more than the premise says. To put an asterisk in region 6 would be to claim that the premise tells us there are pusillanimous sergeants who are not martinets; this too is more than the premise says. All the premise says is that there is at least one individual either in region 5 or in region 6 (although there may be individuals in both places).

The best way to draw the diagram is to use a bar instead of an asterisk. We draw a bar touching region 5 and region 6 but no other regions (Figure 27); this we interpret to mean that there is something somewhere in that space touched by the bar. Thus, according to the diagram, there may or may not be sergeants who are pusillanimous; when the premises are true, the conclusion of the syllogism may or may not be true. We see by the diagram that this **AOO** first-figure syllogism is invalid.

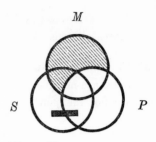

Figure 27

Exercise 7

Determine the mood and figure of each of the following syllogisms and test the validity of each by means of a Venn diagram.

1 All novels by Faulkner are gripping stories. Some novels by Faulkner are novels set in Mississippi. Therefore, some novels set in Mississippi are gripping stories.

2 All chimpanzees that can speak are fascinating creatures. Some university presidents are not fascinating creatures. Hence some university presidents are not chimpanzees that can speak.

3 Some lizards are not dormice, since no dormice are reptiles, and some reptiles are lizards.

4 Some natives of Russia are United States citizens. Therefore,

some natives of Russia are natives of Europe, since some United States citizens are natives of Europe.

5 No mink-lined sneakers are good buys. Some inexpensive articles are not good buys. Therefore, some mink-lined sneakers are not inexpensive articles.

RULES OF THE SYLLOGISM

Venn diagrams provide an efficient and general method for determining the validity of any syllogism. If we were to construct a Venn diagram for each of the 64 possible sets of premises that the 256 possible types of syllogism can have (a tedious but instructive exercise), we would find that the following fifteen forms, based on the notions of mood and figure explained on page 62, are valid from the hypothetical viewpoint.

Figure 1	Figure 2	Figure 3	Figure 4
AAA	EAE	IAI	AEE
EAE	AEE	AII	IAI
AII	EIO	OAO	EIO
EIO	AOO	EIO	

These fifteen forms are also valid from the existential viewpoint. From the existential viewpoint seven additional forms are valid:

Figure 1	Figure 2	Figure 3	Figure 4	Presupposition required
AAI	AEO		AEO	S exist
EAO	EAO			
		AAI	EAO	M exist
		EAO		
			AAI	P exist

In medieval times each valid form of syllogism was given a name, the vowels in the name indicating its mood. Thus **AAA** in the first figure was called *"Barbara"*, and **EAE** in the first figure was called *"Celarent"*. In traditional discussion of the syllogism, the existential viewpoint always was adopted. Some lines of Latin verse were used to help students remember the names of the valid forms:

*Barbara, Celarent, Darii, Ferio*que prioris;
Cesare, Camestres, Festino, Baroco secundae;
Tertia *Darapti, Disamis, Datisi, Felapton,*
Bocardo, Ferison habet; quarta insuper addit
Bramantip, Camenes, Dimaris, Fesapo, Fresison.

These lines omit **AAI** and **EAO** in the first figure, **AEO** and **EAO** in the second, and **AEO** in the fourth. These five forms, though recognized as valid, were looked down upon by medieval logicians. They called these 'weakened' forms, because in each of these five cases a particular conclusion is drawn from premises from which a universal conclusion can validly be derived. Medieval logicians thought it pointless to get a particular conclusion when one could get the universal conclusion instead.

It would be unwise to memorize this list of valid forms; it is far better to remember how to test syllogisms for validity. The Venn diagrams provide one method for testing them. But, on the basis of this list, we can develop another method which does not require pencil and paper. If we study this list of valid forms of syllogism, we can detect certain rules that valid syllogisms obey. One set of rules are these:

1 In any valid syllogism the middle term is distributed at least once.
2 In any valid syllogism no term is distributed in the conclusion unless it is distributed in a premise.
3 No valid syllogism has two negative premises.
4 Any valid syllogism has one negative premise if and only if it has a negative conclusion.

5   No syllogism valid from the hypothetical viewpoint has two
universal premises and a particular conclusion.

If we studied the list of valid forms (which we can justify by
appeal to Venn diagrams), we could prove that each of these rules
is correct. Old-fashioned books on logic used to state such rules
without saying anything about how proof of them could be given.
But these rules are not self-evident and call for proof; using
sixty-four Venn diagrams would be a straightforward way of
proving them.

By studying the list of valid forms, we also could prove some
noteworthy facts about this specific set of rules. Each of the first
four rules states a *necessary* condition for the validity of a
syllogism regarded from the existential viewpoint; taken together,
the conditions stated in these first four rules constitute a *sufficient*
condition[3] for the validity of a syllogism regarded from the existential viewpoint. Moreover, each of the five rules states a necessary condition for the validity of a syllogism regarded from the
hypothetical viewpoint; taken together, these five rules constitute
a sufficient condition for the validity of such a syllogism.

Once we have convinced ourselves of these rules, we may use
them instead of Venn diagrams for checking the validity of specific
syllogisms. To use the rules in testing the validity of a syllogism,
we simply observe whether the syllogism breaks any one of the
rules; if it breaks a rule, it is invalid, whereas if it does not break
any rule, it is valid. A syllogism that violates the first rule is said
to commit the fallacy of *undistributed middle*. A syllogism that
breaks the second rule is said to commit a fallacy of illicit process;

---

[3] By saying that B is a *necessary* condition for C, we mean that nothing
is a case of C without being a case of B. By saying that B is a *sufficient*
condition for C, we mean that anything that is a case of B is a case of C.
For example, being at least thirty years old is a necessary but not a sufficient
condition for being a United States senator. And eating a pint of arsenic
is a sufficient but not a necessary condition for dying.

it is *illicit process of the major* if the major term is distributed in the conclusion but not in the major premise, and it is *illicit process of the minor* if the minor term is distributed in the conclusion but not in the minor premise. No special names need be given to violations of the other rules.

Old-fashioned books usually give also the rule "A syllogism must have only three terms". Violation of this rule was called the fallacy of four terms. It is not necessary to include this rule, since it is part of the definition of a syllogism that it must have just three terms. The fallacy of four terms is a special kind of equivocation (which will be discussed in Chapter 5).

The set of rules stated above has been chosen so as to constitute a brief and easily remembered criterion for the validity of syllogisms. It is instructive to see how further rules can be deduced from the initial set of rules. For example, if we wish to prove that no valid syllogism has two particular premises, we can reason as follows:

Suppose that there were a valid syllogism having two particular premises; its premises would be either (1) two **I** sentences, or (2) two **O** sentences, or (3) an **I** and an **O**. Case 1 is excluded by rule 1, since in two **I** premises the middle term would nowhere be distributed. Case 2 is excluded by rule 3. Case 3 would require the conclusion to be negative, according to rule 4; and in a negative sentence the predicate is distributed, so that by rule 2 the major term would have to be distributed in the major premise. But by rule 1 the middle term also would have to be distributed somewhere in a premise. Yet it is impossible for both the major and the middle term to be distributed, since an **I** and an **O** premise contain only one distributed term altogether. Therefore case 3 is excluded, for it would commit either the fallacy of undistributed middle or the fallacy of illicit process of the major. Hence, the rules imply that there can be no valid syllogism having two particular premises.

Exercise 8

Identify the mood and figure of each syllogism. Test its validity by a Venn diagram. Then check your answer by the rules of the syllogism, and name any fallacy committed that has a name.

1 All juveniles are ineligible to vote. No persons ineligible to vote are eligible to be elected to the school board. Hence, no juveniles are eligible to be elected to the school board.

2 All frogs are amphibians. Hence, some amphibians are not delicious to eat, since some frogs are not delicious to eat.

3 All advocates of socialism are radicals. Some members of the Canadian C.C.F. party are radicals. Therefore, some members of the Canadian C.C.F. party are advocates of socialism.

4 No Christians are polytheists, since no Methodists are polytheists, and all Methodists are Christians.

5 No cars made in the United States are cars with front-wheel drive. Some cars widely sold in the United States are not cars made in the United States. Therefore, some cars with front-wheel drive are widely sold in the United States.

6 Some plays of Shakespeare are histories. No plays commonly read in high schools are histories. Therefore some plays of Shakespeare are not commonly read in high schools.

7 Some people who never read books are college graduates. Some college graduates are well-educated persons. Hence, some well-educated persons are people who never read books.

8 No incubi are poltergeists. All succubi are incubi. Therefore, some succubi are not poltergeists.

Appealing only to the first four rules of the syllogism, prove that the following generalizations hold true of all syllogisms that are valid from the existential viewpoint.

1 If one premise is particular, the conclusion is particular.

2 In the first figure the minor premise is affirmative.

3 In the first figure the major premise is universal.

4 In the second figure the conclusion is negative.

5 In the second figure the major premise is universal.

6 In the third figure the conclusion is particular.

7 In the third figure the minor premise is affirmative.

8 If the major term is the predicate of the major premise, then the minor premise must be affirmative.

9 In the fourth figure, if the conclusion is negative, the major premise must be universal.

10 In the fourth figure, if the minor premise is affirmative, the conclusion must be particular.

Appeal only to the first four syllogistic rules to answer the following questions. Give a proof in each case.

1 In what syllogisms, if any, is the middle term distributed in both premises?

2 Can an invalid syllogism violate all four rules at once?

3 What is the maximum number of rules that an invalid syllogism can violate at once?

4 How many more occurrences of distributed terms can there be in the premises of a valid syllogism than there are in its conclusion?

5 In what valid syllogism is the major term distributed in the major premise but not in the conclusion? Prove that there is just one such syllogism.

6 Can a syllogism be valid from the hypothetical viewpoint but not from the existential viewpoint? Explain.

TRANSLATING INTO CATEGORICAL FORM

So far, we have considered ways of dealing with immediate inferences and syllogisms that are stated in standard form. Very often, however, the arguments met in ordinary discourse are not in standard form, and our logical techniques do not apply to them until we translate them into standard form. For one thing, ordinary arguments usually contain sentences that are not categorical sentences. We cannot begin to apply what we know about the syllogism to such arguments until we have first translated the sentences into equivalent categorical sentences. Any sentence can be translated into categorical form if we exercise ingenuity, and there is always more than one correct way of doing this.[4] Skill at making these translations is useful, for logical relationships between sentences generally are easier to see after the sentences have been expressed in standard categorical form.

First let us examine some of the simpler kinds of cases. "Jaguars are all fast cars" becomes "All Jaguar cars are fast

---

[4] Some philosophers, such as Bertrand Russell, have believed that every assertion has just one essential logical form. They have held, for instance, that a sentence such as "Brutus betrayed Caesar" cannot legitimately be regarded as having the logical form of an **A** sentence; they maintain that this kind of example is essentially relational in form and that the only legitimate way of analyzing it is according to the relational style, which we shall discuss in Chapter 4. But this attitude is misguided. It is only in the context of a specific argument that we can say that a sentence ought to be analyzed as, say, relational rather than categorical. In some other argument the same sentence might properly be analyzed in the opposite fashion.

cars". (Note that it would be misleading to use the translation "All Jaguar cars are fast things". Here the word "fast" has a meaning that is comparative; Jaguars are fast for cars, although they are not fast compared with things like jet planes, rockets, or rays of light.) "Baboons never are courteous" becomes "No baboons are courteous creatures". "There are abstemious Virginians" becomes "Some Virginians are abstemious persons". In each case we try to construct in categorical form a new sentence that is strictly equivalent to the original one.

Sentences containing the verb "to be" in the past tense or future tense can be put into categorical form by moving the tensed verb into the predicate. Thus "Some Elizabethans were great lovers of bear baiting" can become "Some Elizabethans are people who were great lovers of bear baiting"; "No cocker spaniels will be elected to Congress" can become "No cocker spaniels are creatures that will be elected to Congress". These examples illustrate how, in a categorical sentence, the copula is to be understood in a tenseless sense. Also, sentences whose main verbs are verbs other than "to be" can be put into categorical form by transforming the verb into a noun. Thus "No pigs fly" becomes "No pigs are flyers", and "Some men enjoy croquet" can become "Some men are enjoyers of croquet".

Sentences like "Ohio is a state" and "Caesar conquered Gaul" are called *singular* sentences because each speaks about some single individual thing. We cannot translate "Ohio is a state" into "All Ohio is a state" because this has the wrong kind of copula (with "all" the copula should be "are") and because its subject is not a general term. To translate it into "All parts of Ohio are states" would be to alter the meaning. The best way to translate it is this: "Ohio is a state" can become "All things identical to Ohio are states". Thus we get a sentence in proper categorical form that necessarily agrees with the original sentence as regards truth or falsity, since one and only one thing is identical to Ohio (that is,

Ohio itself). Similarly, "Caesar conquered Gaul" can become "All persons identical to Caesar are conquerors of Gaul". This somewhat cumbersome style of translation is required only for singular sentences, however; it would be pointless to translate "All Jaguars are fast cars" into "All things identical with Jaguars are fast cars".

Sometimes we meet sentences that contain no specific indication as to quantity. Occasionally such sentences are really ambiguous, but more often if we think about them we have no trouble seeing that they mean one thing rather than the other. Thus, someone who says "Bachelors are unmarried" surely means "*All* bachelors are unmarried persons"; but someone who says "Visitors are coming" surely means "*Some* visitors are people coming". Similarly, "An elephant is a pachyderm" surely means "All elephants are pachyderms"; but "A policeman is at the door" means "Some policemen are persons at the door".

Another sort of ambiguity can occur when the word "not" is inserted in the middle of a universal sentence. "All my students are not lazy" might mean "All students of mine are people who are not lazy"; or it might mean "It is not the case that all my students are lazy", that is, "Some students of mine are not lazy persons". These two meanings are very different, and so we must distinguish between them; when we meet a sentence constructed in this ambiguous way we simply have to guess what is in the speaker's mind.

Sentences containing the words "only" and "none but" must be handled carefully. Thus, "Only men attend Calvin Coolidge College" does not mean that all men are attenders of Calvin Coolidge College; what it means is "All persons who attend C.C.C. are men". Similarly, "None but women study nursing" does not mean that all women study nursing; it means "All persons who study nursing are women". In general, "Only S are P" means "All P are S", and "None but S are P" also means "All P are S".

But "only some" has a meaning different from "only" by itself; thus "Only some students at the university attend the college" means "Some university students are attenders of the college and some university students are not attenders of the college". In the same vein, "All except employees are eligible" means "All nonemployees are eligible", and it *suggests*, although it does not necessarily *say*, that no employees are eligible. Similarly, "Anyone is eligible unless he is an employee" means "All non-employees are eligible"; it too suggests, although it does not necessarily say, that no employees are eligible. In general, both "All except S are P" and "Anything is P unless it is S" mean "All non$S$ are P".

For some sentences that look quite unlike categorical sentences we may have to devise entirely new terms before we can put them into categorical form. The sentence "Whenever it rains it pours" does not appear to be categorical, but if we think of it as a sentence about *times*, it can become "All times when it rains are times when it pours". Analogously, the sentence "Whither thou goest I will go" can be understood as referring to places, and it can become "All places where thou goest are places where I will go". However, we have to be alert to the intended meanings of sentences like these, for "Wilbur always sleeps in class" does not mean "All times are times when Wilbur is sleeping in class"; what it surely means is "All times when Wilbur is in class are times when he sleeps". Similarly, "She goes everywhere with him" probably does not mean "All places are places to which she goes with him"; much more likely it means "All places he goes are places she goes with him".

Working out translations such as these is necessary as a preliminary to the syllogistic analysis of ordinary reasoning. But it also has an additional intellectual value, in that it encourages us to learn to understand more accurately what ordinary sentences are saying.

Exercise 9

Translate each of the following sentences into categorical form, interpreting its meaning in the way most likely to be intended.

1 No one is always happy.

2 Lead is always heavy.

3 At least one kind of metal is liquid.

4 There aren't any of my friends that I won't help.

5 There are honest politicians.

6 A Scout does a good deed every day.

7 Blessed are the peacemakers.

8 He who takes up the sword shall perish by the sword.

9 All marriages do not end in divorce.

10 Fido barks.

11 None but the lonely heart can know my sadness.

12 Only a woman would drive like that.

13 Whenever I think of Karl Marx I grow angry.

14 He jests at scars who never felt a wound.

15 No friend is better than a fair-weather friend.

16 The unexamined life is not worthy to be lived by man.
                                                    SOCRATES

17 He who knows only his own side of the case, knows little of that.   JOHN STUART MILL

18 Whosoever loveth me loveth my hound. SIR THOMAS MORE

*In each case, (**b**) is a proposed translation of (**a**) into categorical form. Decide whether each translation is correct. If any is incorrect, explain why.*

1 (**a**) American warships are in the Mediterranean.
  (**b**) All American warships are things in the Mediterranean.

2 (**a**) Only the brave deserve the fair.
  (**b**) All brave persons are deservers of the fair.

3 (**a**) A Great Dane is a big dog.
  (**b**) All Great Danes are big dogs.

4 (**a**) Every mistake is not due to ignorance.
  (**b**) All mistakes are things not due to ignorance.

5 (**a**) None but those who love virtue love angling.
  (**b**) All lovers of angling are lovers of virtue.

6 (**a**) It is a wise father that knows his own child.
  (**b**) All wise fathers are knowers of their own children.

7 (**a**) It is sharper than a serpent's tooth to have an ungrateful child.
  (**b**) All persons having ungrateful children are persons who suffer more sharply than do those bitten by serpents' teeth.

8 (**a**) He and she do everything together.
  (**b**) All things are things he and she do together.

TRANSLATING INTO SYLLOGISTIC FORM

Not all arguments can properly be interpreted as syllogisms. However, many arguments not in syllogistic form can be analyzed for validity by being translated into syllogisms. That is, their premises and conclusions admit of being translated into equivalent sentences that constitute syllogisms, and the validity of these arguments stands or falls with that of the syllogisms into which they are translated. By translating such arguments into standard syllogistic form, we make it easier to test their validity by means of Venn diagrams, and we make it possible to test their validity by means of the rules of the syllogism.

There are two different respects in which an argument that can be translated into a syllogism may at first fall short of being in explicit syllogistic form. The argument may at first contain sentences that are not categorical sentences, or it may at first contain more than three terms. We have already discussed translating sentences into categorical form. Now we must consider how to deal with syllogistic arguments that contain too many terms.

Suppose we have an argument that is like a syllogism (that is, it contains three sentences and talks about just three classes of things) but contains too many terms, some of these terms, however, being negations of others. Whenever this happens, we can use immediate inference to eliminate some of the terms, replacing the original sentences by equivalent new ones. For instance, the argument "No millionaires are paupers; no stars of television are nonmillionaires; therefore no stars of television are paupers" as it stands is not in syllogistic form. But we can put it into syllogistic form without difficulty once we notice that two of its terms are negations of each other. The easiest thing to do is to obvert the second premise. We then obtain "No M are P; all S are M; therefore no S are P". This syllogism is **EAE** in the first figure, and since it fulfills all the rules, it is a valid syllogism.

Notice that it would have been an error to have called the original argument invalid because it contains two negative premises. The rule that an argument with two negative premises is invalid applies only to syllogisms in standard form. We must translate this argument into syllogistic form before we attempt to judge it by means of the rules; when we put it into syllogistic form, we find that it is valid.

Immediate inference allows us to reword an argument so as to reduce the number of terms, when some are negations of each other. But sometimes a deeper rewording of the argument is required, if we are to put it into syllogistic form. Where this is so, we must be judicious about selecting our terms, trying to word it so that we have just three terms in all, each of which appears in two different sentences of the argument. For instance, the argument "The car doesn't start easily when the temperature is below zero; it will be below zero tomorrow, and so tomorrow I'll have trouble starting" does not look much like a syllogism. Yet we can put it into syllogistic form if we select our terms judiciously. One way of doing it is this: "All days when the temperature falls below zero are days when the car does not start easily; all days identical to tomorrow are days when the temperature falls below zero; therefore, all days identical to tomorrow are days when the car does not start easily". Here we have **AAA** in the first figure.

Exercise 10

Put each of the following arguments into syllogistic form, state its mood and figure, and then test its validity by means of a Venn diagram and by the rules of the syllogism.

1   Some Mormons are polygamous. All who are not Mormons are not saints. Therefore, some saints are polygamous.

2   All Methodists are puritanical. It is not the case that no Methodists are sinners. Therefore, some sinners are puritanical.

3   All primates are marsupials. Therefore, some salamanders are nonprimates, since every marsupial is a nonsalamander.

4   No priest is married. Some senators are married. Therefore, some who are not priests are senators.

5   All Mexicans are patriotic. Only those who are not slaves are Mexicans. Thus, no slaves are patriotic.

6 Some Sumatrans were not loyal to President Sukarno even though they did not favor the regime of Dr. Sjafruddin Prawiranegara. The proof of this is that none of the followers of Colonel Barlian favored the regime of Dr. Sjafruddin Prawiranegara, yet not all the followers of Colonel Barlian were loyal to President Sukarno.

7 Only an idiot would drink paint thinner. But Wilbur is an idiot, and so he would do it.

8 Wherever the soil is very acid, flowers will not grow. But flowers grow beautifully in your garden, and so the soil cannot be very acid there.

9 You cannot convict somebody of murder just on circumstantial evidence. There is nothing but circumstantial evidence against the butler. Thus the butler cannot be convicted of murder.

RELATED TYPES OF ARGUMENT

The Sorites

We can make use of what we know about syllogisms in order to analyze arguments that consist of chains of syllogisms. When an argument has more than two premises, sometimes two of the premises can be combined to yield a syllogistic conclusion that, when combined with another premise, yields a syllogistic conclusion that, when combined with another premise, . . . yields the final conclusion. An argument of this type is called a *sorites* (from the Greek word for a pile). In order to show that a sorites is valid, we must show how it is possible to pass, by means of a series of valid syllogistic steps, from the premises to the conclusion. We use our ingenuity in order to fit together the links of the chain, testing each link by means of a Venn diagram or by the rules of the syllogism. For example, consider the argument:

Some of my uncles are really worth listening to on military subjects.
No one can remember the battle of San Juan Hill unless he is very old.
No one is really worth listening to on military subjects unless he can
  remember the battle of San Juan Hill.
Therefore, some of my uncles are very old.

This can be symbolized:

Some U are W	(1)
All R are O	(2)
All W are R	(3)
Therefore some U are O	(4)

Here (1) and (3) can be combined to make a syllogism of the form
AII in the first figure whose conclusion, "Some U are R", can
then be combined with (2) to make a syllogism again of the form
AII in the first figure whose conclusion is (4). Thus we show
that the original premises validly yield the desired result.

The method just employed is a method for establishing the
validity of a valid sorites. Suppose, however, that in a given case
we try to pass, by means of syllogistic steps, from the premises to
the conclusion but do not succeed in doing so. This may lead us to
suspect that the sorites is invalid, but just by itself our failure does
not definitely *prove* that the sorites is invalid; perhaps we simply
have not been ingenious enough. To prove that the sorites is
invalid by using our present method, we would have to investigate
every possible sequence in which the premises might be combined,
and we would have to show that *none* of those sequences validly
yields the conclusion.

Further Uses of Venn Diagrams

Some arguments that cannot be translated into syllogisms or
into chains of syllogisms can nevertheless be tested by means of
Venn diagrams. Consider the argument "All who detest Tchaikovsky admire either Bach or Mozart (or both); some who detest

Tchaikovsky do not admire Mozart; therefore, not all who admire Bach admire Mozart". Here we have an argument which is not valid as a syllogism, for if we think of the argument as containing just three terms, its premises are not all in categorical form, while if we think of its premises in categorical form, there are too many terms. But we would be too hasty if we assumed this argument to be invalid just because it is not a valid syllogism; this argument is not supposed to be a syllogism. It is the kind of argument, however, whose validity can be tested by means of a Venn diagram, since it deals with just three classes of individuals and makes appropriately simple assertions about them. We shall indicate on the diagram exactly what the premises say; then by inspecting the diagram we shall be able to tell whether the conclusion follows.

Here we need three circles representing, respectively, those who detest Tchaikovsky, those who admire Bach, and those who admire Mozart. The first premise declares that all individuals inside the *DT* circle are either inside the *AB* or inside the *AM* circles; that is, there are none inside the *DT* circle but outside both *AB* and *AM* circles (Figure 28). The second premise makes the added claim that some individuals inside the *DT* circle are outside the *AM* circle (Figure 29). Inspecting the diagram, we see that the conclusion that not all inside the *AB* circle are inside the *AM* circle validly follows from these two premises.

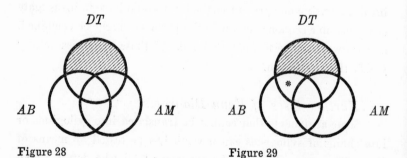

Figure 28   Figure 29

Exercise 11

Use appropriate methods to establish the validity of the argument or to answer the question in each case. Is there any case where the result depends upon whether the existential rather than the hypothetical viewpoint is adopted?

1 Some people are tolerated in polite society even though their manners are not beyond reproach. No one is tolerated in polite society who insists upon drinking the blood of infants. All werewolves insist upon doing just that. Therefore, some people whose manners are not beyond reproach are not werewolves.

2 All the bright students who get high grades are hard-working. Some students who get high grades are either bright or hard-working. Therefore, some students who get high grades are hard-working.

3 No one plays the harpsichord unless he is an intellectual. All dolphins are intellectuals, but they cannot read music. Only those who can read music play the harpsichord. Therefore, dolphins do not play the harpsichord.

4 Every Cypriot is either Turkish or Greek. There are non-Turkish Cypriots. Therefore, some non-Turkish Cypriots are Greek.

5 The regulations of Calvin Coolidge College contain these requirements:
All students must take logic.
All premedical students must take physics.
No one may take physics without taking the calculus.
Only those who do not take the calculus may take logic.
Would you advise a young man who wants to be a doctor to enroll at Calvin Coolidge College?

6 Derive from these three sentences a valid conclusion that follows only from all three sentences together:

Feathers of the moa bird cannot be bought for money.
Nothing is sold by barrow boys but what can be had for a song.
Anything can be bought for money that can be had for a song.

7 Derive a valid conclusion using all these premises:
Any person likely to cause trouble in cramped quarters is dangerous aboard a space capsule.
Infants are always noisy.
All distracting companions are likely to cause trouble in cramped quarters.
No one who would be dangerous aboard a space capsule is suitable as an astronaut for the trip to the moon.
Any noisy person is a distracting companion.

Translate each argument into the form of a syllogism or sorites, and test its validity.

1 Some . . . have . . . expressed themselves in a manner . . . of imagining the whole of virtue to consist in singly aiming, according to the best of their judgment, at promoting the happiness of mankind in the present state; and the whole of vice in doing what they foresee, or might foresee, is likely to produce an overbalance of unhappiness in it: than which mistakes, none can be conceived more terrible. For it is certain, that some of the most shocking instances of injustice, adultery, murder, perjury, and even of persecution, may, in many supposable cases, not have the appearance of being likely to produce an overbalance of misery in the present state; perhaps sometimes may have the contrary appearance.

BISHOP BUTLER, *Analogy of Religion*

2 How can anyone maintain that pain is always evil, if he admits that remorse is painful yet is sometimes a real good?

3 Speculative opinions . . . and articles of faith . . . which are required only to be believed, cannot be imposed on any church by the law of the land. For it is absurd that things should be enjoined by laws which are not in men's power to perform.   And to believe this or that to be true does not depend upon our will.   LOCKE, *A Letter Concerning Toleration*

4   Philosophy must possess complete certitude.   For since philosophy is a science, its content must be demonstrated by inferring conclusions with legitimate sequence from certain and immutable principles.   Now, that which is inferred by legitimate sequence from certain and immutable principles is thereby certain and cannot be doubted. . . . Hence, since there is no room for doubt in philosophy, which is a science, it must possess complete certitude.

WOLFF, *Preliminary Discourse on Philosophy in General*

5   The governments, not only the military ones, but the governments in general, could be, I do not say useful, but harmless, only in case they consisted of infallible, holy people. . . . But the governments, by dint of their very activity, which consists in the practice of violence, are always composed of elements which are the very opposite of holy,—of the most impudent, coarse, and corrupted men.   For this reason every government . . . is a most dangerous institution in the world.

TOLSTOI, "Patriotism and Government"

3. *The Logic of Truth Functions*

ARGUMENTS CONTAINING COMPOUND SENTENCES

We may think of every argument as having two parts. One part consists of those words which make up its logical skeleton, that is, its logical form or structure; the other part consists of those words which are the flesh with which the skeleton is filled out and clothed. For instance, (1) is an argument, and (2) is its logical skeleton:

All spiders are eight-legged.	(1)	All . . . are # # # (2)
No wasps are eight-legged.		No***are # # #
Therefore no wasps are spiders.		∴ no***are . . .

In argument (1) the words "all", "no", and "are" make up the logical skeleton, while the words "spiders", "wasps", and "eight-legged" are the flesh with which the skeleton happens to be filled out. Notice that (1) is a valid argument; it is valid *because* (2) is a valid kind of skeleton. To say that (2) is a valid kind of skeleton or logical form is to say that *any* argument having this same form will have a true conclusion if its premises are true. That is, whatever word or phrase we insert for ". . .", whatever word or phrase we insert for "# # #", and whatever word or phrase we insert for "***", we never can turn (2) into an argument having true premises but a false conclusion.

All the arguments dealt with in Chapter 2 had one important feature in common. They all were like (1) in that their logical skeletons had gaps that were to be filled by single words or phrases which we called general terms and symbolized by means of capital letters. However, not all arguments are like this. Consider argument (3) and its skeleton (4):

This is a wasp or this is a spider. (3)	# # # or . . . (4)
This is not a wasp.	Not # # #
―――――――――――――――――	―――――――――
Therefore this is a spider.	∴ . . . . .

Argument (3) is valid too, but notice the difference between (4) and (2). The gaps in skeleton (4) must be filled not by single words or phrases but by whole sentences. In argument (3) the sentences which happen to fill these gaps are the sentences "This is a wasp" and "This is a spider". Notice also that in analyzing this argument we must think of the first premise not as a categorical sentence but rather as a compound sentence; only by thinking of it in this way can we see what makes the argument valid. We shall now become acquainted with some of the main kinds of arguments that contain compound sentences like this, arguments whose fleshly parts are whole sentences.

Negation

The simplest way of forming a compound sentence is by prefixing the words "It is not the case that". The sentence "It is not the case that wasps are spiders" is a compound sentence, for it contains within itself the simpler sentence "Wasps are spiders". We say that the former sentence is the *negation* of the latter sentence. The single word "not" can be used instead: "Wasps are

not spiders" is another way of expressing the negation of "Wasps
are spiders". But notice that the word "not" is not as reliable in
forming negations as is the phrase "It is not the case that". "Some
wasps are not spiders" is *not* the negation of "Some wasps are
spiders"; the negation of the latter sentence should be expressed
"It is not the case that some wasps are spiders", and that is
equivalent to "No wasps are spiders".

Since the negation (also called the *contradictory*) of a given
sentence should deny just what the sentence says, no less and no
more, it is clear that the negation of the negation of a sentence will
be equivalent to the original sentence itself. This provides us with
one extremely simple form of argument that involves negation
only. From now on, in representing the forms of compound
sentences, we shall stop using cumbersome dots, dashes, and
asterisks; instead, we shall use the letters "p", "q", and "r", which
are to be thought of as doing just the same job, that is, marking
places where sentences may be filled in.

DOUBLE NEGATION

Not (not p)   e.g., It is not the case that wasps are not insects.
∴ p Therefore wasps are insects.

Notice, however, that we cannot use the principle of double
negation indiscriminately to cancel out negations. From "It is not
the case both that there will not be rain and that there will not be
snow" we are not entitled to infer "There will be rain and there
will be snow". This is an example of a misuse of the principle of
double negation.

A MISUSE OF DOUBLE NEGATION

Not (not p and not q)
∴ p and q

Here the mistake is that our premise is the negation of an "and"
sentence rather than the negation of a negation. To avoid

mistakes like this, we need to pay close attention to the logical forms of the expressions with which we deal. The position of a negation can make a great difference to the meaning. As another example, we have to distinguish among

Not (p or q)	e.g., It is not the case that it will either rain or snow.
Not p or q	e.g., It will not rain or it will snow.
Not p or not q	e.g., It will not rain or it will not snow.

Here are three different forms of sentence which say three different things. They are not equivalent; that is, they do not necessarily need to be alike as regards truth or falsity.

Disjunction

A compound sentence consisting of two simpler sentences linked together by "or" (or by "either . . . or . . .", which means just the same) is called a *disjunction* (or an *alternation*). A disjunction is symmetrical, in the sense that "p or q" always is equivalent to "q or p". We can rewrite our earlier skeleton (4) using letters:

DISJUNCTIVE ARGUMENT

p or q	also: p or q	e.g., It will rain or it will snow.
Not p	not q	It will not rain.
∴ q	∴ p	Therefore it will snow.

These forms of disjunctive argument are valid because the first premise tells us that at least one component is true, while the second premise tells us that a certain component is not true; it follows that the other component must be true.

Sometimes there is an ambiguity about the word "or". When we say "p or q", sometimes we mean "p or q but not both". This is called the *exclusive* sense of "or". More often when we say "p or q", we mean "p or q or perhaps both". This is the *nonexclusive* sense of "or". In ordinary conversation, if a gentleman says to a lady in a tone of acquiescence "I'll buy you a Cadillac or a mink coat", he is surely using "or" in the nonexclusive sense, since she cannot accuse him of breaking his promise if he should give her both. Cases of the exclusive sense of "or" occur, though more rarely. If a father says to his child in a tone of refusal "I'll take you to the Zoo or to the beach", then the father can be accused of breaking his word if he takes the child both places.

Ordinarily, unless we have some reason to the contrary, we shall interpret the word "or" in the nonexclusive sense so that we can be sure of not taking too much for granted. Therefore, we regard the following two forms of argument as invalid:

INVALID DISJUNCTIVE ARGUMENTS

p or q	p or q	e.g., **Mary will sing or play.**
p	q	**She will sing.**
∴ not q	∴ not p	**Therefore she will not play.**

These forms would be valid if "or" were understood in the exclusive sense, but they are invalid when "or" is understood in the commoner nonexclusive sense.

Conjunction

A compound sentence consisting of two simpler sentences linked by the word "and" is called a *conjunction*. Sometimes, as in the sentence "They got married and had a baby", the word "and" is used to mean "and then". But other times, as in the sentence "I like cake and I like candy", the word "and" is simply used to join together two assertions. This latter sense of "and" is the more important one for logic. When "and" is used in this weaker sense, conjunctions are symmetrical; that is, "p and q" is then equivalent to "q and p". In English, various other words, such as "but" and "although", often do essentially the same logical job as "and". One absurdly simple but perfectly valid form of conjunctive argument is this:

VALID CONJUNCTIVE ARGUMENT (*simplification*)

p and q

$\overline{\therefore p}$

e.g., **It will rain and snow.**

Therefore it will rain.

The following examples are a more interesting kind of valid conjunctive argument.

VALID CONJUNCTIVE ARGUMENTS

Not (p **and** q)

p

$\overline{\therefore \textbf{not } q}$

e.g., **He will not give her both gems and a car.**

He is giving her gems.

Therefore he will not give her a car.

Not (p **and** q)

q

$\overline{\therefore \textbf{not } p}$

e.g., **It will not both rain and snow.**

It will snow.

Therefore it will not rain.

The following forms, however, are invalid:

INVALID CONJUNCTIVE ARGUMENTS

Not (p **and** q)

Not p

$\overline{\therefore q}$

e.g., **Joe and Ted won't both come.**

Joe won't come.

Therefore Ted will come.

Not (p **and** q)

Not q

$\overline{\therefore p}$

e.g., **He won't give her both love and money.**

He won't give her money.

Therefore he'll give her love.

Conditionals

Another important kind of compound sentence involves the word "if". A sentence consisting of two simpler sentences linked by the word "if" (or by the words "if . . . then ###") is called a *conditional*, or *hypothetical*, sentence. The part that follows the "if" is called the antecedent of the conditional, and the part that follows the "then" is called the *consequent*. In English, conditional sentences may be formulated in a variety of ways so as to be equivalent to "if" sentences. Consider the following formulations, all of which are equivalent:

If Jones is a senator, then he is over thirty.	If p then q
If Jones is a senator, he is over thirty.	If p, q
Jones is over thirty if he is a senator.	q if p
Jones is over thirty provided he is a senator.	q provided p
Jones is a senator only if he is over thirty.	p only if q
Jones is not a senator unless he is over thirty.	Not p unless q
Unless he is over thirty Jones is not a senator.	Unless q, not p

Here, in each sentence, "Jones is a senator" is the antecedent, and "Jones is over thirty" is the consequent. Each of these equivalent sentences claims that the antecedent expresses a *sufficient* condition for the consequent (being a senator is sufficient to guarantee being over thirty) and claims that the consequent expresses a *necessary* condition for the antecedent (being over thirty is necessary to being a senator).

If the antecedent and consequent trade places in a conditional sentence, we obtain the *converse* of our original sentence. Thus "If Jones is over thirty, then he is a senator" is the converse of "If Jones is a senator, then he is over thirty". In general, "if q then p" is the converse of "if p then q". Clearly, the converse is a new and different sentence that need not agree with the original as regards truth or falsity.

If, in a conditional sentence, antecedent and consequent trade places and also each of them is negated, we obtain the *contrapositive* of the original sentence. "If Jones is not over thirty, then he is not a senator" is the contrapositive of "If Jones is a senator, then he is over thirty". In general, "if not q then not p" is the contrapositive of "if p then q". The contrapositive always is equivalent to the original sentence.

Now let us consider some arguments containing conditional sentences.

MODUS PONENS

If p then q	e.g., If Ted comes, Jim goes.
p	Ted is coming.
$\therefore q$	Therefore Jim is going.

MODUS TOLLENS

If p then q	e.g., If Ted comes, Jim goes.
Not q	Jim is not going.
$\therefore$ not p	Therefore Ted is not coming

Somewhat similar, but invalid,[1] is the following:

FALLACY OF AFFIRMING THE CONSEQUENT

If p then q	e.g., If he wants to marry me, he'll give me mink.
q	He is giving me mink.
$\therefore p$	Therefore he wants to marry me.

FALLACY OF DENYING THE ANTECEDENT

If p then q	e.g., If the car runs it has gas.
Not p	The car does not run.
$\therefore$ not q	Therefore the car does not have gas.

Another valid form has three conditional sentences, the consequent of the first being the same as the antecedent of the second:

CHAIN ARGUMENT (*or hypothetical syllogism*)

If p then q	e.g., If Hugo comes, Jay goes.
If q then r	If Jay goes, Wilbur goes.
$\therefore$ if p then r	Therefore if Hugo comes, Wilbur goes.

---

[1] We say that arguments of this form are invalid because, for the present, we are considering only *deductive* reasoning. However, such arguments are not always fallacious when they are intended as *inductive* arguments. In inductive reasoning the speaker claims only that his premises help to make his conclusion reasonable to believe; it may be legitimate to make this weaker claim in connection with some arguments of this form and of other forms that are classified as deductively fallacious.

We can also construct even longer chain arguments with any number of premises. The one requirement for a valid chain argument is that the consequent of the first premise must serve as the antecedent of the next, the consequent of that premise as the antecedent of the next, and so on, while the conclusion must have the first antecedent as its antecedent and the last consequent as its consequent.

Another style of argument involving a conditional premise goes by the name of *reductio ad absurdum* (Latin: "reduction to the absurd"). Suppose, for example, that we want to prove that there is no largest integer (by an integer we mean a positive whole number). We may reason as follows: If there is an integer larger than every other integer, then (because adding one to it will yield a still larger integer) it is not an integer larger than every other integer. From this it follows that there is not a largest integer.

REDUCTIO AD ABSURDUM

If p then not p	e.g., **If there is a largest integer, then there is not a largest integer.**
$\therefore$ **not** p	Therefore it is not the case that there is a largest integer.

This style of reasoning may seem puzzling, because one is inclined to think that a sentence of the form "If p then not p" says something impossible, something necessarily false. However, that is a mistake. A sentence of the form "If p then not p" can very well be true, but only if its antecedent is false. This is why the reasoning is valid: The premise tells us that the truth of the antecedent would carry with it a consequent inconsistent with the truth of the antecedent. Thus the antecedent is 'reduced to absurdity', and this entitles us to conclude that the antecedent is false.

Very similar is a kindred form of *reductio ad absurdum* argument where the premise is a conditional whose consequent is a contradiction:

REDUCTIO AD ABSURDUM *(another form)*

	e.g., If I get home before dark, then I'll both have traveled at 90 miles per hour (for it is 90 miles, and one hour till dark) and not
If *p* then both *q* and not *q*	traveled at 90 miles per hour (for at that speed I'd crash before arriving).
∴ not *p*	Therefore I won't get home before dark.

Here the premise is a conditional whose consequent is necessarily false, but that does not prevent the premise as a whole from being a true sentence. The antecedent is 'reduced to absurdity'; this allows us to infer that it is false.

Dealing with Examples

When we meet an argument that is expressed in ordinary language, we can try to translate it into one of the standard forms with which we are now becoming familiar. If it can be put exactly into one of these forms, we can then tell whether it is valid. For instance, we can handle an example as follows:

Hugo comes only if Jack does not come. ⟶	If *H* then (not *J*)
Hugo is coming. ⟶	*H*
Therefore Jack is not coming. ⟶	(not *J*)

Here the arrows merely connect each sentence with its symbolization. We use capital letters to abbreviate the sentences. (We shall not use the small letters "*p*", "*q*", and "*r*" to abbreviate particular sentences; they will be reserved to represent general logical forms.) This argument is seen to be a case of modus ponens, because its first premise is a conditional and its second premise is the same as the antecedent of the conditional while its conclusion is the same as the consequent of the conditional. Since it is a case of modus ponens, we know that it is valid.

Here is another example:

If John plays, Hugo dances.	⟶ If M then J
If John does not play, Mary will not sing.	⟶ If J then H
Therefore Mary does not sing unless Hugo dances.	⟶ If M then H

Here we have replaced the second premise by its contrapositive, letting double negations cancel out; also we have changed the order of the premises. We are entitled to do these things, because replacing a premise by something equivalent to it does not affect the force of the argument, nor does rearranging the order of the premises. Since this argument is now in the standard form of a chain argument, we know that it is valid.

The Dilemma

The *dilemma* is a type of argument that combines conditional and disjunctive sentences in a special way, which we shall now illustrate.

SIMPLE CONSTRUCTIVE DILEMMA

If p then q	e.g., If he gives her mink, he loves her.
If r then q	If he gives her a Cadillac, he loves her.
p or r	He will give her either mink or a Cadillac.
$\therefore q$	Therefore he loves her.

SIMPLE DESTRUCTIVE DILEMMA

	e.g., If he graduates, he'll have passed physics.
If p then q	If he graduates, he'll have passed biology.
If p then r	Either he won't pass physics or he won't
Not q or not r	pass biology.
$\therefore$ not p	Therefore he will not graduate.

COMPLEX CONSTRUCTIVE DILEMMA

	e.g., If he proposes to Jane, Jane will marry him.
If p then q	If he proposes to Esme, Esme will marry him.
If r then s	Either he will propose to Jane or he will pro-
p or r	pose to Esme.
$\therefore q$ or s	Therefore either Jane or Esme will marry
	him.

COMPLEX DESTRUCTIVE DILEMMA

	e.g., If he's young, he'll be handsome.
If p then q	If he's rich, he'll give presents.
If r then s	Either he won't be handsome or he won't
Not q or not s	give presents.
∴ not p or not r	Therefore either he's not young or he's not rich.

Dilemmas have often been used by debaters, and they were a formidable weapon in the rhetoric of the ancients. Often dilemmas whose overall logical form is valid nevertheless contain logical flaws that prevent them from being good arguments. (This point will be discussed in the section on pure fallacies in Chapter 5.) A valid constructive dilemma is like a double use of modus ponens, while a valid destructive dilemma is like a double use of modus tollens. A dilemma is invalid if it resembles the fallacy of affirming the consequent or of denying the antecedent.

INVALID DILEMMA

	e.g., If Hugo gets all the answers right, he'll pass
If p then q	the test.
If r then not q	If he gets them all wrong, he'll fail the test.
q or not q	He will either pass or fail.
∴ p or r	Therefore he'll either get all the answers right or all the answers wrong.

If your opponent in a debate presents a dilemma whose conclusion you do not want to accept but which you cannot refute, you are said to be 'caught on the horns of a dilemma'. If you succeed in refuting his argument by showing that the disjunctive premise is not true, then you 'escape between the horns of the dilemma'.

Exercise 12

Which of the following sentences are equivalent to "If Clovis loves Mavis, then he will buy her mink"?

1   If Clovis doesn't love Mavis, then he won't buy her mink.

2   Clovis won't buy Mavis mink if he doesn't love her.

3 Clovis will buy Mavis mink unless he doesn't love her.

4 Clovis loves Mavis unless he isn't buying her mink.

5 Clovis isn't buying Mavis mink only if he doesn't love her.

6 Clovis loves Mavis but he isn't buying her mink.

7 Clovis will buy Mavis mink provided he loves her.

8 Clovis loves Mavis only if he'll buy her mink.

9 If Clovis is going to buy Mavis mink, he loves her.

10 If Clovis loves Mavis, he'll buy her mink.

11 Clovis will buy Mavis mink if he loves her.

12 Clovis will buy Mavis mink only if he doesn't love her.

13 In case Clovis doesn't love Mavis, he won't buy her mink.

Abbreviate each argument using the suggested letters, translate it into some familiar form, and state whether it is valid.

1 Either the fuel tank is empty or the gauge is defective. Since the gauge is defective, it follows that the tank is not empty. (T, G)

2 The famous statue of David either is the work of Michelangelo, or it is by Cellini. But it certainly is not by Cellini. Therefore, it must be the work of Michelangelo. (M, C)

3 Clovis is either hard-working or else very lucky. He is hard-working. Hence he is not very lucky. (H, L)

4 Hugo is either lazy or stupid. But the fact is that he is not lazy. Therefore, he is not stupid. (L, S)

5 Either Herbert will stop smoking cigars or his wife will not live with him. His wife is not going to live with him. Therefore, he will not stop smoking cigars. (S, W)

6 There was fog yesterday, or perhaps it was smoke. You say there definitely was no fog? Then it must have been smoke. (*F*, *S*)

7 The orchestra will not play both Brahms and Tchaikovsky; since they are not going to play Brahms, it follows that they will play Tchaikovsky. (*B*, *T*)

8 It is not the case that Hugo would remarry without first getting a divorce. Since he has not got a divorce, he has not remarried. (*R*, *D*)

9 Jasper will not be invited both to the dinner and to the ball. But he will not be invited to the dinner. Hence, he will be invited to the ball. (*D*, *B*)

10 Gerald would not strangle his wife and also poison her. Since he did poison her, it follows that he did not strangle her. (*S*, *P*)

11 If you did not violate the law, your driving license would not be revoked. However, you must have violated the law, since your license has been revoked. (*V*, *R*)

12 If the testimony of the witness was correct, the defendant was guilty. The defendant was, in fact, guilty. Therefore, the testimony of the witness must have been correct. (*T*, *G*)

13 Hugo would be permitted to study the calculus only if he had already taken analytic geometry. Hugo is being permitted to study the calculus. Therefore, he must already have taken analytic geometry. (*C*, *A*)

14 Your car is not safe to drive unless it has good tires. But your car does have good tires, and so it is safe to drive. (*S*, *T*)

15 Harry cannot get a liquor license unless he has political influence. But he has no political influence at all. Therefore, Harry cannot get a liquor license. (*L*, *P*)

16 Morton's insurance will be paid only if he has died. But he has died. Therefore, his insurance will be paid. (*I*, *D*)

17 We get to class only if the car runs; but if the battery is dead, the car does not run. Thus, if the battery is dead, we do not get to class. (*C*, *R*, *B*)

18 If it does not freeze, there will not be ice. And if there is ice, the streets will be slippery. Thus, if it freezes, the streets will be slippery. (*F*, *I*, *S*)

19 If you construct two different circles having the same radius and going through three of the same points, these circles are not different. Therefore, you cannot construct two different circles having the same radius and going through three of the same points. (*C*)

20 If it rains, the driving will be bad, and if it snows, the driving will be bad. It will either rain or snow, and so the driving will be bad. (*R*, *S*, *D*)   *New rule   p · p = p*

21 If prices do not rise, costs do not rise. But costs do rise, if wages rise. Thus, if wages rise, prices rise. (*P*, *C*, *W*)

22 If Mr. Midas doesn't contribute, the fund won't reach its goal. If the canvassers work hard, half the people will contribute. Either Mr. Midas won't contribute or not half the people will. Therefore, either the fund won't reach its goal or the canvassers won't work hard. (*M*, *F*, *C*, *H*)

TRUTH FUNCTIONS

The types of compound sentences that we have been discussing are called *truth-functional* sentences, because they are compounds whose truth or falsity depends on (is a function of) the truth or falsity of the component sentences. Let us consider more carefully the way in which each type of truth-functional sentence depends upon its components.

Negation

The relation between a negation and the sentence negated is simple: They must be opposite as regards truth and falsity. Using the dash as our symbol for negation, we shall write "$-p$" for "not p". We can use the following little table to express the effect of negating a sentence.

p	$-p$
True	False
False	True

We may replace "p" by whatever sentence we please, and the table will show how our chosen sentence is related to its negation.

Disjunction

The relation between a disjunctive sentence and its components also is straightforward. The disjunction is true whenever at least one of its components is true, and it is false otherwise. Here our table must contain four lines, as there are four possible situations to be considered. Using the wedge as our symbol for (nonexclusive) disjunction, we can abbreviate "p or q" as "$p \lor q$".

p	q	$p \lor q$
True	True	True
False	True	True
True	False	True
False	False	False

Here we may replace "p" and "q" by any sentences we please, and the table will show how they are related to their disjunction.

Conjunction

The way in which a conjunctive sentence is related to its components is also clear. The conjunction is true when both its parts are true; otherwise it is false. Using the ampersand as our symbol, we can abbreviate *"p* and *q"* as *"p* & *q"*.

p	q	p & q
True	True	True
False	True	False
True	False	False
False	False	False

The table shows how any two sentences are related to their conjunction. Thus, for instance, the sentence "It will rain and it will get colder" is true if it rains and also gets colder, but it is false if either one or both of these things fail to happen.

Conditionals

To say that a compound sentence is truth-functional is to say that its truth or falsity depends solely upon the truth or falsity of its component sentences. We have just seen that conjunctive sentences are truth-functional. In order to determine whether the sentence "Ted comes and Jim goes" is true or false, all we need to know is whether "Ted comes" is true or false and whether "Jim goes" is true or false. However, not all compound sentences are truth-functional; for instance, in order to discover whether "Ted comes because Jim goes" is true or false, we need to know more than just whether "Ted comes" is true and whether "Jim goes" is true. The difficulty about conditional sentences is that although the words "if-then" are sometimes used in a truth-functional way, they are often used in ways that are not truth-functional.

Let us consider cases where "if . . . then ###" is truth-functional. Suppose a petulant mother exclaims, "If I've told you once, then I've told you a thousand times". If we write *"O"* for "I have told you once" and write *"T"* for "I have told you a thousand times", then the mother's original remark may be expressed "If *O* then *T";* it is equivalent to "not (*O* & not *T*)". This compound sentence is false if *"O"* is true but *"T"* false (if she told him once but did not tell him a thousand times), and it is true otherwise. Construed in this way, the sentence is truth-functional; its truth or falsity depends solely upon the truth or falsity of its parts.

Let us take another similar example and see exactly what truth function "if . . . then ###" expresses. Suppose someone says "If the Cavaliers win today, then I'm a monkey's uncle". What he is saying can be reworded as "It's not the case both that the Cavaliers win today and that I'm not a monkey's uncle". We can draw up a table for this.

C	*M*	*−M*	*C* & *−M*	*−(C & −M)* *if C then M*
True	True	False	False	True
False	True	False	False	True
True	False	True	True	False
False	False	True	False	True

The four horizontal lines of this truth table represent the four possible combinations of truth and falsity for *"C"* and *"M"*. The first two columns of the table show these possibilities and form the starting point. In the first line, where *"C"* and *"M"* both are true, *"−M"* must be false. Hence *"C* & *−M"* has to be false too. Its negation *"−(C* & *−M)"* must therefore be true; "if *C* then *M*", which means the same, will be true too. In the second line, the reasoning is just the same. In the third line, since *"M"* is false, *"−M"* will be true, and *"C* & *− M"* will be true too. Thus *"−(C* & *−M)"* will be false. In the fourth line, since *"C"* is false,

"*C & −M*" must be false too, and so "*− (C & −M)*" must be true.

What has been said in this particular case holds good in general. The rule is: A truth-functional "if . . . then ###" sentence is false when its antecedent is true and its consequent false and is true otherwise. We represent the truth-functional sense of "if . . . then ###" by means of the horseshoe symbol. Thus, "*p ⊃ q*" will be our way of writing a truth-functional conditional. It is clear from what has been said that "*p ⊃ q*" is equivalent to "*− (p & −q)*".

p	q	$p \supset q$
T	T	T
F	T	T
T	F	F
F	F	T

Notice that if we want to express the negation of "*p ⊃ q*" we must look for a sentence whose truth and falsity are always just the opposite of that of "*p ⊃ q*". The negation of "*p ⊃ q*" can be expressed as "*p & −q*". The form "*p ⊃ −q*" is not equivalent to the negation of "*p ⊃ q*", because "*p ⊃ q*" and "*p ⊃ −q*" do not contradict one another. They might both be true, as will happen if "*p*" is false.

p	q	$p \supset q$	$p \,\&\, {-q}$	$p \supset {-q}$
T	T	T	F	F
F	T	T	F	T
T	F	F	T	T
F	F	T	F	T

However, the words "if . . . then ###" are often used in ways that are not truth-functional. Someone might say, "If you drop this vase, then it will break". He means to assert *more* than merely that it is not the case that you will drop it without its breaking. He means to assert also that dropping it *would cause* it to break. Here we may know the truth and falsity of the

component sentences "You will drop this vase" and "It will break",
yet we may still be in doubt about the truth or falsity of "If you
drop it, it will break". Perhaps we agree that you are not going to
drop it and that it is not going to break; yet still we may disagree
about the truth or falsity of "If you drop it, it will break". A
conditional sentence understood in this way is not truth-functional,
and we lose part of its meaning (that is, we are replacing it by
a weaker sentence) if we symbolize it "$D \supset B$".

However, if we make a practice to use the truth-functional
horseshoe to symbolize conditional sentences, we can usually test
arguments very adequately, for the truth-functional horseshoe
expresses that part of the meaning of conditional sentences which
normally is important as regards the validity or invalidity of
arguments in which conditional sentences occur.

This is usually but not invariably so. Here is an example where
we would be led astray by this procedure. The argument "The vase will
not be dropped; therefore, if the vase is dropped, it will break" is a silly
and invalid argument; but if we blindly symbolized it in the form "$-D$,
therefore $D \supset B$" and then tested its validity by the truth-table method
presented later in this chapter, we would get the incorrect answer that
the argument is valid. In order to get correct results when we replace
non-truth-functional conditionals by the corresponding truth-functional
conditionals that they imply, we should keep in mind the following
principles: If an argument is valid, any argument exactly like it except
for having one or more stronger premises must be valid too; and if an
argument is invalid, then any argument exactly like it except for having
a stronger conclusion must also be invalid.

Biconditionals

A compound sentence is called a *biconditional* if it consists of
two simpler sentences linked by the words "if and only if". When
these words are understood in a truth-functional sense, "p if and
only if q" is symbolized "$p \equiv q$". Of course "p if and only if q"
is equivalent to "p if q, and p only if q"; that is, "$p \equiv q$" is

equivalent to "$(q \supset p) \, \& \, (p \supset q)$". Let us draw up a truth table for the latter expression in order to see what the truth table for the former should be.

p	q	$q \supset p$	$p \supset q$	$(q \supset p) \, \& \, (p \supset q)$	$p \equiv q$
T	T	T	T	T	T
F	T	F	T	F	F
T	T	T	F	F	F
F	F	T	T	T	T

The third and fourth columns of this table are obtained from the first two columns, in light of the rule that a conditional is always true except when its antecedent is true and its consequent false. The fifth column is obtained from the third and fourth, in light of the rule that a conjunction is true when and only when both its parts are true. The last column is copied from the fifth; it shows us that the biconditional is true whenever its components are alike as regards truth and falsity, and it is false whenever they differ.

A biconditional says something stronger than does a single conditional. Thus "You'll pass the course if and only if you pass the examination" promises that passing the examination is necessary *and* sufficient for passing the course. In contrast, the conditional sentence "If you pass the examination, then you'll pass the course" merely says that passing the examination is sufficient, and the other conditional "You'll pass the course only if you pass the examination" merely says that passing the examination is necessary.

GROUPING

When we deal with expressions containing several symbols, it is important to pay careful attention to the grouping of the parts. Changing the grouping of its parts sometimes can entirely alter the meaning of an expression. Therefore, to avoid misunderstanding, whenever we write something that is truth-functionally compound, we should be clear about the intended grouping. We shall use parentheses for this purpose.

Notice, for instance, the difference between "$p \,\&\, (q \vee r)$" and "$(p \,\&\, q) \vee r$". The former is a conjunction one part of which is a disjunction; the latter is a disjunction one part of which is a conjunction. They are not equivalent, for a sentence of the first form would not necessarily agree as regards truth or falsity with a corresponding sentence of the second form. Suppose we replace "p" by the sentence "Phyllis comes", replace "q" by the sentence "Queenie comes", and replace "r" by "Rosa comes"; and let us suppose that Phyllis does not come, that Queenie does not come, but that Rosa does come. Then the compound sentence "Phyllis comes, and either Queenie comes or Rosa comes", which is of the form "$p \,\&\, (q \vee r)$", is false (since Phyllis does not come). But the corresponding sentence "Either both Phyllis and Queenie come or Rosa comes", which is of the form "$(p \,\&\, q) \vee r$" is true (since Rosa does come).

Our example shows that "$p \,\&\, (q \vee r)$" is not equivalent to "$(p \,\&\, q) \vee r$". For this reason, it would be improper to write the expression "$p \,\&\, q \vee r$" without parentheses. This expression is ambiguous, because it might have two quite different meanings. One cannot tell whether it is supposed to be a conjunction, one part of which is a disjunction, or a disjunction, one part of which is a conjunction.

Carelessly written sentences in ordinary language, such as "Phyllis comes and Queenie comes or Rosa comes", are ambiguous in just the same confusing way. But if we are careful to use a comma, the meaning is made clear. Thus, "Phyllis comes, and Queenie comes or Rosa comes" has the logical structure "$p \,\&\, (q \vee r)$", while "Phyllis comes and Queenie comes, or Rosa comes" has the logical structure "$(p \,\&\, q) \vee r$". The comma is one of the devices used in ordinary language to indicate groupings which in our symbolism we indicate by means of parentheses. Another device of ordinary language is the use of pairs of words such as "both . . . and . . .", and "either . . . or . . .", for these can prevent ambiguity of grouping even when no punctuation is present.

Exercise 13

Let "R" mean "it rains", let "C" mean "it gets colder", and let "B" mean "the barometer falls". Match each numbered sentence of the second group with the symbolized sentence from the first group that is equivalent to it. (Hint: Each has exactly one natural mate.)

(a) $R \supset C$	(b) $-R \supset C$
(c) $R \supset -C$	(d) $-R \vee C$
(e) $-(R \vee C)$	(f) $-(R \supset C)$
(g) $-(R \& C)$	(h) $-R \& -C$
(i) $-R \equiv C$	(j) $R \equiv C$
(k) $-(R \equiv C)$	(l) $R \equiv (C \& B)$
(m) $(R \& C) \equiv B$	(n) $R \& (C \equiv B)$
(o) $R \supset (C \equiv B)$	(p) $(R \equiv C) \supset B$
(q) $(-R \vee -C) \supset B$	(r) $R \supset (C \& B)$
(s) $R \supset (C \supset B)$	(t) $(R \& C) \supset B$
(u) $(R \supset C) \supset B$	(v) $(R \supset C) \& B$

1   Unless it doesn't rain, it doesn't get colder.

2   It rains only if it gets colder.

3   It neither rains nor gets colder.

4   It doesn't both rain and get colder.

5   It gets colder unless it rains.

6   It rains if and only if it gets colder.

7   That it gets colder if it rains is not the case.

8 It doesn't rain or it gets colder.

9 It is not the case that it rains if and only if it gets colder.

10 If and only if it doesn't rain, it gets colder.

11 It doesn't rain and doesn't get colder.

12 If it rains it gets colder, and the barometer falls.

13 It rains, and it gets colder if and only if the barometer falls.

14 If it rains, then it gets colder only if the barometer falls.

15 It rains if and only if both it gets colder and the barometer falls.

16 If it rains, then it gets colder and the barometer falls.

17 The barometer falls, provided it rains if and only if it gets colder.

18 If it rains and gets colder, then the barometer falls.

19 If it rains, then it gets colder if and only if the barometer falls.

20 It rains and gets colder, if and only if the barometer falls.

21 If it doesn't rain or doesn't get colder, the barometer falls.

22 The barometer falls, provided that it rains only if it gets colder.

Let "A" be short for "Arizona is a western state", let "B" be short for "Bermuda is an island", let "J" be short for "Jordan is a European country", and let "K" be short for "Kalamazoo is the capital of France". Determine whether each of the following is true.

1	$-A$	**2**	$-(-J)$
3	$A \& K$	**4**	$A \& (K \& B)$
5	$B \vee J$	**6**	$K \vee (J \vee A)$
7	$-B \& J$	**8**	$-A \vee -B$
9	$-(J \vee K)$	**10**	$-(J \& -A)$
11	$A \supset K$	**12**	$-A \supset K$

13 $B \supset -J$ 14 $-A \supset -J$
15 $A \equiv J$ 16 $-K \equiv -J$
17 $(B \& J) \equiv (K \vee -A)$ 18 $(A \& B) \supset (J \vee K)$
19 $(B \equiv J) \supset -K$ 20 $(J \supset A) \equiv (A \supset J)$

CONSTRUCTING TRUTH TABLES

Looking back over what we have learned about the various types of compound sentence, we can formulate these rules:

A *negation* always is opposite to the sentence negated as regards truth and falsity.

A *conjunction* is true if and only if both parts are true.

A *disjunction* is true if and only if at least one part is true.

A *conditional* is false when its antecedent is true and its consequent false; otherwise it is true.

A *biconditional* is true if and only if its parts are alike as regards truth or falsity.

In the light of these rules, we shall be able to construct truth tables for more complex sentences, truth tables that will enable us to answer a variety of kinds of logical questions.

If a truth table for a compound sentence is a complete truth table, it must show whether the sentence is true or false in every possible case, that is, in every possible situation as regards the truth and falsity of its component sentences. The number of possible situations that need to be considered (the number of horizontal lines required in the truth table) depends upon the number of distinct simple components.

In the second section of this chapter we wrote a truth table for "$-p$", which needed just two lines. Similarly a truth table for "$(p \vee -p) \& p$" would have just two lines. Where only the letter "p" is present, the only possibilities to be considered are the truth of "p" and the falsity of "p". A truth table for "$p \vee q$" has to have four lines, and so does a truth table for "$(q \& p) \vee (q \vee p)$".

Here *"p"* may be true or false when *"q"* is true and either true or false when *"q"* is false, making four possibilities. If we were dealing with a compound containing three different letters, there would be eight possibilities to consider and so eight lines in the truth table. In general, each additional letter doubles the number of lines required in the truth table.

In constructing a truth table, it is important to be sure that the lines are arranged so as to take account of just the proper possibilities; using a systematic procedure will help. In drawing up the initial columns, let us follow the practice of alternating the entries in the first column ("T" in the first line, "F" in the second line, etc.), pairing the entries in the second column ("T" in the first and second lines, "F" in the third and fourth lines, etc.), alternating by fours the entries in the third initial column ("T" in the first four lines, "F" in the next four lines, etc.), and so on.

When we are dealing with complicated compounds, it often helps to use auxiliary columns, working step by step to reach the final column in which we are interested. For instance, suppose we want a truth table for "$(r \,\&\, q) \supset (p \equiv r)$". Since this contains three letters, we require eight lines. The compound as a whole is a conditional, one part of which is a conjunction and the other part a biconditional. Here it will be wise to use two auxiliary columns, one for the conjunction and one for the biconditional. Then it will be easy to draw up the final column for the conditional as a whole. The table will look like this:

p	q	r	$r \,\&\, q$	$p \equiv r$	$(r \,\&\, q) \supset (p \equiv r)$
T	T	T	T	T	T
F	T	T	T	F	F
T	F	T	F	T	T
F	F	T	F	F	T
T	T	F	F	F	T
F	T	F	F	T	T
T	F	F	F	F	T
F	F	F	F	T	T

Here the three initial columns have been drawn up in a systematic
fashion so as to take account of exactly the right possibilities. The
fourth and fifth columns are auxiliary columns drawn up by
looking at columns 1, 2, and 3. Then from the fourth and fifth
columns we get the sixth column, the one in which we are interested. The sixth column tells us whether the compound is
true or false in each of the eight possible cases. From the table we
obtain the information that our compound is false only if "*p*" is
false and "*q*" and "*r*" are both true.

USES OF TRUTH TABLES

Truth-functional Implication and Validity

A relation of implication that depends solely upon the
truth-functional forms of the sentences concerned is called a
truth-functional implication. Thus to say that a sentence is
truth-functionally implied by one or more other sentences is to say
that, in virtue of their truth-functional forms, it is logically
impossible for the latter all to be true without the former being
true also. An argument whose premises truth-functionally imply
its conclusion is said to be *truth-functionally valid.*

Truth tables provide a method for telling whether truth-
functional implications hold and whether arguments are truth-
functional implications hold and whether arguments are truth-
table containing a column for each sentence involved in the
implication, or for each premise and the conclusion of the argument. Then we inspect the table line by line to see whether there is
any line in which the supposedly implying sentences are all true
and the supposedly implied sentence false, or whether there is any
line in which all the premises of the argument are true and its
conclusion false. If there is such a line, then the implication does
not hold, or the argument is not truth-functionally valid. If there
is no such line, then the implication holds, or the argument is
truth-functionally valid.

All valid arguments of the forms discussed in the first section of this chapter are truth-functionally valid. Each of them can be shown to be truth-functionally valid by means of a truth table. As an example, let us consider modus ponens. A truth table for a particular argument of this form would contain columns for the two premises, say, "$A \supset B$" and "A", and a column for the conclusion "B". Or we can make the table more general in style by expressing the premises as "$p \supset q$" and "p" and the conclusion as "q". When we do it the latter way, the understanding is that the truth table represents *any* argument of the modus ponens form.

Premise	*Conclusion*	*Premise*
p	*q*	*p* $\supset$ *q*
T	T	T
F	T	T
T	F	F
F	F	T

Since there are just two letters occurring in the argument, we need four lines in the table; we have a column for each premise and one for the conclusion. Now, what does the table show? We see that the first line is the only line in which both premises are true, and in the first line the conclusion is true too. There is no possibility of having the premises all true and the conclusion false. This demonstrates that the premises truth-functionally imply the conclusion, that is, that modus ponens is truth-functionally valid.

Let us treat one more example, the simple destructive dilemma. Can we show by means of a truth table that this form of argument is valid? Here we need columns for the premises "$p \supset q$", "$p \supset r$", and "$-q \lor -r$", and we need a column for the conclusion "$-p$". Since there are three letters, the table must have eight lines. The work is easier if we use some auxiliary columns to help us reach the final ones.

p	q	r	$p \supset q$	$p \supset r$	$-q$	$-r$	$-q \vee -r$	$-p$
T	T	T	T	T	F	F	F	F
F	T	T	T	T	F	F	F	T
T	F	T	F	T	T	F	T	F
F	F	T	T	T	T	F	T	T
T	T	F	T	F	F	T	T	F
F	T	F	T	T	F	T	T	T
T	F	F	F	F	T	T	T	F
F	F	F	T	T	T	T	T	T

Here the fourth and fifth columns are for the first two premises, and we get them from the three initial columns, using the rule for the conditional. The sixth and seventh columns are auxiliary ones taken from the initial columns by using the rule for negation. The eighth column is for the third premise, and we derive it from the sixth and seventh. Then we add a column for the conclusion. Inspection of the completed table shows that only in the fourth, sixth, and eighth lines are all premises true, and in each of these lines the conclusion is true. Hence the table shows this form of argument to be truth-functionally valid.

As a final example of this procedure, let us consider the particular argument:

If matter exists, Berkeley was mistaken.
If my hand exists, matter exists.
Therefore either my hand exists or Berkeley was mistaken.

We may symbolize it:

$M \supset B$
$H \supset M$
$\therefore H \vee B$

Let us test the validity of this argument by means of a truth table.

M	B	H	Premise $M \supset B$	Premise $H \supset M$	Conclusion $H \vee B$
T	T	T	T	T	T
F	T	T	T	F	
T	F	T	F		
F	F	T	T	F	
T	T	F	T	T	T
F	T	F	T	T	T
T	F	F	F		
F	F	F	T	T	F

We are concerned only with the question whether it is possible for
the premises both to be true and the conclusion false, and so any
parts of the table that do not help to answer that question may be
left blank. Thus we leave the fifth column blank in the third and
seventh lines, for we are interested only in lines where both
premises are true. We leave the last column blank in the second,
third, fourth, and seventh lines for the same reason. The eighth
line finally gives a definite answer to our question, for in that line
both premises are true and the conclusion is false. This demonstrates that the argument is not truth-functionally valid.

Truth-functional Equivalence

To say that two sentences are equivalent to one another is to
say that they necessarily are alike as regards truth and falsity; to
say that they are *truth-functionally equivalent* is to say that they
are equivalent simply because of their truth-functional form.
Truth tables provide a method for determining whether sentences
are truth-functionally equivalent. Does a sentence of the form
"— $(p \mathbin{\&} q)$" necessarily agree with a corresponding sentence of the
form "$-p \mathbin{\&} -q$" as regards truth or falsity? We can establish the
answer by constructing a truth table containing a column for each
compound. Then we compare these columns line by line; if they
are alike in every line, the equivalence holds, while if the columns

differ in any line, the equivalence does not hold. (Notice that it would be nonsense to say that two compounds are equivalent in some lines but not in others, because being equivalent means being alike as regards truth and falsity in *all* possible cases.)

Let us draw up a table with a column for each of these compounds; let us also include a column for "$-p \vee -q$" so that it can be compared with the others.

p	q	$p \& q$	$-(p \& q)$	$-p$	$-q$	$-p \& -q$	$-p \vee -q$
T	T	T	F	F	F	F	F
F	T	F	T	T	F	F	T
T	F	F	T	F	T	F	T
F	F	F	T	T	T	T	T

Here the third column is obtained from the first two and serves as an auxiliary column from which we get the fourth column. The fifth and sixth columns come from the first and second; from them we obtain the seventh and eighth. With the table complete, we look at it line by line, and we observe that in the second and third lines "$-(p \& q)$" differs from "$-p \& -q$", the former being true and the latter false. Thus a pair of corresponding sentences of these forms would not be equivalent. However, "$-(p \& q)$" and "$-p \vee -q$" are just alike in each line, which shows that any pair of corresponding sentences of these forms would be equivalent. Speaking more concisely, we shall say that "$-(p \& q)$" and "$-p \& -q$" are not equivalent, while "$-(p \& q)$" and "$-p \vee -q$" are.

Not only is "$-(p \& q)$" equivalent to "$-p \vee -q$", but also "$-(p \vee q)$" is equivalent to "$-p \& -q$", as could be shown by another truth table. These two equivalences are known as *De Morgan's laws*, after the nineteenth-century logician De Morgan. All the various equivalences mentioned earlier in this chapter can be demonstrated by means of truth tables. We can show by truth tables that "p" and "$-(-p)$" are equivalent, that "$p \& q$" and

"$q \mathbin{\&} p$" are equivalent, that "$p \supset q$" and "$-q \supset -p$" are equivalent, and so on. The notion of truth-functional equivalence will be useful in connection with reasoning, for when two sentences are truth-functionally equivalent either one may validly be inferred from the other, since if one is true the other must be true too.

Another slightly more complicated principle concerning truth-functional equivalence also is useful in connection with reasoning. This principle may be illustrated as follows: A sentence of the form "$r \supset -(p \mathbin{\&} q)$" has to be equivalent to a corresponding sentence of the form "$r \supset (-p \lor -q)$", because these two compounds are exactly alike except that where the first contains the component "$-(p \mathbin{\&} q)$" the second contains something equivalent to it. The reasoning behind this is that, since the two short compounds are necessarily alike as regards truth and falsity, replacing one by the other in the longer expression cannot alter the truth table for the longer expression; hence the altered longer expression is necessarily the same as the original longer one as regards truth or falsity. This principle holds in general: Any two longer truth-functional compounds are bound to be equivalent if they are exactly alike except that in one of them a component present in the other has been replaced by something equivalent to it.

Tautology and Contradiction

When we draw up a truth table for a compound sentence or formula, usually we find that it is true in some lines and false in other lines. But occasionally we meet extreme cases; occasionally a compound sentence or formula is true in every line of its truth table. Such a compound sentence or formula is called a *tautology*. Also we occasionally meet a compound sentence or formula that is false in every line of its truth table. Such a compound sentence or formula is a kind of *contradiction*. (Note the difference between a contradiction, an expression that is bound to be false, and contradictories, sentences that are negations of each other and are bound to be opposite in truth and falsity.)

Sentences that are tautologies are a special type of necessarily true sentences; they are sentences whose necessary truth results from their truth-functional form. Sentences that are truth-functional contradictions are a special type of necessarily false sentences. A few examples of forms of sentences that are contradictions are "p & $-p$", "$-(p \lor -p)$", and "$p \equiv -p$". Some examples of tautologies are these: "$p \lor -p$" (sometimes described as "the law of excluded middle", because it reflects the fact that any given sentence must be either true or false, there being no third alternative), "$-(p$ & $-p)$" (which is sometimes described as "the law of contradiction", because it reflects the fact that a sentence cannot be both true and false), "$p \supset p$", and "$p \equiv p$".

To every valid truth-functional argument there corresponds a tautology; the tautology is a conditional whose antecedent is the conjunction of the premises of the argument and whose consequent is the conclusion of the argument. For example, the tautology "$[(p \supset q)$ & $p] \supset q$" corresponds to modus ponens. To say that a form of argument is valid is to say that, if its premises are true, then its conclusion must be true. Under such circumstances the corresponding conditional cannot have a true antecedent and a false consequent and so will necessarily be true, a tautology. Thus we can say that a truth-functional argument is valid if and only if its corresponding conditional is a tautology. Hence another way of testing the validity of a truth-functional argument is to form a conditional whose antecedent is the conjunction of the premises and whose consequent is the conclusion and draw up a truth table for this conditional. If the conditional is a tautology, the argument is valid; if not, it is not valid. However, the method described in the preceding section is a bit simpler.

Exercise 14

Test the validity of the argument, or answer the question, by means of a truth table.

1 It will rain if and only if the wind changes. Therefore, it is not the case that it will rain without the wind changing. (*R, W*)

2 If you are convicted of manslaughter or of drunken driving, then your license will be revoked. But you have not been convicted of manslaughter. Therefore, if your license is being revoked, you have been convicted of drunken driving. (*M, D, L*)

3 If you enjoy both Hemingway and Dos Passos, then you would enjoy Faulkner. But you do not enjoy Faulkner. Therefore, if you enjoy Hemingway, you do not enjoy Dos Passos. (*H, D, F*)

4 If you can understand both Plato and Aristotle, you can understand Aquinas. Therefore, if you cannot understand Aquinas, then if you can understand Plato you cannot understand Aristotle. (*P, A, Q*)

5 Is "If Clovis does not marry Wilma, then he will marry Helen" equivalent to "It is not the case that Clovis will both not marry Wilma and not marry Helen"?

6 Is "If costs rise, then either prices and costs both rise or costs rise but prices do not" a tautology?

7 Which of these compounds are tautologies, which are contradictions, and which are neither?

(a) $p \supset (p \vee p)$ **(b)** $p \supset (p \vee q)$

(c) $p \supset -p$ **(d)** $p \mathbin{\&} (q \mathbin{\&} -p)$

(e) $(p \mathbin{\&} q) \equiv (q \supset -q)$ **(f)** $(p \supset q) \vee (q \supset q)$

(g) $(p \mathbin{\&} q) \supset (p \vee q)$ **(h)** $p \vee q$

(i) p

8 Does "$p \supset q$" imply "$p \supset (q \vee r)$"?

9 Is it true that a sentence that is a contradiction implies every sentence? Is it true that a sentence that is a tautology is implied by every sentence?

10 Is the disjunction of a given sentence with itself always equivalent to the given sentence?

DEDUCTIONS

Truth tables provide a perfectly general method for testing the validity of truth-functional arguments. However, if the argument is a lengthy one, and especially if it contains many distinct constituent sentences, the truth-table method may be tedious and long. It is valuable to have a short-cut method to deal more efficiently with involved arguments. We shall now develop a method that involves breaking up long arguments into simpler steps. If we can show how it it is possible to pass, by means of simple valid steps, from the premises to other sentences that follow from them, and then from these to the conclusion, we shall have succeeded in showing that the conclusion follows validly from the premises.

Suppose we have this argument: "Clovis will not both vacation at Sun Valley and buy an Austin-Healey, unless he has inherited money. He will not have inherited money unless his rich grandmother has died. Clovis has bought an Austin-Healey, but his grandmother is hale and hearty. Therefore, Clovis will not vacation at Sun Valley". Since this argument contains four different basic component statements, which we may symbolize "S", "A", "I", and "G", its truth table would require sixteen lines and would be rather tedious. Let us try to pass to the conclusion from the premises by familiar steps. We can symbolize the premises as follows:

1. $(S \ \& \ A) \supset I$ *Premise*
2. $I \supset G$ *Premise*
3. $A \ \& -G$ *Premise*

We can make a useful first move by separating one part of the conjunction of line 3:

4. $-G$ *From 3 by conjunctive simplification*

Next we can put together lines 4 and 2, using modus tollens:

5. $-I$ *From 2, 4 by modus tollens*

Then we can use modus tollens again:

6. $-(S \ \& \ A)$ *From 5, 1 by modus tollens*

And from this we can get the desired conclusion:

7. A *From 3 by conjunctive simplification*
8. $-S$ *From 6, 7 by conjunctive argument*

Here we have broken up the involved argument into simple valid steps. Thus we succeed in showing that the conclusion follows from the premises. When arranged in a coherent order like this, the steps are said to constitute a *deduction*. Each line in the deduction must either be a premise or be clearly justified by means of some standard principle.

In more advanced studies of symbolic logic, it is usual to select some very small group of standard principles for justifying steps and then to insist upon using no others. In that way, greater elegance and economy are achieved, thereby enhancing the theoretical interest of the deductions that are constructed. For our elementary purposes, however, that sort of elegance is not so important. Let us therefore include among our principles for use in deduction all those principles with which we have so far become acquainted, and also a few new ones. This broad though inelegant approach will mean that our deductions will be comparatively easy to construct; it will spare us the irritation sometimes felt by beginners using elegantly economical deductive rules when they find that certain moves, which they see to be perfectly valid, nevertheless are not directly sanctioned by the rules.

Let us arrange our principles under three headings. First are our standard elementary forms of valid argument; we always may write any new line in a deduction if that new line follows from earlier lines by one of these forms of argument. Next are equivalences; we always are justified in adding a new line if it is equivalent to some preceding line. Finally, we shall allow ourselves to add any tautology as a new line; the justification for this is that tautologies are necessarily true. Let us now draw up a list of principles.

Truth-functional principles for use in deduction

ELEMENTARY FORMS OF VALID ARGUMENT

Modus ponens:	$p \supset q$, p; **therefore** q
Modus tollens:	$p \supset q$, $-q$; **therefore** $-p$
Chain argument:	$p \supset q$, $q \supset r$; **therefore** $p \supset r$
Disjunctive	$p \vee q$, $-p$; **therefore** q
arguments:	$p \vee q$, $-q$; **therefore** p
	p; **therefore** $p \vee q$ (*disjunctive addition*)
Conjunctive	$-(p \,\&\, q)$, p; **therefore** $-q$
arguments:	$-(p \,\&\, q)$, q; **therefore** $-p$
	$p \,\&\, q$; **therefore** p (*simplification*)
	$p \,\&\, q$; **therefore** q (*simplification*)
	p, q; **therefore** $p \,\&\, q$ (*adjunction*)
Reductio	$p \supset -p$; **therefore** $-p$
ad absurdum:	$p \supset (q \,\&\, -q)$; **therefore** $-p$
Dilemmas:	$p \supset q$, $r \supset s$, $p \vee r$; **therefore** $q \vee s$
	(*complex constructive*)
	$p \supset q$, $r \supset s$, $-q \vee -s$; **therefore** $-p \vee -r$
	(*complex destructive*)
	$p \supset q$, $r \supset q$, $p \vee r$; **therefore** q
	(*simple constructive*)
	$p \supset q$, $p \supset r$, $-q \vee -r$; **therefore** $-p$
	(*simple destructive*)

EQUIVALENCES

Any expression may validly be inferred from any other that is equivalent to it. We shall use the following equivalences:

"p" and "$p \lor p$" and "$p \mathbin{\&} p$" all are equivalent.

"$p \supset q$" and "$-p \lor q$" and "$-(p \mathbin{\&} -q)$" all are equivalent.

"$p \equiv q$" and "$(q \supset p) \mathbin{\&} (p \supset q)$" are equivalent.

Double negation: "p" and "$-(-p)$" are equivalent.

Contraposition: "$p \supset q$" and "$- q \supset -p$" are equivalent.

Commutation: "$p \lor q$" and "$q \lor p$" are equivalent.

"$p \mathbin{\&} q$" and "$q \mathbin{\&} p$" are equivalent.

Association: "$p \lor (q \lor r)$" and "$(p \lor q) \lor r$" are equivalent.

"$p \mathbin{\&} (q \mathbin{\&} r)$" and "$(p \mathbin{\&} q) \mathbin{\&} r$" are equivalent.

Distribution: "$p \mathbin{\&} (q \lor r)$" and "$(p \mathbin{\&} q) \lor (p \mathbin{\&} r)$" are equivalent.

"$p \lor (q \mathbin{\&} r)$" and "$(p \lor q) \mathbin{\&} (p \lor r)$" are equivalent.

De Morgan's laws: "$-(p \lor q)$" and "$-p \mathbin{\&} -q$" are equivalent.

"$-(p \mathbin{\&} q)$" and "$-p \lor -q$" are equivalent.

Exportation: "$(p \mathbin{\&} q) \supset r$" and "$p \supset (q \supset r)$" are equivalent.

TAUTOLOGIES

Since a tautology is necessarily true, we may add any tautology we please as a line in a deduction, provided we are prepared to show by a truth table that it is a tautology. Some examples of tautologies are:

$p \lor -p$ $p \equiv p$ $(p \mathbin{\&} q) \supset (p \lor q)$

$-(p \mathbin{\&} -p)$ $p \supset (p \lor q)$ ⋅

$p \supset p$ $(p \mathbin{\&} q) \supset p$ ⋅

                                                          ⋅

This list of principles perhaps looks tediously long, but the advantage of having a good many principles is that they make deductions easier to construct; all the principles in this list are standard logical principles worth being acquainted with. We have already met the elementary valid forms of argument; if any of them seem strange or dubious, their validity can be proved by means of truth tables. Under the heading of equivalences are some principles that we have met and also some new ones. If any of these seems strange or dubious, again truth tables can be used. (It

is also illuminating to invent sentences illustrating these principles.) We may justify a line in a deduction by pointing out that it
can be obtained from some preceding line by replacing one expression by another that is equivalent to it; that is the use of these
equivalences. Our third heading is tautologies; since a tautology
is necessarily true, we may write it anywhere as a line in a
deduction. If there is any doubt about whether a given expression
is a tautology, its truth table should be constructed to settle the
question.

Now let us examine another example of a deduction in which
more of these principles are employed. Let us suppose that we are
given an argument having three premises, which we shall symbolize
as lines 1, 2, and 3, and a conclusion which we symbolize as line
11 (although we do not know at first that the conclusion will be the
eleventh line; we know that only after finishing the deduction).

1.	$A \lor (B \ \& \ C)$	*Premise*
2.	$A \supset D$	*Premise*
3.	$D \supset C$	*Premise*
4.	$A \supset C$	*From 2, 3 by chain argument*
5.	$-A \supset (B \ \& \ C)$	*From 1 by equivalence of "$p \lor q$" to "$-p \supset q$"*
6.	$-C \supset -A$	*From 4 by contraposition*
7.	$-C \supset (B \ \& \ C)$	*From 6, 5 by chain argument*
8.	$(B \ \& \ C) \supset C$	*Tautology*
9.	$-C \supset C$	*From 7, 8 by chain argument*
10.	$-(-C)$	*From 9 by reductio ad absurdum*
11.	C	*From 10 by double negation*

In constructing the deduction, our strategy could have been
the following: Looking at the premises, we see that the second and
third can be put together to form a chain argument, yielding
line 4. Wondering how to combine line 4 with anything else, we
notice that line 1 might possibly combine with line 4. If line 1 is
rewritten as a conditional instead of a disjunction, it will be more
likely to combine with line 4, and so we make use of the fact that

"$p \lor q$" is equivalent to "$-p \supset q$". (This is essentially the same as the principle that "$p \supset q$" is equivalent to "$-p \lor q$", the only difference being that we have used the principle of double negation to shift the negation signs.) Now, if line 4 is replaced by its contrapositive, we obtain a standard chain argument whose conclusion is line 7. This is close to what we want, but we still need to separate out the "C" which is contained in the consequent of line 7. If we choose an appropriate tautology, we can do this, and so we write line 8 and then get line 9 by another chain argument. Line 9 gives the desired conclusion by *reductio ad absurdum*.

In order to construct a proof such as this, we must use a little ingenuity; we have not mastered any mechanical method that will automatically tell us what steps we should take. But if we are familiar with the main types of elementary forms of valid argument, with the main types of equivalences, and with simple sorts of tautologies, we find that only a very little ingenuity is required to proceed step by step.

Exercise 15

State the justification for each step that is not a premise in each of the following deductions. Mention what specific principle is used and what earlier lines, if any, are involved at each step.

1
1. $D \& E$ *Premise*
2. $D \supset F$ *Premise*
3. D
4. F

2
1. $J \supset K$ *Premise*
2. $-(K \& L)$ *Premise*
3. $-K \lor -L$
4. $K \supset -L$
5. $J \supset -L$

3
1. $(A \supset B) \lor C$ *Premise*
2. $-C \& -B$ *Premise*
3. $-C$
4. $A \supset B$

4
1. $(A \supset B)$
   $\supset (-C \supset D)$
2. $-B \supset D$ *Premise*
3. $A \supset -D$ *Premise*

3 5. $-B$
6. $-A$

4 4. $-(-D) \supset -A$
5. $D \supset -A$
6. $-B \supset -A$
7. $A \supset B$
8. $-C \supset D$
9. $-(-C) \vee D$
10. $C \vee D$

Construct the following deductions.

1 From the premises "$-(F \& G)$" and "G" and "$H \supset F$", deduce the conclusion "$-H$".

2 From the premises "$-(M \vee P)$" and "$N \supset P$", deduce the conclusion "$-N$".

3 From the premises "$A \supset B$" and "$(B \& C) \supset D$", deduce the conclusion "$C \supset (A \supset D)$".

4 From the premises "$S \equiv (T \vee U)$" and "$-(T \vee U)$" and "$U \supset (T \& W)$", deduce the conclusion "$-(S \& W)$".

Symbolize each argument, using the suggested letters. Then construct a deduction to show it is valid.

1 If the patient had no fever, then malaria was not the cause of his death. But malaria or food poisoning was the cause of his death. The patient had no fever. Therefore, food poisoning must have been the cause of his death. (F, M, P)

2 Hubert will be expelled from the university if he has violated the honor code. Either Hubert was telling the truth about his recent activities or he has violated the honor code. Hubert was not telling the truth about his recent activities. Therefore Hubert will be expelled from the university. (E, V, T)

3 Had Franklin D. Roosevelt been a socialist, he would have been willing to nationalize industries. Had he been willing to nationalize industries, this would have been done during the

Depression. But no industries were nationalized during the Depression. Hence, Roosevelt must not have been a socialist. (*R, W, D*)

4 If either the husband or the wife paid the premium that was due, then the policy was in force and the cost of the accident was covered. If the cost of the accident was covered, they were not forced into bankruptcy. But they were forced into bankruptcy. Therefore, the husband did not pay the premium that was due. (*H, W, P, C, B*)

SHOWING INVALIDITY

If an argument is not valid, it will not be possible to construct a deduction that moves step by step from the premises to the conclusion. But the fact that we have failed to construct a deduction for an argument by no means demonstrates that it is invalid; perhaps we have not worked intelligently enough. Suppose we work on an argument, trying unsuccessfully to construct a deduction for it; we may eventually suspect that perhaps the argument is not valid. In such a situation we could resort to a truth table. But it is valuable also to have a short-cut method of demonstrating that an argument is invalid.

To say that an argument is invalid is to say that it is possible for the premises all to be true yet the conclusion false. This gives us the clue to a short-cut method of demonstrating invalidity. If we can find a way of assigning truth and falsity to the constituent letters so that the premises all will be true but the conclusion false, this will demonstrate that the argument is invalid.

Suppose we have an argument whose three premises are symbolized "$A \supset (B \vee C)$", "$(C \& D) \supset E$", and "$-E$", and whose conclusion is symbolized "$-A$". We shall not be able to pass, by valid steps, from these premises to this conclusion. Let us try instead to show that the argument is invalid. We want to see whether it is logically possible for the premises all to be true and the conclusion false. If the conclusion is false, "*A*" must be true; if "*A*" is true, then either "*B*" or "*C*" (or both) must be true in order that the first premise be true. Also, in order that the third premise be true, "*E*" must be false; if "*E*" is false, then "*C*" and "*D*" cannot both be true, in order that the second premise be true. Let us try letting "*A*" be true, "*E*" false, "*B*" and "*C*" both true, and "*D*" false. This proves to be one satisfactory way of assigning truth and falsity to the constituent letters, for this is a way of making the premises all true and the conclusion false. Thus we have shown that there is a logically possible way for the premises all to be true while the conclusion is false; hence the argument is shown to be invalid. This method is like finding in the truth table for the argument one single line that suffices to show the argument invalid.

Exercise 16

Use the short-cut method to show that each of the following arguments is invalid.

1 $A \supset B$
    $C \supset D$
    $\therefore A \supset C$

2 $R \supset S$
    $T \supset -S$
    $S \vee -S$
    $\therefore R \vee T$

3 $A \supset B$
    $C \supset D$
    $-A \vee -C$
    $\therefore -B \vee -D$

4 $F \vee G$
    $F \supset H$
    $G \supset J$
    $\therefore H \& J$

5 $A \supset (B \vee C)$
    $B \supset (D \& E)$
    $D \supset (E \supset F)$
    $-(A \& F)$
    $\therefore A \equiv C$

Show that each argument is valid or that it is invalid.

1 If the rudder does not break and the fuel holds out, the ship will get safely to port and no one will drown. If the fuel holds out but the rudder breaks, then the ship can be steered by means of its propellers. If the ship can be steered by means of its propellers, it will get safely to port. If the rudder does not break, then the fuel will hold out. Therefore, the ship will get safely to port. (*R, F, P, D, S*)

2 Hugo left a message for Clovis but none for Esme, or he left a message for Esme but none for Reggie. If Hugo left a message for Clovis, then he was seen by the landlady. But the landlady did not see Hugo. Therefore, Hugo left no message for Reggie. (*C, E, R, L*)

3 If Bulgaria is hostile toward Yugoslavia or Greece, then Bulgaria is serving Russia's interests. Bulgaria is serving Russia's interests if and only if it cooperates with both Czechoslovakia and Rumania. Therefore, if Bulgaria does not cooperate with Rumania, it will not be hostile toward Yugoslavia. (*Y, G, S, C, R*)

4 If Wilbur joined the Navy he got seasick, and if he joined the Army he got bored. If he was either seasick or bored, then he was unhappy. But he was not unhappy. Therefore, Wilbur did not join either the Navy or the Army. (*N, S, A, B, U*)

A set of sentences is called consistent *if and only if it is possible that all of them may be true together. You can show that a set of sentences is consistent by finding a way of assigning truth and falsity to the letters so as to make all the compound sentences true together. You can show that a set of sentences is inconsistent by deducing from them a contradiction. Discover whether each of these sets of sentences is consistent or inconsistent.*

1 If Jones is telling the truth, then Smith is not guilty. If Brown is telling the truth, then Jones is not doing so. Brown is telling the truth, and Smith is not guilty. (*J, S, B*)

2 If Ted and Jim come, then Bob will go. If Fred comes, then Jim comes. Fred goes and Jim comes. Bob does not go. (*T, J, B, F*)

3 The company earns more profit if and only if its domestic sales increase or its export sales increase. Its export sales increase if and only if its domestic sales do not increase. (*P, D, E*)

Analyze the structure of each of the following truth-functional arguments.

1 "I hope, Marianne," continued Elinor, "you do not consider Edward as deficient in general taste. Indeed, I think I may say that you cannot, for your behaviour to him is perfectly cordial, and if *that* were your opinion, I am sure you could never be civil to him."   JANE AUSTEN, *Sense and Sensibility*

2 Murder and treachery cannot be good without regret being bad: regret cannot be good without treachery and murder being bad. Both, however, are supposed to have been foredoomed; so something must be fatally unreasonable, absurd, and wrong in the world. It must be a place of which either sin or error forms a necessary part. From this dilemma there seems at first sight no escape.

WILLIAM JAMES, "The Dilemma of Determinism"

3 With respect to every reality external to myself, I can get hold of it only through thinking it. In order to get hold of it really, I should have to be able to make myself into the other, the acting individual, and make the foreign reality my own reality, which is impossible. For if I make the foreign reality my own, this does not mean that I become the other through knowing his reality, but it means that I acquire a new reality, which belongs to me as opposed to him.

KIERKEGAARD, *Concluding Unscientific Postscript*

4 Either to disinthrone the King of Heav'n
We war, if war be best, or to regain
Our own right lost: him to unthrone we then
May hope, when everlasting Fate shall yield
To fickle Chance, and *Chaos* judge the strife:

The former vain to hope argues as vain
The latter: for what place can be for us
Within Heav'n's bound, unless Heav'n's Lord supreme
We overpower?   MILTON, *Paradise Lost*

5 If man lacked free judgment of will, how would that be good
for which justice itself is commended when it condemns sins
and honors deeds rightly done? For that which was not done
by the will would be neither sinfully nor rightly done. And
according to this if man did not have free will, both punishment and reward would be unjust. However, there must have
been justice in both punishment and reward, since it is one of
the goods which are from God. Therefore, God must have
given man free will.   ST. AUGUSTINE, *De Libero Arbitrio*

4. *Quantification*

In Chapter 2 we met the quantifiers "all" and "some" in categorical sentences. Now we shall see how to use symbols in place of quantifier words. We shall also see how these quantifier symbols can be combined with truth-functional symbols so as to provide a very powerful symbolic language by means of which a much wider range of sentences and arguments can be analyzed. The development of this general theory of quantification is one of the most important achievements of modern symbolic logic.

THE SYMBOLISM OF QUANTIFICATION

Let us begin with a sentence in ordinary language and see how it can be expressed in the symbolism of quantification. Consider the sentence

There exists at least one liquid that is a metal. (1)

We can reword this as

There exists at least one thing such that it is liquid and it is
   a metal.   (2)

and as

There exists at least one thing x such that x is liquid and x is
   a metal.   (3)

The letter "x" in (3) is called a *variable*. There is nothing
mysterious about its significance, however, for it functions as a
pronoun, the way "it" did in (2), enabling us to see that in the
different parts of the sentence the speaker is talking about the same
thing rather than about different things. Now we introduce the
symbol "$(\exists x)$", which is called an *existential quantifier* and which
corresponds to the words "There is at least one thing x such that".
This enables us to rewrite (3) in the form

$(\exists x)(x$ is liquid & x is a metal)   (4)

This sentence is called an *existential quantification,* because it
starts with an existential quantifier which is attached to the whole
of the rest of the sentence. Sentence (4) can be read in various
equivalent ways besides (1), (2), and (3). All the following
readings also are permissible:

There is something such that it is liquid and is a metal.
Something is liquid and is a metal.
Some liquids are metals.
There are liquid metals.
Liquid metals exist.

    Next let us consider another sentence in ordinary language
and see how it can be expressed using another quantificational
symbol. Consider the sentence

Each thing is either solid or not solid.   (5)

We can reword this as

Each thing is such that either it is solid or it is not solid.   (6)

and as

Each thing x is such that either x is solid or x is not solid.   (7)

Again the variable *"x"* is merely doing the job of a pronoun. Now we introduce the symbol *"(x)"*, which is called a *universal quantifier* and which corresponds to the words "Each thing x is such that". This enables us to rewrite (7) in the form

(x) $(x$ is solid v x is not solid)   (8)

This sentence is called a *universal quantification,* because it starts with a universal quantifier which is attached to the whole of the rest of the sentence. Sentence (8) can be read in various equivalent ways; besides (5), (6), and (7), all the following readings are possible:

Each thing is solid or not solid.
Anything is solid or not solid.
Everything is either solid or not solid.
All things are either solid or not solid.

So far, we have used just the letter *"x"* as a variable. But other variables, such as *"y"* and *"z"*, can equally well be used in quantifications. The sentence "$(\exists y)$ $(y$ is liquid & y is a metal)" is equivalent to (4). Both of them say that there is something such that *it* is liquid and *it* is a metal. The sentence "(z) $(z$ is solid v z is not solid)" is equivalent to (8). Both of them say that each thing is such that *it* is solid or *it* is not solid. When the quantifier is "$(\exists x)$" or "(x)", we say that *"x"* is the *variable of quantification;* when the quantifier is "$(\exists y)$" or "(y)", we say that *"y"* is the variable of quantification; and so on.

In the cases that we have considered thus far, the quantifier has been attached to the whole of the rest of the sentence. In these cases we put parentheses around all the rest of the sentence to show that it all falls within what we call the *scope* of the quanti-

fier. Attaching the quantifier to the whole remainder of the
sentence means that every occurrence of the variable of quantification within the rest of the sentence has to be thought of as a
pronoun referring back to that quantifier.

However, quantifiers are not always attached in this way;
sometimes we have a quantifier that is attached only to a portion of
the sentence. For example, the sentence

Either something is solid or everything is liquid.

can be reworded

**Either there is something x such that x is solid or each thing x is such
that x is liquid.**

and can be put into quantificational symbolism as

$$(\exists x)(x \text{ is solid}) \vee (x)(x \text{ is liquid}) \tag{9}$$

Here sentence (9) considered as a whole is not a quantification;
rather it is a disjunction whose components are quantifications.
The parentheses show us that the "x" within "$(x$ is solid$)$" is to
be thought of as a pronoun referring to the first quantifier, while
the "x" in "$(x$ is liquid$)$" is to be thought of as a pronoun referring
to the second quantifier. Thus the scope of the first quantifier does
not overlap that of the second quantifier, and the two quantifications that form parts of the disjunction are completely separate.
Therefore it would be equally correct to write (9) in the equivalent
form:

$$(\exists y)(y \text{ is solid}) \vee (z)(z \text{ is liquid}) \tag{10}$$

Because each quantification is self-contained, we get equivalent
results whether we use different variables in the two quantifications, as in (10), or use the same variable throughout, as in (9).

All the variables we have considered so far have been func-
tioning as pronouns referring to quantifiers. Variables are said

to be *bound* by their quantifiers when they occur in this way. A variable that does not refer to any quantifier is said to be *free*. Consider the expressions:

x is solid ∨ x is liquid
(∃x) (x is solid) ∨ x is liquid
(y) (y is solid ∨ x is liquid)

There are two free occurrences of "x" in the first expression, and there is one free "x" in each of the others. Expressions like these are neither true nor false, for nothing has been decided about what these free occurrences of "x" are supposed to refer to; "x" here is like a pronoun without an antecedent. An expression is not true or false so long as it contains any free occurrences of variables.

Exercise 17

Translate each of the following sentences into the symbolism of quantification.

1 Something is a pig and can fly.

2 Everything is either physical or mental.

3 There is nothing mental.

4 There is something such that it is mental and it is immortal.

5 It is not the case that something mental is immortal.

6 Anything is physical if and only if it is not immortal.

Which of the following expressions are true-or-false sentences? Which of the variables are free and which are bound?

1 (x) (x is male ∨ x is female)

2 (x) (x is male) ∨ y is female.

3 x is male ∨ y is female.

4 (x) $(x$ is male$)$ ∨ x is female.

5 $(\exists y)$ $(y$ is mental$)$ & z is immortal.

6 $(\exists y)$ $(y$ is mental$)$ & y is immortal.

7 $(\exists y)$ $(y$ is mental & y is immortal$)$

SOME NONEQUIVALENCES AND EQUIVALENCES

To say that two sentences are equivalent is to say that they necessarily are alike as regards truth and falsity. Considering some pairs of sentences that are not equivalent will help us better to understand how quantifiers work. In dealing with sentences involving quantifiers, we need to notice how much of what follows the quantifier falls within the scope of the quantifier. For example, the sentences

Something is liquid and is solid.   (1)
Something is liquid and something is solid.   (2)

are definitely not equivalent, as is shown by the fact that (1) is false but (2) is true. In the symbolism of quantification, we use parentheses to indicate the distinction:

$(\exists x)$ $(x$ is liquid & x is solid$)$ (3)
$(\exists x)$ $(x$ is liquid$)$ & $(\exists x)$ $(x$ is solid$)$ (4)

Here (3) is a way of symbolizing (1), and (4) is a way of symbolizing (2). Each quantifier governs all and only what is inclosed within the parentheses that immediately follow it. In (3) the quantifier embraces within its scope all that follows, and the whole expression is the existential quantification of a conjunction. In (4) we have two separate quantifiers each with a briefer scope; here the whole thing is a conjunction of two existential quantifications.

Similarly with universal quantifiers, we must distinguish between

$(x)\,(x$ is solid $\lor\;x$ is not solid)   (5)

$(x)\,(x$ is solid) $\lor\;(x)\,(x$ is not solid)   (6)

These sentences are not equivalent. Sentence (5) is the universal quantification of a disjunction, and it truly says that each thing is solid or not solid; sentence (6) is the disjunction of two universal quantifications, and it falsely says that either everything is solid or everything is nonsolid.

We must also pay attention to the positions of negation signs. It makes a difference whether a negation sign occurs outside or within the scope of a quantifier, and we must distinguish between

$-(x)\,(x$ is solid)   (7)

$(x)-(x$ is solid)   (8)

Sentence (7) is the negation of a universal quantification, and thus it truly says that not everything is solid. Sentence (8) is the universal quantification of a negation, and it falsely says that everything is nonsolid.[1]

Furthermore, we must beware of assuming that negation signs flanking a quantifier will merely cancel out; we must distinguish between

$-(\exists x)-(x$ is solid $\lor\;x$ is liquid)   (9)

$(\exists x)\,(x$ is solid $\lor\;x$ is liquid)   (10)

These are not equivalent. Sentence (9) falsely says that nothing is neither solid nor liquid, while sentence (10) truly says that something is either solid or liquid.

However, some simple and important equivalences involve pairs of negation signs. Consider the existential quantification "$(\exists x)\,(x$ is liquid)". Is there any equivalent way in which this

[1] Whenever there would be ambiguity without them, we use parentheses or brackets to enclose all that falls within the scope of a quantifier. But instead of writing "$(x)\,[-(x$ is solid)$]$" we write simply "$(x)-(x$ is solid)", as there is no danger of misunderstanding here. In the absence of parentheses or brackets, we always interpret the scope of the quantifier as being as short as would make sense.

thought can be expressed? To say that there is at least one liquid amounts to denying that everything is such as not to be liquid. Thus "$(\exists x)(x$ is liquid)" is equivalent to "$-(x)-(x$ is liquid)". And the underlying principle is perfectly general: If an existential quantifier is replaced by a universal quantifier flanked with negation signs, the new sentence is equivalent to the old one.

Next consider the sentence "$(x)(x$ is solid)". Is there any equivalent way in which this can be expressed? To say that each thing is solid amounts to denying that there exists even one thing that is not solid. Thus "$(x)(x$ is solid)" is equivalent to "$-(\exists x)-(x$ is solid)". The underlying principle is perfectly general: Whenever a universal quantifier is replaced by an existential quantifier flanked with negation signs, the new sentence is equivalent to the old one.

By similar reflection, we can see that "$-(x)(x$ is solid)" is equivalent to "$(\exists x)-(x$ is solid)" and that "$-(\exists x)(x$ is liquid)" is equivalent to "$(x)-(x$ is liquid)". Here too the principles involved are perfectly general. When a negation sign immediately followed by a universal quantifier is replaced by an existential quantifier immediately followed by a negation sign, the new sentence is equivalent to the old. And when a negation sign immediately followed by an existential quantifier is replaced by a universal quantifier immediately followed by a negation sign, again the new sentence is equivalent to the old. These two principles of equivalence can be summarized by saying that a negation sign may be 'passed through' a quantifier, either forward or backward, provided that the type of quantifier is changed (i.e., from universal to existential, or vice versa).

These various kinds of elementary quantificational equivalence also have some further consequences. We remember that it is a basic fact about truth-functionally compound sentences that any two such sentences have to be equivalent if they are exactly alike except that in one of them a component present in the other has been replaced by something equivalent to it. This means that, for instance, we can employ our knowledge of the equivalence of "$-(x)(x$ is liquid)" to "$(\exists x)-(x$ is liquid)" in order to conclude that a longer sentence such as "$(\exists y)(y$ is solid) $\supset -(x)$ $(x$ is liquid)" must be equivalent to "$(\exists y)(y$ is solid) $\supset (\exists x)-(x$ is liquid)". Here the latter two sentences are truth-functional compounds (both are conditionals) and are exactly alike except that a component of one has been replaced in the other by something equivalent to it. Since the two longer sentences are exactly alike in overall form and since each component of the former necessarily agrees with the corresponding component of the latter as regards truth or falsity, the two longer sentences must agree as regards truth or falsity (i.e., they are equivalent). We shall make use of these principles of equivalence in a later section.

TRANSLATING WORDS INTO SYMBOLS

Now let us try translating words into symbols. We shall start by putting the four traditional forms of categorical sentence into quantificational symbols. Let us write "Sx" as short for "x is a Swede". ("Sx" can also be read "x is Swedish" or "x comes from Sweden"; it does not matter whether we use noun, adjective, or verb here.) Let us write "Px" for "x is a Protestant". ("Px" can also be read "x is Protestant" or "x accepts Protestantism".) The **A** sentence "All Swedes are Protestants" is equivalent to "Each thing is such that if it is a Swede then it is a Protestant". Thus, the **A** sentence can be expressed in symbols as

$(x)(Sx \supset Px)$ **(A)**

The **E** sentence "No Swedes are Protestants" means the same as "Each thing is such that if it is a Swede then it is not a Protestant", and it can be written in symbols as

$(x)(Sx \supset -Px)$ **(E)**

The **I** sentence "Some Swedes are Protestants" means "Something is a Swede and a Protestant", and it is written in symbols as

$(\exists x)(Sx \& Px)$ **(I)**

The **O** sentence "Some Swedes are not Protestants", meaning "Something is a Swede and is not a Protestant", becomes

$(\exists x)(Sx \& -Px)$ **(O)**

The **A** and **O** sentences have to be contradictories, as do the **E** and **I**. This indicates that an alternative way of symbolizing the **A** sentence would be to write the **O** preceded by a negation sign; that is, "$(x)(Sx \supset Px)$" and "$-(\exists x)(Sx \& -Px)$" have to be equivalent. It is easily seen that this makes sense, for "$(x)(Sx \supset Px)$" is equivalent to "$(x)-(Sx \& -Px)$" in virtue of the meaning of the horseshoe, and that in turn is equivalent to "$-(\exists x)$ $(Sx \& -Px)$" in virtue of the principle about passing a negation sign through a quantifier. Similarly, an alternative way of symbolizing the **E** would be to write the **I** preceded by a negation sign; "$(x)(Sx \supset -Px)$" must be equivalent to "$-(\exists x)(Sx \& Px)$".

It is necessary to avoid the mistake of supposing that "Some S are P" could be rendered as "$(\exists x)(Sx \supset Px)$". Remembering how the conditional is related to disjunction, we see that "$(\exists x)(Sx \supset Px)$" is equivalent to "$(\exists x)(-Sx \vee Px)$"; the latter says merely that there exists at least one thing that is either a non-Swede or a Protestant. But this is a very weak statement; the existence of at least one stone would be enough to make it true (for stones are non-Swedes). This shows that "$(\exists x)(-Sx \vee Px)$" and, with it, "$(\exists x)(Sx \supset Px)$" mean something far weaker than the meaning of "Some S are P".

A kindred mistake is supposing that "No S are P" can be rendered as "$(x)-(Sx \supset Px)$". To see that this is a mistake, let us rewrite the conditional in terms of disjunction, getting

"$(x) - (-Sx \lor Px)$". Using De Morgan's law, we can rewrite this as "$(x)(Sx \& -Px)$". But this says that everything is both an S and a non$P$. This is a very strong statement, far stronger than that of "No S are P". Thus "$(x) - (Sx \supset Px)$" cannot be equivalent to "No S are P".

So far, we have been symbolizing relatively simple sentences. We can handle a much richer variety of sentences if we extend our symbolism in two ways. For one thing, we shall use capital letters followed by more than one variable to symbolize relations between things. Thus we can write "Ixy", for example, to mean "x influences y". Here it is important to notice that the order of the variables "x" and "y" in the expression "Ixy" is in one respect of no significance: "Ixy" can be put into words either as "x influences y" or as "y is influenced by x". But in another respect the order makes an essential difference: "Ixy" is not interchangeable with "Iyx", for the former means "x influences y" whereas the latter means "y influences x". Also, we shall allow one quantifier to occur within the scope of another. Thus we can write such symbolized sentences as the following:

$(\exists x)(\exists y)Ixy$ (1)

$(x)(y)Ixy$ (2)

$(\exists x)Ixx$ (3)

$(x)Ixx$ (4)

Here (1) means that there is something such that there is something it influences; in other words, something influences something. Example (2) means that each thing is such that each thing is influenced by it; that is, everything influences everything. Notice that (2) does not mean merely that everything influences everything *else;* it means that everything influences everything, including itself. Example (3) means that something influences itself. Example (4) means that everything influences itself.

Now that we are allowing one quantifier to occur within the

scope of another, we must notice that sometimes the order of
the quantifiers can affect the meaning of the sentence. Thus
"$(x)(\exists y)\ Ixy$" means that everything influences something; that
is, each thing is such that there is something or other it influences.
If we change the order of the quantifiers, we get "$(\exists y)(x)\ Ixy$",
which means that there is some one thing that everything influences. These two sentences are not equivalent, for the first says
that, whatever we select, there is always at least one thing that it
influences, whereas the second says that there is at least one thing
such that whatever we pick influences it. The second sentence says
more and logically implies the first; the first sentence says less and
might be true even if the second were not.

Let us now get some practice in translating words into
quantificational symbols. In dealing with examples, it is usually
best to proceed step by step, moving gradually toward the symbolic
formulation. Let "P" mean "is a person" (so that "Px" means "x
is a person", "Py" means "y is a person", etc.), and let "R" mean
"resembles" (so that "Rxy" means "x resembles y", "Ryx" means "y
resembles x", and so on). We shall now symbolize four sentences;
working downward from each original sentence, we move step by
step toward a symbolization of it.

Everyone resembles someone.
Each person resembles someone.
Each x is such that, if x is a person, x resembles someone.
$(x)(Px \supset x$ resembles someone$)$
$(x)(Px \supset$ there is someone x resembles$)$
$(x)[Px \supset (\exists y)\ (y$ is a person & x resembles $y)]$
$(x)[Px \supset (\exists y)(Py \ \& \ Rxy)]$

Someone resembles everyone.
There is a person who resembles every person.
$(\exists x)(x$ is a person & x resembles every person$)$
$(\exists x)(Px \ \&$ each person is resembled by $x)$
$(\exists x)[Px \ \& \ (y)(Py \supset Rxy)]$

Someone resembles someone.
There is a person who resembles someone.
$(\exists x)(Px \ \& \ x \text{ resembles someone})$
$(\exists x)[Px \ \& \ (\exists y)(Py \ \& \ Rxy)]$

Everyone resembles everyone.
$(x)(Px \supset x \text{ resembles everyone})$
$(x)(Px \supset \text{ everyone is resembled by } x)$
$(x)(Px \supset \text{ each person is resembled by } x)$
$(x)[Px \supset (y)(Py \supset Rxy)]$

These are not the only correct ways of symbolizing the original sentences, but they are the easiest ways. When a true-or-false sentence is properly symbolized, every occurrence of a variable in it must fall within the scope of the proper quantifier. Free variables never occur in the symbolization of sentences like these.

The following is an argument of medieval vintage and is an example of a valid argument whose validity cannot be established either by syllogistic or by truth-functional methods:

All circles are figures.
Therefore, whoever draws a circle draws a figure.

We are not yet in a position to show that the argument is valid, but we can now symbolize its premise and conclusion. The premise becomes

$(x)(Cx \supset Fx)$

Symbolizing the conclusion is more difficult and is best done step by step. Two initial steps can be

Each thing is such that if it is a drawer of a circle then it is a drawer of a figure.
$(x)(x \text{ is a drawer of a circle} \supset x \text{ is a drawer of a figure})$

In order to exhibit the connection between the premise and the conclusion of the argument, we must introduce into our version of the conclusion the letters "C" and "F" that we used in the premise. Otherwise we would not bring out those aspects of the logical structure that are germane to the validity of the argument. We can do this as follows:

(x)[(x is a drawer of something that is a circle) $\supset$ (x is a drawer of something that is a figure)]

(x)[(something is a circle & x draws it) $\supset$ (something is a figure & x draws it)]

(x)[$(\exists y)(Cy$ & x draws $y) \supset (\exists y)(Fy$ & x draws $y)$]

Now if we use "D" to express the relation "draws", we have

(x)[$(\exists y)(Cy$ & $Dxy) \supset (\exists y)(Fy$ & $Dxy)$]

Thus we have symbolized both the premise and the conclusion of the argument in such a way as to exhibit the logical structure involved in the reasoning. In the next section we shall develop a method by means of which the validity of an argument like this can be established.

Exercise 18

Translate each of the following sentences into symbolic form. Do any of them contradict each other? Are any equivalent?

1   There is someone whom everybody fears.

2   Everybody fears someone or other.

3   Everybody is feared by someone or other.

4   Nobody fears everybody.

5   Nobody fears nobody.

6   Someone does not fear everyone.

7   Nobody fears anybody.

8   Someone does not fear anyone.

Let "S" mean "sailor", let "G" mean "girl", and let "H" mean "has". Translate each of the following into words.

1 $(x)(Sx \supset -Gx)$

2 $(\exists x)(Gx \& -Sx)$

3 $(\exists x)[Sx \& (\exists y) \ Hxy]$

4 $(\exists x)[Sx \& (\exists y)(Gy \& Hxy)]$

5 $(x)[Sx \supset (\exists y)(Gy \& Hxy)]$

6 $(\exists x)[Sx \& (y)(Gy \supset Hxy)]$

7 $(\exists x)[Gx \& (y)(Sy \supset Hxy)]$

8 $(y)[Gy \supset (\exists x)(Sx \& Hxy)]$

9 $(x)[Sx \supset (y)(Gy \supset Hxy)]$

Give a clear reason why each of the following translations is not correct.

1 No sailors are girls. $(x)-(Sx \supset Gx)$

2 Every sailor has a girl. $(x)Sx \supset (\exists y)(Gy \& Hxy)$

3 There is a sailor who has every girl. $(\exists x)[Sx \supset (y)(Gy \supset Hxy)]$

4 There is a girl who is every sailor's. $(\exists y)[Gy \& (x)(Sx \& Hxy)]$

5 Every girl is some sailor's. $(\exists x)[Sx \& (y)(Gy \supset Hxy)]$

Symbolize the following:

1 Every problem is solvable by some method or other.

2 There is a method by which every problem is solvable.

3 There is a post office in every city.

4 If anything is damaged, someone will have to pay for it.

5 Someone will have to pay for everything that is damaged.

6 If something is damaged, someone will have to pay a fine.

7 If any automobiles are solid gold, then some automobiles are expensive.

8 If all trespassers are violators of the law and only hoboes are trespassers, then if there are any trespassers some hoboes are violators of the law.

9 If all teachers are perfectionists and no students are hard-working, then some teachers will be frustrated.

10 If any student is careless, then if all teachers are perfectionists, he will be censured.

11 There is a disease that any doctor can cure; therefore, every doctor can cure some disease or other.

12 There is a politician whom everyone likes; therefore, there is a politician who likes himself.

PROVING VALIDITY OF ARGUMENTS

Neither Venn diagrams nor truth tables provide a method that is sufficient for establishing the validity of quantificational arguments. To do this we need a more powerful method. We shall use an extended version of the method of deduction that was developed in the preceding chapter.

Suppose we are interested in the argument "There is something that causes everything; therefore, each thing has some cause or other". This argument can be symbolized "$(\exists x)(y)Cxy$, therefore $(y)(\exists x)Cxy$". To claim that the argument is valid is to claim that it is impossible for the premise to be true but the conclusion false. This amounts to the same thing as claiming that the sentence "$(\exists x)(y)Cxy \,\&\, -(y)(\exists x)Cxy$" is a contradiction (that is, inconsistent, necessarily false). If we had a way of showing that the latter sentence is a contradiction, we would thereby have a way of showing that the original argument is valid.

How can we show a sentence to be a contradiction? The *reductio ad absurdum* reasoning mentioned in Chapter 3 gives a hint. Suppose we could show that from a sentence some other sentence that is definitely a contradiction validly follows. This would mean that the former sentence could be true only if the latter were, and since the latter is a contradiction and cannot be true, the former cannot be true either and must be a contradiction also. Going back to our example, if we can show that some obvious contradiction follows validly from "$(\exists x)\ (y)\,Cxy\ \&\ -(y)\ (\exists x)Cxy$", then we shall have shown that our original argument "$(\exists x)\,(y)\,Cxy$, therefore $(y)\,(\exists x)\,Cxy$" is a valid argument. We need to develop some rules of deduction that will enable us to do this.

Let us introduce the letters "a", "b", "c", etc., which we shall employ as *names* for particular things in the universe. We must regard each letter as naming just one thing, at least during the course of any one deduction (although a letter might name different things in different deductions). By a universal quantification, we mean an expression that starts with a universal quantifier whose scope is all the rest of the expression. A universal quantification such as "$(x)\,(x$ is physical$)$", which we might write "$(x)Fx$", says that everything is physical; thus from the universal quantification we are entitled to infer "Fa", "Fb", "Fc", etc. Here we are simply making use of the idea that what is true of everything must be true of each particular thing.

Here the singular sentence "Fa" is called an *instance* of the universal sentence "$(x)Fx$". In general, an instance is anything that we get from a quantification by removing the quantifier and inserting a name in place of the variable. (The name is to be inserted in *all* those places where the variable of quantification occurred.) Even if we do not know what the various letters mean, we still can tell that "$Fa \supset Ga$" is an instance of "$(z)\,(Fz \supset Gz)$", that "Hbc" is an instance of "$(x)Hxc$", that "$(\exists y)Rcyc$" is an instance of "$(z)\,(\exists y)Rzyz$", and also that "$(\exists y)Rcyc$" is an instance of "$(z)\,(\exists y)Rzyc$". However, "$Fa \supset Gx$" is not an instance of "$(x)\,(Fx \supset Gx)$", for the name has not replaced all occurrences of the variable of quantification.

This rule of *universal instantiation* is perfectly general: It says that from any universal quantification we may validly deduce any instance of it. Notice, however, that the rule does not entitle us to infer *"Fa ⊃ P"* from *"(x)Fx ⊃ P"*. This case is improper and does not accord with the rule, because the expression with which we start is not a universal quantification; the quantifier does not govern the whole of the expression. (Here *"P"* is to be thought of as a letter of the kind we used in the preceding chapter; it is short for some whole sentence.) To see that this case is improper, think of the sentence "If everything is physical, Plato was mistaken", which may be symbolized *"(x)Fx ⊃ P"*, and think of the sentence "If this book is physical, Plato was mistaken", which may be symbolized *"Fa ⊃ P"*. The first could be true even if the second is false, which shows that the second cannot follow validly from the first.

An expression is called an existential quantification if it starts with an existential quantifier whose scope is all the rest of the expression. An existential quantification *"(∃x)Fx"* says that there is at least one thing that is an *F*. Now let us take the letter *"a"* and arbitrarily use it as a name to refer to this thing (or to one of these things) that is supposed to be an *F*. If we understand *"a"* in this way, we may derive *"Fa"* from *"(∃x)Fx"*. Here too we can employ the notion of an instance: Anything is an instance of an existential quantification if it can be derived from the quantification by dropping the initial quantifier and inserting a name in all the places where the variable of quantification occurred.

The rule of *existential instantiation* tells us that from any existential quantification we may infer any instance of it, with one qualification. If we are to avoid fallacious reasoning, this rule has to be hedged with a restriction. We shall formulate the restriction as follows: When the instance is inferred by means of existential

instantiation, the name being introduced into the instance must be
one that has not previously been used in the deduction. Before we
discuss this restriction more fully, let us first see how the rules are
used.

In order to establish the validity of the argument
"$(\exists x)(y)Cxy$, therefore $(y)(\exists x)Cxy$", which we were considering
previously, we wanted to derive some obvious contradiction from
"$(\exists x)(y)Cxy \, \& -(y)(\exists x)Cxy$". We now are in a position to do
this. Let us draw up our work in the form of a deduction. We
shall use our two quantificational rules, the quantificational equivalences from earlier in this chapter, and also the truth-functional
principles from Chapter 3.

1.	$(\exists x)(y)Cxy \,\&$ $-(y)(\exists x)Cxy$	*Premise*
2.	$(\exists x)(y)Cxy$	*From 1 by conjunctive simplification (conj. simp.)*
3.	$(y)Cay$	*From 2 by existential instantiation (E.I.)*
4.	$-(y)(\exists x)Cxy$	*From 1 by conj. simp.*
5.	$(\exists y)-(\exists x)Cxy$	*From 4 by quantificational equivalence (quant. equiv.)*
6.	$-(\exists x)Cxb$	*From 5 by E.I.*
7.	Cab	*From 3 by universal instantiation (U.I.)*
8.	$(x)-Cxb$	*From 6 by quant. equiv.*
9.	$-Cab$	*From 8 by U.I.*
10.	$Cab \,\& -Cab$	*From 7, 9 by conjunctive adjunction (conj. adj.)*

Looking at the deduction as a whole, we see that in the last line we
have derived a definite contradiction of the form "$p \,\& -p$".
Conclusions of this form are the clearest and most obvious of
contradictions, and so we shall use them as the standard type of
contradiction, always trying to obtain a conclusion of this form as
the last line of a quantificational deduction. In this deduction
the contradiction was validly derived from the first line, and so the
first line must be a contradiction too. This shows that our original
argument was valid. Here then is our method for showing the
validity of valid quantificational arguments.

Going back now to the rule of existential instantiation, we see that there must be some kind of restriction upon it. A sentence such as "$(\exists x)Fx$" says that at least one thing is F, and if we think of the letter "a" as naming such a thing, then we may infer "Fa". But clearly it is important here that "a" be a name which has not previously been assigned some other special sense elsewhere in the same deduction. Invalid reasoning can easily occur if we neglect this restriction and allow a single letter to be assigned more than one special sense in the course of a deduction. For example, the expression "$(\exists x)Fx\ \&\ (\exists x)-Fx$" is not a contradiction but the following deduction purports to show that it is:

1.	$(\exists x)Fx\ \&\ (\exists x)-Fx$	*Premise*
2.	$(\exists x)Fx$	*From 1 by conj. simp.*
3.	Fa	*From 2 by E.I.*
4.	$(\exists x)-Fx$	*From 1 by conj. simp.*
5.	$-Fa$	*From 4 by E.I.*
6.	$Fa\ \&\ -Fa$	*From 3, 5 by conj. adj.*

This deduction claims to show that a contradiction follows from the first line and therefore that the first line is a contradiction. But that is not so, and the deduction is illegitimate. The fallacy is that in getting line 3 we have chosen to think of "a" as naming a particular thing that is F, but in line 5 we think of the same letter "a" as naming a particular thing that is non$F$. It is illegitimate to assume that the thing that was the F is the thing that is the non$F$; there is no reason why they need be the same thing. The mistake lies in line 5, where the name introduced into the instance ought to have been a name that had not occurred before in the deduction.

Here is another example to illustrate how this restriction is needed to prevent fallacious reasoning. The sentence "There is something that causes everything" does not follow from "Each thing is caused by something or other", yet here is a deduction that purports to show that it does follow:

1. $(x)(\exists y)Cxy \;\&\; -(\exists y)(x)Cxy$ *Premise*
2. $(x)(\exists y)Cxy$ *From 1 by conj. simp.*
3. $(\exists y)Cay$ *From 2 by U.I.*
4. Cab *From 3 by E.I.*
5. $-(\exists y)(x)Cxy$ *From 1 by conj. simp.*
6. $(y)-(x)Cxy$ *From 5 by quant. equiv.*
7. $-(x)Cxb$ *From 6 by U.I.*
8. $(\exists x)-Cxb$ *From 7 by quant. equiv.*
9. $-Cab$ *From 8 by E.I.*
10. $Cab \;\&\; -Cab$ *From 4, 9 by conj. adj.*

By apparently deducing a contradiction from the conjunction of "$(x)(\exists y)Cxy$" with the negation of "$(\exists y)(x)Cxy$", this deduction purports to show that the latter validly follows from the former. This is fallacious, and so we must think over the steps in the deduction to see what is wrong. In line 3 we let the letter "a" refer to an individual object, any object we please. Then in line 4 we let the letter "b" refer to an object related to the object a. Our choice of a was completely free, but our choice of b was not; b has to be an object to which a bears the C relation. So far it is all right. Then in line 7 we chose object b again; this is still all right, for line 6 is true of everything and so must be true of b. But in line 9 we chose a again, and this is the mistake. In line 9 we should have chosen a particular object not bearing the C relation to b. Line 8 guarantees us that there is at least one such object, but we have no guarantee that a is such an object. The letter "a" is not used for the first time in line 9, for "a" was previously introduced to refer to the object chosen in line 3. We have no right to assume that the sense assigned to "a" in line 9 is compatible with the sense previously assigned to "a" in line 3. We can avoid this sort of fallacy in deductions by insisting upon the restriction that the name introduced by means of existential instantiation must always be a new name that has not previously been used in the deduction.

Let us conclude this section by returning to the medieval argument symbolized at the end of the preceding section. We now are able to demonstrate its validity by means of a deduction.

1. $(x)(Cx \supset Fx)$ $\& -(x)[(\exists y)(Cy \& Dxy)$ $\supset (\exists y)(Fy \& Dxy)]$	*Premise*
2. $-(x)[(\exists y)(Cy \& Dxy)$ $\supset (\exists y)(Fy \& Dxy)]$	*From 1 by conj. simp.*
3. $(\exists x)-[(\exists y)(Cy \& Dxy)$ $\supset (\exists y)(Fy \& Dxy)]$	*From 2 by quant. equiv.*
4. $-[(\exists y)(Cy \& Day)$ $\supset (\exists y)(Fy \& Day)]$	*From 3 by E.I.*
5. $(\exists y)(Cy \& Day)$ $\& -(\exists y)(Fy \& Day)$	*From 4 by equivalence*
6. $(\exists y)(Cy \& Day)$	*From 5 by conj. simp.*
7. $Cb \& Dab$	*From 6 by E.I.*
8. $-(\exists y)(Fy \& Day)$	*From 5 by conj. simp.*
9. $(y)-(Fy \& Day)$	*From 8 by quant. equiv.*
10. $-(Fb \& Dab)$	*From 9 by U.I.*
11. $(x)(Cx \supset Fx)$	*From 1 by conj. simp.*
12. $Cb \supset Fb$	*From 11 by U.I.*
13. Cb	*From 7 by conj. simp.*
14. Fb	*From 12, 13 by modus ponens*
15. Dab	*From 7 by conj. simp.*
16. $Fb \& Dab$	*From 14, 15 by conj. adj.*
17. $(Fb \& Dab) \& -(Fb \& Dab)$	*From 16, 10 by conj. adj.*

Looking back over this deduction, we see that the steps are correct and that the deduction establishes the validity of the original argument. It should be emphasized that there can also be other correct series of steps that will establish the desired result.

But you may wonder how the deduction was invented. The rules of deduction tell us many kinds of steps that we *may* perform, but they do not tell us what we *must* do to finish the deduction; for that, some trial-and-error work will be needed. The aim in constructing the deduction is to reach a last line of the

form "p & $-p$"; anything of that form will do. Now, if we are
to obtain that sort of obvious contradiction here, it is likely that
we shall need different instances, some of which contain the same
names. (If we introduce a new name into each new instance, we
are not likely to obtain any contradiction.) For this reason, it is
wise, insofar as possible, to perform E.I. before we perform U.I.
Doing so allows us to introduce into the U.I. instance the same
name that previously we introduced into the E.I. instance, thus
improving the chances of obtaining a contradiction. This is why
in the earlier lines of the deduction we elect to deal first with the
right-hand part of line 1, upon which we can perform E.I., rather
than with the left-hand component, upon which we would have to
perform U.I. Then in lines 10 and 12, when we finally perform
U.I., we choose the previously used name "b" which seems to offer
most promise of yielding a contradiction.

   Our principles for use in quantificational deductions follow:

Principles for use in quantificational deductions

   I. We may use any of the principles of truth-functional deduction
   that were listed in Chapter 3.

   II. QUANTIFICATIONAL RULES OF INFERENCE

   Universal instantiation (U.I.): From any universal quantification
   we may validly infer any instance of it.
   Existential instantiation (E.I.): From an existential quantification
   we may validly infer any instance of it, provided that the name
   being introduced into the instance is new to the deduction.

   III. QUANTIFICATIONAL EQUIVALENCES

   (From a sentence we may validly infer any sentence equivalent
   to it.)
   1. Two sentences are equivalent if they are exactly alike except
       that, where the first contains a negation sign immediately fol-
       lowed by a universal quantifier, the other contains an existential
       quantifier immediately followed by a negation sign; e.g., "$- (x)$
       Fx" is equivalent to "$(\exists x) - Fx$".
   2. Two sentences always are equivalent if they are exactly alike
       except that, where the first contains a negation sign immediately

followed by an existential quantifier, the second contains a universal quantifier immediately followed by a negation sign; e.g., "$- (\exists x)\ Fx$" is equivalent to "$(x) - Fx$".

Two more quantificational equivalences will be added later.

Exercise 19

Each of the following is a correct deduction. Explain the justification for each step, and state what the deduction shows.

1
1. $(x)(Sx \supset Px)$
   $\& (\exists x)(Sx \& -Px)$
2. $(\exists x)(Sx \& -Px)$
3. $Sa \& -Pa$
4. $(x)(Sx \supset Px)$
5. $Sa \supset Pa$
6. Sa
7. Pa
8. $-Pa$
9. $Pa \& -Pa$

2
1. $(x)Fx \& -(y)Fy$
2. $-(y)Fy$
3. $(\exists y)-Fy$
4. $-Fa$
5. $(x)Fx$
6. Fa
7. $Fa \& -Fa$

3
1. $[(x)(Mx \supset -Px)$
   $\& (x)(Sx \supset Mx)]$
   $\& -(x)(Sx \supset -Px)$
2. $-(x)(Sx \supset -Px)$
3. $(\exists x)-(Sx \supset -Px)$
4. $-(Sa \supset -Pa)$
5. $(x)(Mx \supset -Px)$
   $\& (x)(Sx \supset Mx)$
6. $(x)(Mx \supset -Px)$
7. $Ma \supset -Pa$
8. $(x)(Sx \supset Mx)$
9. $Sa \supset Ma$
10. $Sa \& Pa$
11. Sa
12. Ma
13. $-Pa$
14. Pa
15. $Pa \& -Pa$

4
1. $(\exists x)[Gx \& (y)(Gy$
   $\supset Hxy)] \&$
   $-(\exists x)(Gx \& Hxx)$
2. $(\exists x)[Gx \& (y)(Gy$
   $\supset Hxy)]$
3. $Gb \& (y)(Gy \supset Hby)$
4. $(y)(Gy \supset Hby)$
5. $Gb \supset Hbb$
6. $-(\exists x)(Gx \& Hxx)$
7. $(x)-(Gx \& Hxx)$
8. $-(Gb \& Hbb)$
9. Gb
10. Hbb
11. $-Hbb$
12. $Hbb \& -Hbb$

5   1. $(\exists z)[-Rzz \& (y)Rzy]$
     2. $-Rcc \& (y)Rcy$
     3. $(y)Rcy$
     4. Rcc
     5. $-Rcc$
     6. $Rcc \& -Rcc$

6   1. $-(x)[(y)Fy \supset Fx]$
     2. $(\exists x)-[(y)Fy \supset Fx]$
     3. $-[(y)Fy \supset Fa]$
     4. $(y)Fy \& -Fa$
     5. $(y)Fy$
     6. Fa
     7. $-Fa$
     8. $Fa \& -Fa$

Explain the justification of each legitimate step. If any step is illegitimate, explain why and consider whether the deduction could be rearranged so as to demonstrate the same result legitimately.

1   1. $(x)Fx \& -(y)Fy$
     2. $(x)Fx$
     3. Fa
     4. $-(y)Fy$
     5. $(\exists y)-Fy$
     6. $-Fa$
     7. $Fa \& -Fa$

2   1. $(\exists x)(\exists y)Rxy \&$
        $-(\exists x)Rxx$
     2. $(\exists x)(\exists y)Rxy$
     3. $(\exists y)Ray$
     4. $-(\exists x)Rxx$
     5. $(x)-Rxx$
     6. $-Raa$
     7. Raa
     8. $Raa \& -Raa$

USING THE METHOD

Questions These Deductions Can Answer

Our method of deduction enables us to demonstrate that a quantificational sentence is a contradiction. We do so by showing that from the given sentence a truth-functional contradiction of the form *"p & −p"* validly follows. As we have already seen, this method can be used to answer questions about the validity of arguments, because any question about the validity of an argument (or about an implication) can be rephrased as a question about whether·some sentence is a contradiction.

If we want to test the validity of a quantificational argument, we put the premise into conjunction with the negation of the conclusion, and we try to show that this conjunction is a contradiction. When we have an argument with more than one premise, we can also use this method. However, now we must form a conjunction of all the premises, put this into conjunction with the negation of the conclusion, and see whether this is a contradiction. If it is, that shows that it is impossible for the conclusion to be false provided all the premises are true; that is, it shows that the premises imply the conclusion and the argument is valid.

Another question we can handle is whether a quantificational sentence is necessarily true in virtue of its quantificational form. This question can be rephrased as a question about a contradiction. That is because a given sentence is necessarily true if and only if its negation is a contradiction. For instance, a sentence of the form "$(x)(Fx \supset Fx)$" is necessarily true if and only if the corresponding sentence of the form "$-(x)(Fx \supset Fx)$" is a contradiction. This provides a method of demonstrating the necessary truth of a quantificational sentence: We form the negation of the given sentence and then show that this negation is a contradiction.

Strategy in Using the Rules

In constructing deductions, we must use a little strategy in order to avoid being balked by the restriction on the rule of existential instantiation. The restriction requires that any name introduced by means of E.I. must be a new name. We should not let this restriction prevent us from getting the legitimate results that we want. For example, suppose we are trying to show by deduction that a syllogism of the type **AII** in the first figure is valid. Symbolizing the premises and putting them into conjunction with the negation of the conclusion, we have the following:

1 $[(x)(Mx \supset Px) \& (\exists x)(Sx \& Mx)] \& -(\exists x)(Sx \& Px)$

We might then attempt to deduce a contradiction from this by proceeding as follows:

2. $(x)(Mx \supset Px) \& (\exists x)(Sx \& Mx)$	*From 1 by conj. simp.*
3. $(x)(Mx \supset Px)$	*From 2 by conj. simp.*
4. $Ma \supset Pa$	*From 3 by U.I.*
5. $(\exists x)(Sx \& Mx)$	*From 2 by conj. simp.*

But now we are in trouble. We cannot properly obtain "*Sa & Ma*" from line 5 by E.I., for the name "*a*" already has been used in the deduction, and no other instance would yield a contradiction. Here the solution is to take our steps in a different order. We perform E.I. first, and then U.I.

1. $[(x)(Mx \supset Px) \& (\exists x)(Sx \& Mx)] \& -(\exists x)(Sx \& Px)$	
2. $(x)(Mx \supset Px) \& (\exists x)(Sx \& Mx)$	*From 1 by conj. simp.*
3. $(\exists x)(Sx \& Mx)$	*From 2 by conj. simp.*
4. $Sa \& Ma$	*From 3 by E.I.*
5. $(x)(Mx \supset Px)$	*From 2 by conj. simp.*
6. $Ma \supset Pa$	*From 5 by U.I.*
7. $-(\exists x)(Sx \& Px)$	*From 1 by conj. simp.*
8. $(x)-(Sx \& Px)$	*From 7 by quant. equiv.*
9. $-(Sa \& Pa)$	*From 8 by U.I.*
10. Ma	*From 4 by conj. simp.*
11. Pa	*From 6, 10 by modus ponens*
12. Sa	*From 4 by conj. simp.*
13. $Sa \& Pa$	*From 11, 12 by conj. adj.*
14. $(Sa \& Pa) \& -(Sa \& Pa)$	*From 9, 13 by conj. adj.*

Here we get the contradiction we want, because we have arranged the sequence of steps so that we do not violate the restriction. As was mentioned at the end of the preceding section, it always is wise to perform E.I. before U.I., insofar as that is possible.

As another example of strategy, let us consider how we could show that the sentence "There is something such that if something is physical then it is physical" is necessarily true. We may symbolize it "$(\exists x)[(\exists y)Fy \supset Fx]$". To show that it is necessarily true, we must derive a contradiction from its negation.

1.	$-(\exists x)[(\exists y)Fy \supset Fx]$	
2.	$(x)-[(\exists y)Fy \supset Fx]$	*From 1 by quant. equiv.*
3.	$-[(\exists y)Fy \supset Fa]$	*From 2 by U.I.*
4.	$(\exists y)Fy \& -Fa$	*From 3 by equivalence*
5.	$(\exists y)Fy$	*From 4 by conj. simp.*

At this point in the deduction we are prevented from reaching "Fa" as the next line, for that would violate the restriction. And here we cannot perform the existential instantiation first, because the existential quantifier is buried within the scope of the universal quantifier. (The rule of existential instantiation allows removal of an existential quantifier only when it stands at the beginning of the expression and governs the whole.) Here the problem of strategy is momentarily puzzling. The solution is to use another name and then go back and obtain a second instance from the universal quantification so as to produce the contradiction.

6.	Fb	*From 5 by E.I.*
7.	$-[(\exists y)Fy \supset Fb]$	*From 2 by U.I.*
8.	$(\exists y)Fy \& -Fb$	*From 7 by equivalence*
9.	$-Fb$	*From 8 by conj. simp.*
10.	$Fb \& -Fb$	*From 6, 9 by conj. adj.*

In inventing deductions like these, we have to use trial and error, experimenting with various possibilities until we find a combination of steps that will yield the needed result.

Arguments Containing Singular Sentences

A sentence containing a proper name or other phrase that purports to apply to exactly one individual is called a singular sentence. Such sentences can be translated into categorical form, as we saw in Chapter 2. But quantificational symbolism offers a better way of treating them, for we can use the letters *"a"*, *"b"*, *"c"*, etc., as names. Thus, for instance, "All philosophers are wise; Socrates is a philosopher; therefore Socrates is wise" can be symbolized as *"(x)(Px ⊃ Wx), Pa, therefore Wa"*. Here *"a"* refers to Socrates. We can demonstrate the validity of the syllogism thus:

1. $[(x)(Px \supset Wx) \& Pa] \& -Wa$
2. $(x)(Px \supset Wx) \& Pa$ *From 1 by conj. simp.*
3. $(x)(Px \supset Wx)$ *From 2 by conj. simp.*
4. $Pa \supset Wa$ *From 3 by U.I.*
5. Pa *From 2 by conj. simp.*
6. Wa *From 4, 5 by modus ponens*
7. $-Wa$ *From 1 by conj. simp.*
8. $Wa \& -Wa$ *From 6, 7 by conj. adj.*

Exercise 20

In each case construct a quantificational deduction to show that the example is logically correct.

1 "Something is bigger than something" validly follows from "Everything is bigger than something".

2 If there is something such that everything is bigger than it, then for each thing there is something than which it is bigger.

3 "Nothing is bigger than anything" contradicts "Something is bigger than something".

4 All these jewels are valuable. Whatever gets lost will have to be paid for. Therefore, if everything valuable gets lost, then all these jewels will have to be paid for.

5 There is a subject that is liked by any student who likes any subject at all. Every student likes some subject or other. Therefore, there is a subject that is liked by all students.

6 Every logical problem is challenging. Anyone who solves anything challenging deserves credit. Someone clever solved certain logical problems. Therefore, someone clever deserves credit.

7 The regulations of a certain ship state that any barber aboard this ship must shave all and only those aboard the ship who do not shave themselves. Therefore, according to these regulations there is no barber aboard this ship.

8 Every elephant is bigger than any mouse. Dumbo is an elephant. Mickey is a mouse. Therefore, Dumbo is bigger than Mickey.

9 No human person is his own father. Therefore, a person who is father of every human person is not human.

10 Infinity is bigger than every countable number. Therefore, infinity is not a countable number, since no number is bigger than itself.

EXTENDING THE METHOD

Although our method already enables us to handle many kinds of examples, it still is not complete. There are other kinds of examples with which we are not yet in a position to deal. The difficulty is this. In using the method to derive a contradiction, we need to be able to obtain instances of the various quantifications that occur in the first line. The rules of U.I. and E.I. allow us to obtain an instance from a quantification only when the quantifier is at the very beginning and governs the whole expression. Hence we have to derive from the first line new lines that will have quantifiers at the beginning governing the whole lines; from these lines we in turn obtain our instances. When the first line is a conjunction of quantifications or their negations, the truth-functional rule of conjunctive simplification together with the quantificational equivalences suffice to enable us to derive the new lines needed, each having at its beginning a quantifier that governs the whole. But where the first line contains quantifications that are linked together in ways other than mere conjunction, the rule of conjunctive simplification is powerless.

Consider the quantificational sentence "Either everything is solid and not solid or everything is liquid and not liquid", which may be symbolized "$(x)(Sx \, \& -Sx) \lor (y)(Ly \, \& -Ly)$". This sentence is a contradiction, but so far we do not have any way of showing it to be a contradiction. If we write this as the first line of a deduction, there is no rule permitting us to take any useful step beyond the first line. We shall now extend our method by adding to it a pair of further principles of equivalence that will enable us, in cases like this, to obtain the needed further lines, each having at the beginning a quantifier governing all the rest.

Consider the two sentences:

Either each thing is mental, or Berkeley's philosophy is mistaken.
Each thing is such that either it is mental or Berkeley's philosophy is mistaken.

If we write "M" for "mental" and "B" for the whole sentence "Berkeley's philosophy is mistaken", we can symbolize the two sentences thus:

$(x)Mx \lor B$
$(x)(Mx \lor B)$

The first sentence is a disjunction one component of which is a universal quantification, while the second sentence is a universal quantification of a disjunction. The two sentences are equivalent, however, for each is true if and only if either everything is mental or Berkeley's philosophy is mistaken. The underlying principle of equivalence here can be stated in more general terms: Any disjunction, one part of which is a universal quantification, may be rewritten in the equivalent form of a universal quantification of a disjunction. Returning to our earlier example, we now can carry out the desired deduction.

1. $(x)(Sx \& -Sx) \lor (y)(Ly \& -Ly)$
2. $(x)[(Sx \& -Sx) \lor (y)(Ly \& -Ly)]$ *From 1 by quant. equiv.*
3. $(Sa \& -Sa) \lor (y)(Ly \& -Ly)$ *From 2 by U.I.*
4. $(y)[(Sa \& -Sa) \lor (Ly \& -Ly)]$ *From 3 by quant. equiv.*
5. $(Sa \& -Sa) \lor (La \& -La)$ *From 4 by U.I.*
6. $(Sa \& -Sa) \supset (Sa \& -Sa)$ *Tautology*
7. $(La \& -La) \supset (Sa \& -Sa)$ *Tautology*
8. $Sa \& -Sa$ *From 5, 6, 7; dilemma*

Here we twice make use of our new principle of quantificational equivalence, first in line 2 and again in line 4. In each case we take a universal quantifier that governed only one component of a disjunction and move it so that it governs the whole disjunction.

Still another kind of example that our method does not yet enable us to handle is illustrated by the sentence "Either something is liquid and is not liquid or something is solid and is not solid", which may be symbolized "$(\exists x)(Lx \& -Lx) \lor (\exists y)(Sy \& -Sy)$". This sentence is a contradiction, but here again we cannot show that it is so, for our rules do not yet enable us to take any useful step beyond the first line. We need one more principle of equivalence.

To understand this last principle of equivalence, consider these sentences:

Either something moves or Zeno's philosophy is correct.
Something is such that either it moves or Zeno's philosophy is correct.

Writing "M" for "moves" and "Z" for the whole sentence "Zeno's philosophy is correct", we can symbolize these as follows:

$(\exists x)Mx \lor Z$
$(\exists x)(Mx \lor Z)$

The first sentence is a disjunction one component of which is an existential quantification, while the second sentence is an existential quantification of a disjunction. They are equivalent, however, for each is true if and only if either at least one thing moves or Zeno's philosophy is correct. The underlying principle of equivalence here can be stated in general terms: Any disjunction, one part of which is an existential quantification, may be rewritten in the equivalent form of an existential quantification of a disjunction. Returning to our example, we now can complete the desired deduction.

1. $(\exists x)(Lx \& -Lx) \lor (\exists y)(Sy \& -Sy)$
2. $(\exists x)[(Lx \& -Lx) \lor (\exists y)(Sy \& -Sy)]$ *From 1 by quant. equiv.*
3. $(La \& -La) \lor (\exists y)(Sy \& -Sy)$ *From 2 by E.I.*
4. $(\exists y)[(La \& -La) \lor (Sy \& -Sy)]$ *From 3 by quant. equiv.*
5. $(La \& -La) \lor (Sb \& -Sb)$ *From 4 by E.I.*
6. $(La \& -La) \supset (La \& -La)$ *Tautology*
7. $(Sb \& -Sb) \supset (La \& -La)$ *Tautology*
8. $La \& -La$ *From 5, 6, 7; dilemma*

Here we twice make use of our newest principle of quantificational equivalence, first in line 2 and again in line 4. In each case we take an existential quantifier that governed only one component of a disjunction and move it so that it governs the whole disjunction.

These principles of quantificational equivalence for use in deductions involve negation and disjunction, and so by themselves they do not tell us how to deal with lines in which quantifications are linked by the conditional or other truth-functional compounds. However, the conditional or any other truth-functional compound can be equivalently expressed using nothing but conjunction, negation, and disjunction; thus we are able to take the steps we need. For example, the sentence "If everything is liquid or not liquid, then something is solid and not solid" is shown to be a contradiction in the following manner:

1. $(x)(Lx \lor -Lx) \supset (\exists y)(Sy \& -Sy)$
2. $-(x)(Lx \lor -Lx) \lor (\exists y)(Sy \& -Sy)$ *From 1 by equivalence*
3. $(\exists y)[-(x)(Lx \lor -Lx) \lor (Sy \& -Sy)]$ *From 2 by quant. equiv.*

4. $-(x)(Lx \vee -Lx) \vee (Sa \& -Sa)$	*From 3 by E.I.*
5. $(\exists x)-(Lx \vee -Lx) \vee (Sa \& -Sa)$	*From 4 by quant. equiv.*
6. $(\exists x)[-(Lx \vee -Lx) \vee (Sa \& -Sa)]$	*From 5 by quant. equiv.*
7. $-(Lb \vee -Lb) \vee (Sa \& -Sa)$	*From 6 by E.I.*
8. $(-Lb \& Lb) \vee (Sa \& -Sa)$	*From 7 by equivalence*
9. $(Sa \& -Sa) \supset (Sa \& -Sa)$	*Tautology*
10. $(-Lb \& Lb) \supset (Sa \& -Sa)$	*Tautology*
11. $Sa \& -Sa$	*From 8, 9, 10; dilemma*

Here we make use of a truth-functional equivalence to obtain line 2 and start the deduction.

In light of what has been said in this section, we can now add two further principles of quantificational equivalence to the list on p. 156. These additional principles belong under heading III of the list. It is necessary to mention, however, that in discussing these two principles of equivalence we have taken it for granted that the sentences with which we are concerned do not contain any free variables. These principles would have to be restated in narrower form if they were to hold good for sentences containing free variables; but we are not concerned with that sort of sentence.

ADDITIONAL PRINCIPLES OF QUANTIFICATIONAL EQUIVALENCE

3. **Any disjunction, one component of which is a universal quantification, may be rewritten in the equivalent form of a universal quantification of a disjunction; e.g., "$(x)Mx \vee B$" is equivalent to "$(x)(Mx \vee B)$".**

4. **Any disjunction, one component of which is an existential quantification, may be rewritten in the equivalent form of an existential quantification of a disjunction; e.g., "$(\exists x)Mx \vee Z$" is equivalent to "$(\exists x)(Mx \vee Z)$".**

Exercise 21

In each case, construct a deduction showing that a sentence symbolized in the given way would be a contradiction.

1    $-[-(x)Ax \vee (y)Ay]$

2 $-[(\exists z)Bz \supset (\exists x)Bx]$

3 $(\exists x)(Ax \supset Ax) \supset (y)-(By \supset By)$

4 $(\exists z)-(Az \vee -Az) \equiv (y)(Ay \equiv Ay)$

5 $(\exists x)(Ax \vee Bx) \,\&\, -(\exists x)(-Bx \supset Ax)$

6 $-\{(x)(\exists y)(Bx \supset Cxy) \vee (\exists x)[Bx \,\&\, -(\exists y)Cxy)]\}$

7 $(x)[Ax \supset (\exists y)Cxy] \equiv (\exists z)[Az \,\&\, (y)\, -Czy]$

8 $(\exists x)[Bx \,\&\, (y)-By] \vee (z)[Bz \equiv -(\exists y)By]$

NEGATIVE DEMONSTRATIONS

The method of quantificational deduction that we have been using is a method for bringing out contradictions; we have been using it also to establish the validity of quantificational arguments and to detect necessarily true quantificational sentences. But can this method be used to demonstrate that a quantificational sentence is *not* a contradiction? In one special kind of case it is possible to do so: Specifically, if it can be shown that the negation of a sentence is a contradiction, this will suffice to demonstrate that the given sentence is not a contradiction. However, suppose we start with a sentence that is not a contradiction and whose negation is not a contradiction either. Can we demonstrate that a sentence of this kind is not a contradiction? The mere fact that we have tried to deduce a truth-functional contradiction from it and have not been successful does not prove that there is no contradiction; perhaps we have not worked intelligently enough. Our method of deduction simply does not offer a general way of demonstrating the negative fact that a quantificational sentence is not a contradiction.

Consider the sentence "There is something that is a unicorn only if it is herbivorous, and all unicorns are nonherbivorous". It may be symbolized "$(\exists x)(Ux \supset Hx) \,\&\, (x)(Ux \supset -Hx)$". Suppose we want to learn whether it is a contradiction. If we try to use our method of deduction, we find that even after working long and hard we do not deduce a truth-functional contradiction. But this lack of success means merely that we have established nothing. Can we show more definitely that the sentence is not a contradiction?

If a sentence of the form "$(\exists x)(Ux \supset Hx)$ & $(x)(Ux \supset -Hx)$" is not a contradiction, this means that some sentences of this form are true. If we find at least one sentence of this form that is definitely true, we shall thereby demonstrate that our original sentence is not a contradiction. Or, to put it more accurately, we shall have demonstrated that our original sentence is not a contradiction on account of having this quantificational form; we have not dealt with and have not removed the possibility that it might be a contradiction for some other reason, although in this example there is no other reason that merits consideration.[2]

Let us try then to discover a sentence of this same form that is very clearly true. This can best be done if we seek a sentence dealing with things concerning which very clear and definite assertions can be made. Numbers are probably the best subject matter for this purpose. Let us see whether we can discover a way of *reinterpreting* the letters "U" and "H" so that "$(\exists x)(Ux \supset Hx)$ & $(x)(Ux \supset -Hx)$" becomes a true sentence about numbers. Let us reinterpret "U" to mean "odd number" and "H" to mean "even number". Under this reinterpretation, "$(\exists x)(Ux \supset Hx)$ & $(x)(Ux \supset -Hx)$" turns into the sentence "There is at least one number such that if it is odd then it is even, and every number is such that if it is odd then it is not even". (Here we are thinking of numbers as being the only objects under discussion;

---

[2] Being a contradiction on account of its quantificational form is a sufficient though not a necessary condition for a sentence being a contradiction. A sentence like "Some wealthy persons are not rich" is a contradiction even though its quantificational form—presumably, "$(\exists x)(Wx$ & $-Rx)$"— is not what makes it so.

we are limiting our 'universe of discourse' to numbers.) This
sentence is a conjunction, and its first component is definitely
true, since there is at least one number, for instance 2, such that
if it is odd then it is even. (Remember that this is the truth-
functional sense of "if—then".) The second component of the
conjunction is definitely true too, since no odd numbers are even.
Thus the sentence as a whole is definitely true. This shows that
our original sentence is not a contradiction (at least, not on
account of its quantificational form).

So far, we have discussed a procedure for showing that a
quantificational sentence is not a contradiction. This same procedure can be employed to show that an argument is not valid in
virtue of its quantificational form. For example, suppose the
question is whether the argument "Everything attracts something;
therefore something is attracted by everything", being symbolized
"$(x)(\exists y)Axy$, therefore $(\exists y)(x)Axy$", is valid. We can show
that it is an invalid argument if a reinterpretation of "A" can turn
the premise into a definitely true sentence and turn the conclusion
into a definitely false one.

To do this, let us again talk about numbers, and let us think of
numbers as being the only things to which we shall refer for the
moment. (We limit our 'universe of discourse' to numbers.) Let
us reinterpret "A" to mean "smaller than". Then "$(x)(\exists y)$
Axy" comes to mean "Each number is smaller than some other",
while "$(\exists y)(x)Axy$" becomes "There is a number than which
every number is smaller". The former sentence is definitely
true whereas the latter is definitely false, thus showing the invalidity of the original argument, or, more accurately, showing
that the original argument is not valid on account of its quantificational form.

Finally, we shall note one further sort of negative result that
can be established by this procedure of reinterpreting quantificational sentences. Suppose the question now is whether two quan-

tificational sentences are equivalent. Consider, for example, the sentences

If something is not for the best, then Leibniz's philosophy is mistaken.
Something is such that if it is not for the best then Leibniz's philosophy is mistaken.

Writing "B" for "for the best" and "L" for the sentence "Leibniz's philosophy is mistaken", we can symbolize these:

$(\exists x) - Bx \supset L$
$(\exists x)(-Bx \supset L)$

Perhaps we start by trying to demonstrate that the two sentences are equivalent. To say that two sentences are equivalent is to say that they are necessarily alike as regards truth and falsity. This means that each must validly follow from the other. We could attempt to construct two deductions, one showing that the first sentence validly follows from the second, and another showing that the second sentence validly follows from the first. In this case, however, we would be unable to complete both deductions. Encountering difficulty, we could change our approach and seek to show instead that the two sentences are not equivalent. How can we do this?

One way of showing that they are not equivalent is to reinterpret the letters "B" and "L" so that we obtain two new sentences having the very same forms but definitely differing as regards truth and falsity. In doing this, let us again treat of numbers. We reinterpret "B" to mean "even" and reinterpret "L" to mean "2 is smaller than 1". Then we obtain two new sentences:

If something is not an even number, then 2 is smaller than 1.
Something is such that if it is not an even number then 2 is smaller than 1.

The first sentence is definitely false, because it is a conditional with true antecedent and false consequent. The second sentence is

definitely true, because there is at least one thing, say the number
4, such that if it is not an even number then 2 is smaller than 1.
(Here again we recall the truth-functional sense of "if—then".)
Thus we have found two sentences definitely different as regards
truth and falsity but having the very same forms as the original
two sentences. This shows that our original two sentences are not
equivalent; at any rate, they are not equivalent in virtue of their
quantificational form.

Exercise 22

*Show that sentences of each of the following forms are not
contradictions on account of their quantificational form.*

1 $(x)(-Gx \supset Gx)$

2 $(\exists x)(Fx \supset -Fx)$

3 $(\exists x)(\exists y)Rxy \; \& -(x)(\exists y)Rxy$

*Show that arguments of the following forms are not valid on
account of their quantificational form.*

1 $(\exists x)(\exists y)Rxy$, therefore $(\exists x)(y)Rxy$

2 $(x)[(Fx \& Gx) \supset Hx]$, therefore $(x)[(Fx \lor Gx) \supset Hx]$

3 $(x)Fx \supset (\exists y)Gy$, therefore $(x)[Fx \supset (\exists y)Gy]$

4 $(x)Fx \supset (\exists y)Gy$, therefore $Fa \supset (\exists y)Gy$

Show that each of the following statements is correct.

1 Sentences of the forms "$(x)(\exists y)Rxy$" and "$(x)-(\exists y)Rxy$"
are not equivalent to negations of each other.

2 Sentences of the form "$(x)(\exists y)Rxy \lor (x)(\exists y)-Rxy$" are
not necessarily true.

3 The following regulations of the Warren G. Harding University do not involve a contradiction:

Students who study the same subject must not room together; every student who is a dormitory resident must have a roommate; no law student may have a roommate who is studying a different subject than he is.

5. *Fallacies*

Logicians normally give their attention to logically correct types of reasoning and do not devote much effort to cataloguing the myriad forms of logical error, for the former prove to be of much greater theoretical interest than the latter. When we are concerned with the practical aspect of logic, however, some discussion of logical errors is worthwhile. The efficient way of improving our ability to tell the difference between good and bad reasoning is to look at examples of the bad as well as the good.

A *fallacy* is a logical mistake in reasoning. The term "fallacy" is often loosely applied to any sort of mistaken belief or untrue sentence. "It's a fallacy to believe that handling a toad causes warts", people say; here the thing being called a fallacy is just a belief, not an inference. In logic the term "fallacy" is restricted to mistakes in reasoning. When there are premises and a conclusion that, through some logical error, is mistakenly thought to be proved by them, then and only then is there a fallacy in the logical sense. Innumerable kinds of logical mistakes can be made in reasoning. Some kinds are more tempting and more likely to deceive than others, and many of these have specific names.

The great advantage of a name for something is that it enables us to keep the thing clearly in mind and helps us to recognize it when we meet it. In this sense, knowing the name gives us a sort of power over the thing. By learning the names of some of the commoner kinds of fallacies and by having a general scheme for classifying them, we are able to recognize fallacies more readily and to think more clearly about them. We shall use the scheme of classification shown in the table on the following page. It embodies some of the traditional terminology for fallacies but in reorganized form. This classification covers fallacies in both deductive and inductive reasoning, although for the present we shall limit our examples to fallacies that arise in deductive reasoning.

In thinking about the classification of fallacies, let us recall that the purpose of constructing arguments is to prove conclusions that are in some way unknown or doubtful or that have been challenged and called into question. A speaker can prove a conclusion only if his argument contains premises (1) that are capable of all being true, (2) that are such that the speaker and his hearers can know them to be true without being aware of whether the conclusion is true, and (3) from which the conclusion follows. The neglect of any one of these three requirements for a successful proof gives rise to a separate category of fallacies.

Neglect of the third requirement gives rise to the fallacies of *non sequitur* (Latin: "it does not follow"). These fallacious arguments are fallacies in the most obvious sense of the term, for their logical defect is that they have an insufficient link between premises and conclusion.

Neglect of the second requirement gives rise to reasoning that is fallacious in a more subtle sense. If the premises are related to the conclusion in such an intimate way that the speaker and his

hearers could not have less reason to doubt the premises than they
have to doubt the conclusion, then the argument is worthless as a
proof, even though the link between premises and conclusion may
have the most cast-iron rigor. Fallacies of this second category are

Classification of fallacies

GENERAL TYPE			SOME SPECIFIC FORMS
Inconsistency			$\vdots$
Petitio Principii			Fallacy of complex question $\vdots$
Non *Sequitur*	*Pure Fallacies*	*Formal fallacies in deduction*	Undistributed middle Illicit process Affirming the consequent Denying the antecedent $\vdots$
		Pure inductive fallacies	Forgetful induction Hasty induction Slothful induction
	Fallacies of Ambiguity	*Equivocation*	Fallacy of four terms Composition, division $\vdots$
		Amphiboly	$\vdots$

	Fallacies of Irrelevance (ignoratio elenchi)		ad hominem abusive
			                            circumstantial
			                            tu quoque
			ad baculum
			ad verecundiam
			ad misericordiam
			black-and-white thinking $\vdots$

called fallacies of *petitio principii* (Latin : "begging the question").

Finally, neglect of the first requirement gives rise to the remaining category of fallacies. If someone uses as premises sentences that necessarily could not all be true at once, then his reasoning certainly cannot establish his conclusion, even though the link between premises and conclusion is as rigorous as can be. When someone reasons from a set of premises that necessarily could not all be true, he is committing a fallacy of *inconsistency*.

Using our scheme for classifying fallacies, we shall have to keep in mind that often a fallacious argument may be classified in more than one way. Perhaps when interpreted in one fashion it commits one fallacy, while under some other legitimate interpretation it would be regarded as committing some different fallacy. (We shall meet examples of this sort presently.) But every fallacious argument should admit of being classified in at least one place in our scheme. Also we should note that an argument may fall under some general heading without being an example of any specifically named form of fallacy under that heading ; the dots at various places in the table indicate where there are further specific types of fallacies, many of them without special names.

INCONSISTENCY

Suppose someone reasons in the following way : "Franklin is 20 miles due north of Jefferson. There is a straight road that starts at Franklin and goes through Adamston to Sperryville. Jefferson is 20 miles due west of Adamston. Sperryville is northeast of Jefferson. Therefore, Jefferson is nearer to Franklin than to Sperryville".

There is something wrong with this argument, even though the speaker may not have noticed it. The trouble here is not that there is any insufficiency about the link between premises and conclusion ; instead, the trouble is with the premises themselves.

They cannot all be true. To use premises that are not all true always is a mistake, but it is not always a logical mistake. In this case, however, the premises do not merely happen to be not all true; they necessarily are not all true. It would be contradicting oneself to accept all four of these premises. Therefore, in this case a logical error, a fallacy of inconsistency, is being committed. In general, anyone commits a fallacy of inconsistency if he reasons from premises that necessarily could not all be true.

Should we say that an argument of this sort is invalid? No. For to call an argument invalid is to say that it is possible for its premises to be true while its conclusion is false, and that possibility does not arise here. An argument whose premises cannot all be true is an argument incapable of having premises all true but conclusion false. Thus this sort of argument is perfectly valid; yet it is logically defective all the same, as we have seen.

THE PETITIO PRINCIPII

An argument is called a *petitio principii* (or begging of the question) if the argument fails to prove anything because it somehow takes for granted what it is supposed to prove. Suppose someone says "Jones is insane, you know", and we reply, "Really? Are you sure?", and he responds, "Certainly, I can prove it. Jones is demented; therefore he is insane". This is a valid argument in the sense that, if the premise is true, the conclusion must be true too; but the argument is unsatisfactory, for it does not really prove anything. The premise is merely another statement of the conclusion, so that anyone who doubted the truth of the conclusion surely ought to be equally doubtful about the truth of the premise, and the argument would be valueless for the purpose of convincing him of the truth of the conclusion. Thus the argument takes for granted just what it is supposed to prove; it begs the question.

Consider a longer chain of reasoning:

"We must not drink liquor."

"Why do you say that?"

"Drinking is against the will of Allah."

"How do you know?"

"The Koran says so."

"But how do you know that the Koran is right?"

"Everything said in the Koran is right."

"How do you know that?"

"Why, it's all divinely inspired."

"But how do you know?"

"Why, the Koran itself declares that it is divinely inspired."

"But why believe that?"

"You've got to believe the Koran, because everything in the Koran is right."

This chain of reasoning is a more extended case of begging the question; the speaker is reasoning in a large circle, taking for granted one of the things that he professes to be proving.

One specific form of *petitio principii*, or begging the question, has a special name of its own: the fallacy of *complex question*. This is the fallacy of framing a question so as to take for granted something controversial that ought to be proved.

Suppose Mr. White is trying to prove that Mr. Black has a bad character, and White asks Black the famous question, "Have you stopped beating your wife yet?". If Black answers "Yes" to this question, White will argue that Black is admitting to having been a wife-beater, while if he answers "No", then White will argue that Black is admitting to still being a wife-beater. The questioner has framed his question in such a way as to take for granted that Black has a wife whom he has been beating. The fallacy is that this is a controversial proposition that is at least as doubtful as is the conclusion (that Black has a bad character) supposedly being established. It is not proper in this debate just to take for granted this controversial proposition; it needs to be proved, if White is to make use of it at all.

However, it would also be legitimate to regard the fallacy of complex question as a kind of fallacy of ambiguity. In the example we could say that the answer "No" is ambiguous, for it could mean either "No, I'm still beating my wife" or it could mean "No, I haven't stopped because I never started".

An argument committing the fallacy of begging the question usually does so on account of its premises. Thus far in our discussion we have spoken as though that were the only way in which this fallacy could be committed. However, it also is possible for an argument to beg the question in a subtler way, on account of its logical form. Such arguments rarely occur in ordinary discourse, but they are of philosophical interest.

Suppose someone argues: "All syllogisms conforming to the five rules of the syllogism are valid; some syllogisms conforming to the five rules are in the mood **AII,** third figure; therefore, some syllogisms in the mood **AII,** third figure, are valid". Here there is nothing especially objectionable about the premises. But the peculiarity is that the argument itself is in the mood **AII,** third figure. Consequently anyone who had any doubt about the truth of the conclusion ought to be at least equally doubtful about the validity of this argument. Hence the argument is ineffectual for proving its conclusion and deserves to be classified as a *petitio principii*.

THE NON SEQUITUR: PURE FALLACIES

We call an argument a *non sequitur* if its conclusion does not follow from its premises. The fallacies of *non sequitur* form the largest category, which we shall subdivide into three types. First we shall consider what, for want of a better name, may be called *pure* fallacies. These are *non sequitur* fallacies in which the source of the error is purely some misunderstanding of logical principles themselves. The principles of deductive reasoning are distinctly different from those of inductive reasoning. Therefore, in treating this type of fallacy, we need to classify the deductive and the inductive cases separately; this is not necessary with regard to the other sorts of fallacy. For the present, we shall not discuss the inductive cases of pure fallacies but shall focus our attention upon the deductive cases.

In deduction, pure fallacies are *formal* fallacies. These are *non sequiturs* fallacious because of defects in their logical form. The victim of such a fallacy commits a logical error because he fails to notice the difference as regards validity between the deductively invalid form of the argument and some rather similar deductively valid form. He symbolizes the argument correctly (if he is using symbols) but fails to recognize the invalidity of the form. When someone commits a formal fallacy, his mistake is not that of misinterpreting the logical form of the argument (as would be the case if he symbolized the argument incorrectly) ; instead, his mistake is that of believing the logical form to be deductively valid when it is not. Thus, for example, when people are taken in by the fallacy of affirming the consequent, the likeliest source of confusion is their failure to notice how this form differs from modus ponens as regards validity.

A more complicated example occurs if someone argues: "If men are not really evil, then it is unnecessary to have police to prevent crime. And if men are really evil, then police will be ineffectual in preventing crime. Now, either men are not evil or they are evil. Therefore, police are either unnecessary or ineffectual". The argument is in the form of a valid dilemma; but even though the dilemma is valid, there is something amiss about the thinking here. The trouble is that the second premise is an absurd oversimplification; it is absurd to believe that either all men are free of evil or else that all men are evil. But what would lead anyone to accept a premise like this? By what sort of reasoning would one arrive at the premise itself? The line of thought leading to the second premise can best be regarded as committing a formal fallacy. The fallacy lies in thinking that from the necessary truth "Every man is such that either he is evil or he is not evil" we may validly infer "Either every man is evil or every man is not evil". It is the formal fallacy of supposing that, from a universal sentence whose parts are disjunctions, we may infer a corresponding disjunction both of whose parts are universal. This is a mistake arising from misunderstanding a principle about logical form.

THE NON SEQUITUR: FALLACIES OF AMBIGUITY

A quite different sort of *non sequitur* occurs when we make the mistake of incorrectly interpreting the logical form of an argument. The language in which the argument is expressed leads us to misunderstand the logical structure of the argument, and we incorrectly translate the argument into a valid form, when actually its form is invalid. We shall distinguish between two different ways in which the language of an argument may tempt us to make this mistake.

Perhaps some one word or phrase in the argument is used in two different senses. In this case, if we do not notice these different senses, we may carelessly assume that they are the same; thus we misinterpret the logical form of the argument. It is called a fallacy of *equivocation* if some definite word or phrase is ambiguous.

Some fallacies of equivocation have special names of their own. In an argument that is intended to be a syllogism but that really contains four terms instead of three, we have the *fallacy of four terms*. For example, the argument "No designing persons are to be trusted; architects are people who make designs; therefore, architects are not to be trusted" is a crude specimen of this fallacy. Here the terms "designing person" and "person who makes designs" are used by the speaker as if they meant the same, but of course they do not have the same sense at all; the first term refers to people who hatch evil schemes, while the second term refers to people who draw blueprints. The argument is intended to be a syllogism but is not really one for it has no middle term. In this example the equivocation is very obvious and the fallacy easy to detect, but sometimes fallacies of this sort are more hidden and insidious.

Next we shall consider the fallacies of composition and division, two special forms of equivocation that involve an improper sort of reasoning from part to whole or from whole to part. This may occur in syllogisms or in other kinds of argument.

Suppose someone reasons: "No man can sing as loud as an organ plays; the Glee Club are men; therefore, the Glee Club cannot sing as loud as an organ plays". This is intended to be a syllogism of the form **EAE** in the first figure. If it really were **EAE** in the first figure, it would have to be valid. Since it certainly is not valid, something is wrong. The second premise talks about the Glee Club *distributively;* that is, it says something about individual members of the Glee Club considered singly (that each individual member is a man). The conclusion, however, talks about the members of the Glee Club *collectively;* that is, it says something about the members of the Glee Club considered as a whole unit, not about each of them considered singly.

This argument cannot correctly be translated into a syllogism, for we cannot word it so as to consist of categorical sentences containing just three terms. If we put the premises into categorical form, they become "No men are singers louder than organs" and "All groups identical to the Glee Club are groups consisting of men", with more than three terms; if we use just three terms, we cannot put the premises into categorical form. The equivocation between "the Glee Club" understood distributively and "the Glee Club" understood collectively causes the speaker to reason fallaciously from a fact about individual members of the group to a conclusion about the group as a unit. This is called the *fallacy of composition*.

Another legitimate interpretation would be to regard the fallacy of composition as a formal fallacy. It would be a formal fallacy if the speaker is clear about how to symbolize the argument correctly but thinks it a valid logical principle that whatever holds true of each member of a group must hold true also of the group considered as a whole. If this is the case, the mistake is caused by a pure misunderstanding of logical principles.

A kindred example is this: "Accidents are frequent; getting struck by lightning is an accident; therefore getting struck by lightning is frequent". Here again we have an argument probably intended to be a valid syllogism, but it is invalid, and the mistake is due to equivocation. The trouble is that the first premise talks about accidents collectively; it says that the whole class of accidents is a class such that at almost any moment some of its members are occurring. The second premise, however, talks about accidents distributively, for it says that each individual case of getting struck by lightning is an individual case of an accident. Here equivocation arises because the word "accidents" is used in these two senses, collective and distributive. This causes the speaker to reason fallaciously from a fact about the whole to a conclusion about a part. This is called the *fallacy of division*.[1] Notice, however, that it is not always fallacious to reason from

---

[1] The fallacy of division also could legitimately be interpreted as a formal fallacy. It would be a formal fallacy if the speaker is clear about what the premises say but thinks it a valid logical principle that whatever holds true of a group considered as a whole must hold true also of each part of that group. Then the mistake would be caused by a pure misunderstanding of logical principles.

part to whole or from whole to part; normal valid syllogisms in a sense do this and do it legitimately. The fallacies of composition and division are improper because, when they do this, they confuse the collective with the distributive sense of terms.

Another fallacy of equivocation may be called *illicit obversion.* It arises when terms that are not really negations of one another are used as though they were. If someone reasons "All child-murderers are inhuman; therefore no child-murderers are human", he is guilty of this fallacy. The example purports to be obversion; but it is not correct obversion, for the predicate has not really been negated. The term "human" is not the negation (or contradictory) of the term "inhuman", for "inhuman" means cruel rather than nonhuman. If we correctly obverted the sentence "All child-murderers are inhuman" we would get "No child-murderers are nonhuman". It would be the same type of fallacy if someone were to argue "No rocks are alive; therefore all rocks are dead". Here again the obversion is incorrect, for "alive" and "dead" are not contradictory terms; instead they are merely contraries.

In general, two terms are *contradictories* (or negations) of each other if and only if one or the other but not both of the terms must apply to each thing; while two terms are *contraries* of each other if and only if at most one of them applies to each thing and neither applies to some things. The terms "alive" and "dead" are contraries rather than contradictories because there are some things, such as rocks, that are neither alive nor dead. (To call a thing dead is to imply that it once was alive.) The proper contradictory of "alive" is "lifeless", and so the sentence "No rocks are alive" has as its correct obverse "All rocks are lifeless".

Another logically interesting kind of equivocation arises from confusion about the distinction between words and what they represent. Were someone to argue: "Much ancient history is contained in the Bible; the Bible is a phrase of eight letters;

therefore, much ancient history is contained in a phrase of eight letters", he would be making a crude mistake of this kind. The trouble is that the first premise talks about (mentions) the Bible, a lengthy book, whereas the second premise talks about (mentions) the words "The Bible", a short phrase. The argument is confusing because it is written in such a way as to use the very same two-word expression to mention the book and to mention the name of the book. We can avoid this sort of confusion if we form the habit of using quotation marks when we want to mention words. Let us always write

"The Bible" is a phrase of eight letters.

instead of

The Bible is a phrase of eight letters.

If we follow this practice, we shall be less likely to confuse the name of a thing with the thing itself.

There are far too many kinds of equivocation to discuss them all, but we shall consider one more kind, which arises from confusion among the various senses of the verb "to be". The sense of "is" and "are" with which we have mainly been concerned is the sense in which these verbs are used for *predication,* that is, when the verb is followed by a general term, as in "Sugar is a food" or "Crows are black birds". There is a second important sense of "to be", however, in which it means *identity.* In this sense the verb is followed by a singular term, as in "Boise is Idaho's capital" or "12 is the sum of 5 and 7". Here "is" means absolute identity; Boise is the very same thing as Idaho's capital, and 12 is the very same number as the sum of 5 and 7.

The forms of inference that are valid with the "is" of identity differ, of course, from those which hold for the "is" of predication. Three usually valid forms of inference employing the "is" of identity are the following:

FORMS OF IDENTITY REASONING

$x = y$	e.g., **Scott is the author of** *Waverly.*
Fx	**Scott wrote** *Ivanhoe.*
$\therefore Fy$	**Therefore the author of** *Waverly* **wrote** *Ivanhoe.*

$x = y$	e.g., **Boise is Idaho's capital.**
$\therefore y = x$	**Therefore Idaho's capital is Boise.**

$x = y$	e.g., **Boise is Idaho's capital.**
$y = z$	**Idaho's capital is Idaho's largest city.**
$\therefore x = z$	**Therefore Boise is Idaho's largest city.**

The first of these three forms involves the principle that whatever is true of a thing must also be true of anything identical to it. The second involves the principle of the symmetry of identity: the principle that an identity sentence remains true when its items are transposed. The third involves the principle of the transitivity of identity: the principle that when the identity relation holds between a first thing and a second and between a second and a third, then it must hold also between the first and the third.

For the sake of accuracy, we must notice that the first of these three forms of identity reasoning is not valid without qualification. For ordinary cases it is valid, but there are exceptions. These exceptions fall into three groups.

1. It is not valid where the name in the second premise is mentioned rather than used. For example, it would be invalid to argue:

Boise is Idaho's capital.
"Boise" is a five-letter word.
Therefore "Idaho's capital" is a five-letter word.

2. It is not valid where the name occurs in the second premise within a sentence saying that something is necessary, not necessary, possible, not possible, or the like. Thus it would be invalid to argue:

Nine is the number of planets.
Necessarily, nine is greater than seven.
Therefore, necessarily, the number of planets is greater than seven.

Also belonging to this group of exceptions are kindred cases where the second premise declares that something is provable or unprovable in a certain way, knowable or unknowable by certain means, and the like.

3. It is not valid where the name occurs in the second premise within the scope of a verb that expresses some psychological attitude such as believing, desiring, fearing, or the like. It is invalid to argue:

Matilda is Hugo's future wife.
Hugo fears that Matilda will reject his proposal of marriage.
Therefore Hugo fears that his future wife will reject his proposal of marriage.

But aside from these three exceptions, this form of identity reasoning is reliable.

These forms of identity reasoning are clear enough and simple enough so that fallacies are not likely to arise in connection with them except when there is misunderstanding regarding the sense of the verb "to be". But suppose someone were to reason as follows: "Time is money; time is measured in seconds; and so money is measured in seconds". This argument is intended to be a case of the first of the three forms of identity reasoning, and so it has a confusing air of correctness about it. But the fallacy arises because the first occurrence of "is" in this argument is not the true "is" of identity. When we say "Time is money", we do not mean that time is just the same thing as money; we mean only that time is as good as money or that time can be exchanged for money. Here the word "is" is used in a metaphorical sense which is strictly neither the "is" of predication nor the "is" of identity.

Again, suppose that someone argues: "God is love; love is an emotion; therefore God is an emotion". Again the argument apes our first form of identity reasoning. Here too the fallacy is one of equivocation, for the premise "God is love" is not meant as an identity sentence. People who say "God is love" mean that God personifies love or exhibits love; again the "is" is used in some metaphorical sense. The moral of this is that we must be alert against fallacies arising from confusion among the different senses of "to be".

So far in this section, we have been considering equivocation, the type of ambiguity arising when a single word or phrase is used in more than one sense. We shall conclude our discussion of ambiguity by noting that sometimes the logical form of an argument is misinterpreted not because any single word is ambiguous but because the grammar of a whole sentence is ambiguous and allows of more than one interpretation. This type of ambiguity traditionally has been called *amphiboly*. An example occurs in Shakespeare's *Henry VI* when the spirit prophesies "The Duke yet lives that Henry shall depose". Henry infers from this prophecy that he is going to depose a Duke. However, a better conclusion to have inferred would have been that a Duke was going to depose Henry. (It is easier for a prophet to stay in business if he makes his predictions amphibolous.)

Throughout this section we have been considering logical mistakes that can arise owing to ambiguity. It would be incorrect, however, to conclude that ambiguity is always bad. Ambiguous language sometimes has a vivid flavor which can be admirable, if we are not misled by it. Ambiguity, like vagueness, is objectionable only insofar as it confuses people and causes them to commit fallacies in their reasoning.

THE NON SEQUITUR: FALLACIES OF IRRELEVANCE

The third kind of *non sequitur* arises when something about an argument tempts us simply to overlook the fact that there really is no connection between the premises and the conclusion. The argument excites us somehow, and we are misled into thinking that the premises support the conclusion, when actually they have nothing to do with the point supposedly being proved. Fallacies of this sort are called *fallacies of irrelevance,* or fallacies of *ignoratio elenchi* (Latin and Greek: ignorance of the connection).

One important type of fallacy of this kind is the *ad hominem* fallacy. An argument is *ad hominem* (Latin: "to the man") if it is directed at an opponent in a controversy, rather than being directly relevant to proving the conclusion under discussion. For example, suppose someone argues: "Of course Karl Marx must have been mistaken in maintaining that capitalism is an evil form of economic and social organization, bound to harm the working class. Why, he was a miserable failure of a man who couldn't even earn enough money to support his family". This is an *ad hominem* argument, for it attacks Marx the man, instead of offering direct reasons why his views are incorrect. This is the *abusive* form of the *ad hominem* argument.

Another form of the *ad hominem* argument occurs if a speaker produces reasons why his opponent might be expected to believe the conclusion, rather than reasons why the conclusion is true. Suppose members of Congress are debating whether the United States should spend money to promote birth control by artificial means in populous underdeveloped countries. Senator Brown happens to be a Catholic but supports the proposal, while Senator Green, who is not a Catholic, opposes it because he is against spending money for any purpose. Suppose Senator Green argues with Senator Brown, saying "This birth-control proposal is contrary to your religious principles, so that ought to prove to you that it's a bad proposal". Here Green is appealing to religious principles in which he himself does not believe; he has not offered any direct reason why the proposal is bad but instead has given a reason why Brown might have been expected to regard the proposal as bad. This is called the *circumstantial* form of *ad hominem* argument.

A third form of the *ad hominem* argument occurs when a speaker, trying to show that he is not at fault, argues that his opponent has said or done things just as bad as those of which he, the speaker, is accused. For example, suppose Wilbur has accused Hugo of driving a car that is not safe, because it has no brakes. Hugo, aiming to refute the accusation, might reply "Who are you to talk? On your car the doors won't even latch, and you tie them shut with bits of string". This is the *tu quoque* (Latin: "you're another") form of the *ad hominem* argument.

We must notice, however, that not all *ad hominem* arguments are logically fallacious. The abusive form of *ad hominem* argument says that, because a man has some weakness or defect, his views are incorrect. This is often but not always a worthless line of reasoning; sometimes it can be quite a good argument and not a fallacy at all. For instance, the fact that Professor Smith is a stupid, maladjusted man of paranoid tendencies increases the probability that his views on economic theory are unsound, for we know from past experience that economic theory is a difficult subject and that intelligent men of balanced judgment are more likely to have sound views about it. Perhaps we still ought to read Professor Smith's books, if we have time, before we definitely dismiss his views, but this information about his personality certainly is not irrelevant to the question whether his views are correct. We have here an inductive argument, which is not conclusive but is logically respectable (unlike the argument concerning Karl Marx, which is silly, for we know of no correlation between a man's earning power and the soundness of his views on social philosophy).

The circumstantial form of *ad hominem* argument also can be of some value, though never as a direct proof of the conclusion. Pointing out to Senator Brown that his views on legislation are inconsistent with his religious principles may be worthwhile, for if his views contradict one another, they cannot both be right. To point this out does not show which view is mistaken, but it shows that Senator Brown needs to change one opinion or the other.

Even the *tu quoque* form of *ad hominem* reasoning is not always worthless; it can be of real intellectual value in helping us form a consistent view of the comparative depravity of different individuals.

Another quite different fallacy of irrelevance is the appeal to unsuitable authority (the argument *ad verecundiam*). If we appeal to some admired or famous person as if he were an authority on a certain question when really he is not, we are making this fallacious appeal to authority. It is not always illogical to appeal to authorities; but we should not trust an authority outside his special proven field of competence. We are not entitled to appeal to persons as authorities unless there are good reasons for believing them to be authorities. A beautiful movie star may be an authority on how to look attractive to the opposite sex, but she is not necessarily an authority on which cigarette tastes best or is most healthful. A famous and beloved general may once have been an expert on military strategy, but this does not necessarily make him now an authority on education, economics, or morality.

The appeal to force is another fallacy of irrelevance (also called the *ad baculum* argument, which is Latin for "appeal to the stick"). By threatening a person we may succeed in winning him over to our point of view; but we must not think that a threat constitutes a logically valid argument. Usually a threat is not presented as an argument at all. We have the *ad baculum* fallacy only when the threat is treated as if it were a proof. A robber who says "Give me your money or I'll blow your brains out" is not committing the fallacy of appeal to force. He is not committing any fallacy at all, for he is not reasoning; he is just giving an order and stating an intention. However, a dictator who says "My opinions are right, because I'll imprison anyone who disagrees with me" perhaps would be committing the fallacy; he might be treating a threat as though it were a logical reason in favor of a conclusion.

Even if cases in which anyone really thinks that a threat can serve as a logical reason are very rare or nonexistent, the traditional phrase *"ad baculum* argument" is a good phrase to have in our vocabulary. We can use it to refer to the procedure of people who abandon reasoning and resort to force, or threats of force, in trying to get their way. In this looser sense, the *ad baculum* 'argument' is not really an argument and is not a fallacy in reasoning; instead, it is an abandonment of reasoning. (And it is often but not always wrong to abandon reasoning in favor of force.)

The appeal to pity, or appeal for mercy (*ad misericordiam* argument), is the fallacy of arguing that a certain conclusion must be true because otherwise someone whom there is reason to pity will be made more miserable. An appeal to pity or a plea for mercy is not a fallacy unless it is claimed to be a logical reason for believing some conclusion. The *ad misericordiam* fallacy is committed by the employee who argues "Please, Boss, you can see that my work is worth higher wages; I've got many hungry wives and children to feed". And a criminal would be committing this fallacy if he tried to offer evidence about his unhappy childhood as a reason why the court should believe that he did not perform the killings of which he stands accused. (However, it would be no fallacy for him to offer evidence about his unhappy childhood in trying to show that he deserves to be treated leniently.)

We conclude with what is perhaps the most common of all fallacies of irrelevance, the fallacy of *black-and-white thinking*. A wife may say to her husband "So you think the soup is too cold, do you? Well, I suppose you would like to have had it scalding hot then, instead". The second remark is presented as if it followed logically from the first, yet there is no logical connection whatever. But people find it very easy to fall into this sort of thinking in extremes, especially in the heat of controversy.

Exercise 23

Identify and explain any fallacies that occur.

1 Nothing is better than filet mignon. But tripe is better than nothing. Therefore tripe is better than filet mignon.

2 Nietzsche said that Christian morality was shallow and wrong. But that must be untrue, for Nietzsche was a maladjusted man who eventually went insane.

3 Recently we interviewed 147 local voters to find out their opinions of how the President is handling his job: 113 approved his handling of domestic affairs, 89 approved his handling of foreign affairs, and 51 approved of both. We conclude that the President has considerable support among these voters.

4 Members of the jury, you must convict the defendant. For when I asked him "Did you voluntarily kill the deceased?" he answered "No". Thus he himself confesses that he is guilty of involuntary manslaughter.

5 No baboons are interesting persons. Therefore, all baboons are uninteresting persons.

6 Sociology 77 is a great course; you can get "A" without doing any work at all. I'm sure, because Hugo Lebeau told me, and he really knew all about courses. Pity the Dean suspended him after only one semester; grade-point deficiency, I think they said.

7 Of course she doesn't dislike me. She told me that she doesn't. And I know she wouldn't lie to me about it, for she always tells the truth to people she likes.

8 Virginia gentlemen all have good manners. But these fellows are from Ohio, and so they're bound to have bad manners.

9 It's always socialistic for government to take over any job from free, private enterprise; to do so stifles people's initiative and forces everyone down to a stagnant dead level. Now, I'm not talking about things like education—we couldn't leave that to private enterprise, because many poorer children could not get adequate schooling if there were no state-supported schools. But I do say that socialism of any form is always harmful, and that's why government must leave medicine entirely in private hands.

10 All the works of Shakespeare cannot be read in a day. Therefore, the play *Hamlet,* which is one of the works of Shakespeare, cannot be read in a day.

11 Come now, Mr. Barber, I'm sure you'll agree that $3 is the fair price to charge for haircuts. One barber on the other side of town did try charging less than our Protective Association recommends, but you recall how his shop mysteriously burned down.

12 A whale is a sea creature. Hence, a small whale is a small sea creature.

13 You think I ought to study more, instead of averaging sixty hours a week at parties? That's absurd, because you know as well as I do that one can't get an all-round education by spending one's every waking hour grinding away at those dreary textbooks.

14 Buggy-whip makers are unemployed workers. Unemployed workers are everywhere this year. So buggy-whip makers are everywhere this year.

15 The American Indians accuse the United States government of being unjust to them. We can dismiss this accusation by pointing out that the Indians were extremely cruel to some of the early settlers.

16 Crime, communism, and juvenile delinquency are on the rise throughout our nation. Therefore, we ought to abolish the Federal income tax.

17 Three out of four doctors recommend the ingredients in Manacin. Therefore, Manacin is a medicine that most doctors approve.

18 Aluminum is strong. Alcoa is aluminum. Therefore, Alcoa is strong.

19 The German philosopher Kant held that all the supposedly logical proofs of the existence of God were fallacious. Therefore, Kant must have been an atheist.

20 To call you an animal is to speak the truth. To call you a jackass is to call you an animal. Therefore, to call you a jackass is to speak the truth.

21 Members of the jury, the defendant stands accused of bigamy. Bigamy is a cruel and vicious crime, which strikes at the very foundation of our whole cherished institution of the family. How essential the family is to our American way of life! But the institution of the family will be destroyed if bigamy goes unpunished. Therefore, you must convict the defendant.

22 This dog is yours, and this dog is a mother; therefore, this dog is your mother.

23 Safflower is a weed. Weeds are abundant. Therefore safflower is abundant.

24 Since we know that all self-contradictory sentences are untrue, it follows that all self-consistent sentences must be true.

25 The Rolls Royce is the world's finest automobile. Therefore you necessarily get the most for your money when you buy a Rolls.

Identify and explain any fallacies that occur.

1 "It is proved," Pangloss used to say, "that things cannot be other than they are, for since everything was made for a purpose, it follows that everything is made for the best purpose."

VOLTAIRE, *Candide*

2 If a friend of yours requests you on his deathbed to hand over his estate to his daughter, without leaving his intention anywhere in writing . . . or speaking of it to anybody, what will you do? You no doubt will hand over the money; perhaps Epicurus himself would have done the same. . . . Do you not see that . . . even you Epicureans, who profess to make your own interest and pleasure your sole standard, nevertheless perform actions that prove you to be really aiming not at pleasure but at duty . . . ?   CICERO, *De Finibus*

3 Everything that is in motion must be moved by something else. If therefore the thing which causes it to move be in motion, this too must be moved by something else, and so on. But we cannot proceed to infinity in this way, because in that case there would be no first mover, and in consequence neither would there be any other mover; for secondary movers do not cause movement except they be moved by a first mover, as, for example, a stick cannot cause movement unless it is moved by the hand. Therefore it is necessary to stop at some first mover which is moved by nothing else. And this is what we all understand God to be.   ST. THOMAS AQUINAS, *Summa Theologica*

4 From the moment when private property in movable objects developed, in all societies in which this private property existed there must be this moral law in common: Thou shalt not steal. Does this law thereby become an eternal moral law? By no means. In a society in which the motive for stealing has been done away with, in which therefore at the very most only lunatics would ever steal, how the teacher of morals would be laughed at who tried solemnly to proclaim the eternal truth: Thou shalt not steal!   ENGELS, *Anti-Dürhing*

5 We are what we all abhor, *Anthropophagi* and Cannibals, devourers not onely of men but of our selves; and that not in an allegory, but a positive truth; for all this mass of flesh which we behold, came in at our mouths; this frame we look upon, hath been upon our trenchers; in brief, we have devour'd our selves.
                    SIR THOMAS BROWNE, *Religio Medici*

AVOIDING AMBIGUITY: DEFINITIONS

When we encounter words that cause confusion because their meanings are ambiguous, it is often helpful to define them. A traditional way of characterizing the definition of a word is to say that the definition is a verbal formulation of its meaning. However, the word "meaning" itself is ambiguous. Thus a general term may be said to mean each individual thing to which it applies (for example, the general term "man" means Socrates, Caesar, and each other man). This is called *extensional* meaning, and the totality of things to which the general term applies is called the extension of the term. But also a general term may be said to mean those characteristics which anything must possess in order that the term correctly apply to it (for example, the term "bachelor" means being a man and being unmarried). This is called *intensional* meaning, and the totality of characteristics which anything would have to possess in order that the term apply to it is called the intension of the term. A definition of a general term tries to specify the intension; the definition does not tell us what the extension is.

From another point of view, however, we can characterize definitions without employing the term "meaning". We may say that a definition of a word is a recipe for paraphrasing the word, that is, for transforming sentences containing the word into equivalent sentences that contain other expressions instead. Recipes of this kind are of especial practical value when they tell us how to paraphrase ambiguous, confusing, or unfamiliar words, replacing them with clearer or more familiar words.

The most fundamental way of explaining a word is to give examples. Sometimes we do this by pointing to visible examples. When a child asks "What's a dog?", we respond by pointing to Fido, Rover, and Bruno. Some philosophers have called this procedure "ostensive definition", but it is better to call it merely ostensive teaching of words. This ostensive procedure differs from definition in that it gives no recipe for paraphrasing the word. Although explaining a word by giving examples often can be indispensably valuable, it is not the same as giving a definition. Sometimes a definition is much more helpful than a list of examples.

In ordinary discourse we often express definitions in ways that do not clearly show that they are definitions. Wishing to define the word "dormouse", a speaker may say "A dormouse is a small hibernating European rodent resembling a squirrel". The hearer is then expected to realize that the speaker is intending to define the word "dormouse", rather than intending to make an ordinary statement about dormice (as he would be doing if he said "Dormice are rather prolific animals"). A careful speaker can make his intention clearer by stating his definition in such a way as to leave no doubt that it is a definition. If he says "The word 'dormouse' means 'small hibernating European rodent resembling a squirrel' ", then he has made it perfectly clear that he is defining the word. Moreover, here he has given what is called an *explicit* definition, that is, a definition in which the *definiendum* (the expression being defined) is declared to be replaceable by another explicitly given expression, the *definiens* (that which does the defining).

Not all definitions are explicit ones. In a dictionary many words have to be defined not by giving one exact equivalent but by giving several partial synonyms. Thus "honesty" may be defined as "refraining from lying, cheating, or stealing; being truthful, trustworthy, upright, sincere, fair, straightforward or chaste". Here the meaning of the definiendum is adequately if not rigorously explained, but this is not an explicit definition, for we are not given some one other word or phrase that always means just the same as the definiendum.

In logic and mathematics, rigorous definitions that are not explicit definitions sometimes are used. For example, if we wish to define the biconditional symbol we can say "$p \equiv q$" is defined as "$(q \supset p)$ & $(p \supset q)$". This is called a *definition in context;* it supplies a rule enabling us to rewrite any expression containing the biconditional sign so that it will contain the horseshoe and ampersand instead. If we already understand the horseshoe and ampersand, this definition shows us exactly what the biconditional sign means. But this is not an explicit definition, for the whole expression containing the biconditional sign must be rearranged completely; we do not just remove one sign and put some other sign in its place.

Definitions that are useful in preventing ambiguity may be subdivided into two types. Some of them serve the purpose of describing the meaning that a word already has in language. We might call definitions of this type *analytical* definitions. In giving this kind of definition of a word, the speaker does not aim to change its meaning; he aims only to characterize the meaning it already has. Dictionary definitions are of this type. When a definition has this purpose, we can properly ask whether the definition is correct or incorrect.

In order to be correct in its description of the meaning of a word, an analytical definition must not be *too broad;* that is, it must not embrace things that do not really belong. (To define "pneumonia" as "disease of the lungs" would be too broad, for there are many lung diseases besides pneumonia.) Also, in order to be correct in its description of the meaning of a word, an analytical definition must not be *too narrow;* that is, it must not exclude things that really belong. (To define "psychosis" as "schizophrenia" would be too narrow, for there are other kinds of psychoses.) Sometimes an incorrect definition errs by being too broad in one respect and also too narrow in some other respect (for instance, defining "liberalism" as "the view that the power of the government should be increased").

Furthermore, analytical definitions should be clear enough to be understood by those for whom they are intended; otherwise they are of little use. When in his dictionary Dr. Johnson defined a net as "any thing made with interstitial vacuities", his definition was of little use, for his readers would not have understood the definiens as well as they already understood the definiendum; the definition uses murky words to explain a relatively clear one and so is of negligible value.

Finally, a definition cannot serve much useful purpose if it is circular, that is, if the definiendum occurs within the definiens in such a way that no one could understand the definiens who did not already understand the definiendum. For example, to define "straight line" as "the line along which a ray of light travels when it goes straight" is circular and uninformative.

Traditional logic used to prescribe additional rules for definitions, including the rule that definitions should be given by genus and species and the rule that a definition ought not to be negative. However, these rules need not always be obeyed. To be sure, in giving a definition, it often is helpful to proceed by genus and species, that is, first saying what general kind of thing the word means and then saying what the specific form is. But not all legitimate definitions follow this pattern. Also, it is often wise to avoid definitions couched in negative terms ("A lion is a big cat; not a tiger, not a leopard, not an ocelot"), for such definitions are likely to be too broad. But some negative definitions are perfectly legitimate.

A second kind of definition useful in preventing ambiguity is the *stipulative definition,* whose purpose is to declare how a speaker intends that a certain word, phrase, or symbol shall be understood ("Let '*S*' mean 'Samoans' "; "Let 'heavy truck' mean 'truck that can carry a load of 5 tons or more' "; etc.). Perhaps the expression being defined is one that previously had no meaning, or perhaps it had a different or a vaguer meaning. At any rate, the point of the stipulative definition is that the expression now is deliberately endowed with a particular meaning. Obviously, a stipulative definition cannot be of much use if it is unclear or circular. However, we do not have to worry about whether it is too broad or too narrow, for that sort of correctness cannot pertain to stipulative definitions. A stipulative definition is arbitrary, in the sense that it expresses only the speaker's intention to use the word in the stipulated manner, and he is, after all, entitled to use it however he pleases, so long as he does not cause confusion.

In order to avoid causing confusion, however, a stipulative definition should not assign to a word that already has an established meaning some new meaning that is likely to be confused with it. Consider the following dialogue:

BLACK: Justice Tompkins is a Communist, you know. He ought to be impeached.

WHITE: He is? I agree that we should not have Communists on the bench. But how do you know he's one?

BLACK: It's obvious. He ruled against prayer in public schools, and according to my definition—surely I'm entitled to use words as I please—anyone who does that is a Communist. Therefore, he ought to be impeached.

Here the stipulative definition is used to promote ambiguity rather than to prevent it. In the ordinary sense of the word "Communist", White agrees with Black that judges ought not to be Communists. But Black offers no evidence that the judge is a Communist in this sense. All that Black shows is that the judge is a 'Communist' in the peculiar, special sense of having ruled against prayer in public schools; from that, nothing follows about whether the judge ought to be impeached. Black is causing confusion by failing to keep distinct these two very different senses of the word; this happens because he fails to recognize the difference here between a stipulative and an analytical definition.

Confusion can be caused in another way by a stipulative definition if a word or symbol that purports to name some individual thing (such a word or symbol being a singular term) is introduced even though it is not known that there is any such thing. Suppose I say "Let 'n' stand for the largest whole number". And then I go on to use this symbol "n" in making supposed assertions about this largest whole number. Here I am guilty of constructing a confused definition, for there is no largest whole number; hence, I have no right to introduce and use a symbol for this nonentity.[2] I may become badly confused if I assume that this definition is enough to entitle me to start talking about this largest whole number as if it existed. There is no such number, and a mere definition cannot create a number or any other object.

The two kinds of definitions mentioned so far both aim to inform us about verbal usage. The stipulative definition expresses a speaker's intention henceforth to use his definiendum in a certain way, and the analytical definition describes the way in which the definiendum already is used in language. These two kinds of definitions are valuable in helping to prevent ambiguity.

It would be a mistake, however, to suppose that everything called a definition belongs to one of these two kinds. In fact, the profoundest and most valuable definitions usually do not fit tidily into either kind. When Newton defined force as the product of mass times acceleration, when Einstein defined simultaneity of distant events in terms of the transmission of light rays, and when Whitehead and Russell defined zero as the class of all empty classes, these important definitions expressed stipulations about how Newton, Einstein, and Whitehead and Russell proposed to use their terms. But these definitions did not merely do this; they

---

[2] The situation is different with regard to general terms. It is all right to define the general term "unicorn" as "horse with a horn in its forehead". There are no unicorns, but the definition tells us that, if there were any horse with a horn in its forehead, it would be called a unicorn. We can use the general term "unicorn" even though there are no unicorns; but we must beware of using the singular term "n" unless we know that there is such a number.

also reflected previously established usage. What these definitions did was to propose new verbal usages growing out of the previously established usages: new usages that, it was felt, perfected tendencies of thought implicit in the old usages and thereby offered improved scope for the development of theoretical insight into the subject matter being treated.

Not only in technical scientific fields but also in more literary spheres we find definitions that do not fit tidily into the two categories of stipulative and analytical. We might give them the name *revelatory* definitions. For example, when Pater defined architecture as frozen music, he was not trying to describe how the word "architecture" is used in our language. (He took it for granted that his readers would know what kinds of constructions are considered architecture.) Nor was he proposing some arbitrary new usage. We should not censure his definition merely on the ground that it is unhelpful for the purpose of preventing ambiguity; that is not the purpose of this kind of definition. This definition is a metaphor, and it suggests a new way of looking at architecture, comparing the structural organization of the parts of a building with the structural organization of the parts of a musical composition. In trying to decide whether the definition is a good one or not, we must reflect about the extent and validity of this comparison between music and buildings; the definition is a good one if the comparison is illuminating.

Or again, when a writer on psychoanalysis says that man is to be defined as the neurotic animal, this definition does not have the purpose of explaining the meaning of the word "man" to someone unfamiliar with it. Instead, its purpose is to call attention to something about men that the writer thinks is of fundamental importance in making men what they are and in accounting for the differences between the life of men and the life of animals. The definition is a good one if it achieves this. These revelatory definitions have no relation to the elimination of ambiguity; they are mentioned only to indicate that analytical and stipulative definitions are not the only kinds of definition.

Traditional philosophers, in line with Aristotle and scholasticism, emphasized what were called *real definitions*. Like the definitions we are calling revelatory, real definitions were not supposed to explain words but rather to describe the basic natures of things. It was believed, however, that there must be only one proper real definition of each species of natural being. For instance, it was held that the real definition of man is that he is the rational animal. According to this traditional point of view, it would have been thought incorrect to define man as the tool-using animal or the animal with language, let alone as the neurotic animal. The weakness of this traditional view is that it fails to recognize how a given term may be defined in different yet equally legitimate ways to serve different purposes.

People sometimes think that one always should define one's terms at the beginning of any discussion. This idea should not be carried too far. No speaker could be under an obligation to define all his terms. (He could never finish the task of defining *all* the terms he uses, unless he allowed his definitions to be circular.) Moreover, we have a fairly adequate understanding of the meanings of many words that we have never bothered to define and also of many words that we perhaps would not know how to define adequately even if we tried. Thus, it would be foolish to try indiscriminately to define all our terms before proceeding with our thinking. However, it is often helpful, and even essential, to seek definitions of particular words that are harmfully ambiguous (or harmfully vague).

This is especially true with regard to discussions in which confusion is caused by failure to notice the different meanings of a term. A *verbal dispute* is a dispute arising solely from the fact that some word is being used with different meanings; this kind of dispute can be settled merely by giving the definitions that clarify the situation (though to say this is not to say that such disputes always are *easy* to settle).

The American philosopher William James gives a classic example of such a dispute.[3] Suppose there is a squirrel on the trunk of a tree, and a man walks around the tree. The squirrel moves around the tree trunk so as to stay out of sight, always facing the man but keeping the tree between them. Has the man gone around the squirrel or not? Some of James's friends disputed hotly for a long time about this question. Here is a purely verbal dispute; it can be settled by pointing out that in one sense the man has gone 'around' the squirrel, for he has moved from the north to the west and then to the south and east of the squirrel's location, but in another sense the man has not gone 'around' the squirrel, for the squirrel has always been facing him. Once we have pointed out these two different senses of the word, we have done all that can reasonably be done; there is nothing more worth discussing (though this does not ensure that discussion will cease). With a verbal dispute like this, giving definitions is the way to resolve the dispute. But it would be utterly wrong to assume that all disputes are verbal in this way. There are many serious problems for the settling of which definitions are not needed, and there are many other problems where, if definitions help, they mark only the beginning of the thinking needed to resolve the issue.

Exercise 24

Discuss the purpose and adequacy of the definition proposed or considered in each of the following examples.

1   A mammal may be defined as a four-legged land animal that suckles its young.

2   A square is defined as a plane rectilinear figure having sides of equal length that meet at right angles.

---

[3] William James, *Pragmatism*, Lecture II.

3 Lying means saying something that is not so.

4 Belonging to the Caucasian race means having parents both of whom belonged to the Caucasian race.

5 Intelligence may be defined as that which intelligence tests measure.

6 By pleasure we mean the absence of pain in the body and of trouble in the soul.   EPICURUS

7 And so, Lord, do thou, who dost give understanding to faith, give me so far as thou knowest it to be profitable, to understand that thou are that which we believe. And, indeed, we believe that thou art a being than which nothing greater can be conceived.   ST. ANSELM, *Proslogium*

8 By *Original Sin,* as the phrase has been most commonly used by divines, is meant *the innate, sinful depravity of the heart.*
                    JONATHAN EDWARDS, *Doctrine of Original Sin*

9 "What is Optimism?" asked Cacambo.
"It's the passion for maintaining that all is right when all goes wrong with us," replied Candide.   VOLTAIRE, *Candide*

10 True happiness consists in decreasing the difference between our desires and our powers, in establishing a perfect equilibrium between the power and the will.   ROUSSEAU, *Emile*

11 *To acquire a knowledge of the world* might be defined as the aim of all education.   SCHOPENHAUER, "On Education"

12 Life itself is *essentially* appropriation, injury, conquest of the strange and weak, suppression, severity, obtrusion of its own forms, incorporation, and at the very least, putting it mildest, exploitation. . . . Life *is* precisely Will to Power.
                    NIETZSCHE, *Beyond Good and Evil*

13 These three elements, then, go to constitute any religion. A religion must teach some moral code, must in some way inspire a strong feeling of devotion to that code, and in so doing must

show something in the nature of things that answers to the
code or that serves to reinforce the feeling.

JOSIAH ROYCE, *The Religious Aspect of Philosophy*

14 Consider yellow, for example. We may try to define it, by
describing its physical equivalent; we may state what kind of
light-vibrations must stimulate the normal eye, in order that
we may perceive it. But a moment's reflection is sufficient to
shew that those light-vibrations are not themselves what we
mean by yellow. *They* are not what we perceive. Indeed we
should never have been able to discover their existence, unless
we had first been struck by the patent difference of quality
between the different colours. The most we can be entitled to
say of those vibrations is that they are what corresponds in
space to the yellow which we actually perceive.

G. E. MOORE, *Principia Ethica*

15 We reject the subjectivist view that to call an action right, or a
thing good, is to say that it is generally approved of, because it
is not self-contradictory to assert that some actions which are
generally approved of are not right, or that some things which
are generally approved of are not good.

A. J. AYER, *Language, Truth and Logic*

*In which of the following cases does there occur confusion that
could be remedied by giving definitions or by correcting definitions that are given? Explain each case.*

1 Our senses lead us to imagine that things like stones, floors, and
furniture are solid objects. But modern science has made the
startling discovery that these are not really solid objects at all:
They consist of swarms of atoms whirling through mostly
empty space. The floor is no more solid than is a swarm of bees.
How deceptive the senses are!

2 HUGO: Why do you go around telling everyone that I stole this
car? My friends have become suspicious of me, and I may lose

my job. But you know perfectly well that I bought this car, you lying slanderer.

CLOVIS: Please don't excite yourself, my dear fellow. You bought that car for a ridiculously low price, and according to my definition that is stealing. So of course when people ask me about you, I tell them that you're a thief.

3 It is possible to prove that the physical universe came into being only a finite length of time ago. Let *e* be the earliest event in the history of the physical universe. Now, there cannot have been any physical happening earlier than *e*, since *e* is by definition the earliest such event. And as every two points in time are separated by only a finite interval, *e* cannot have occurred more than a finite length of time ago. Thus the history of the physical universe does not go back infinitely far into the past.

4 Sometimes you hear it said that people are less religious nowadays than they used to be, because so many do not attend any church or practice any traditional religion. But I maintain that this idea is mistaken. Perhaps relatively fewer people do attend churches now than did a century ago; but this just means that their religion has changed, not that they have no religion. Everyone is necessarily religious, for religion is best defined as *ultimate concern*. Whatever a man's ultimate concern is, that is his religion. Perhaps nowadays more people have baseball, television, or the pursuit of money as their religion; but at any rate, people are not less religious now than they used to be.

5 WHITE: Brown is a real gentleman. He always opens the door for a lady, he dresses elegantly, and his manners are polished.

BLACK: He is not a gentleman at all. He was caught cheating at cards, he has repeatedly lied to his employer, and he once accepted a bribe.

6 HUGO: This bag contains a bomb. You can hear it ticking. If we don't do something, it will explode and destroy our building.

CLOVIS: Nonsense, it's not a bomb. The bag just happens to contain an old alarm clock and some waterlogged firecrackers. There is no danger at all.

In each case discuss the soundness of Black's criticism of White's argument.

1 WHITE: If you are rich, you can afford a skiing holiday in Switzerland. But I see you cannot afford that. So this tells me you're not rich.

BLACK: Your argument is no good, because the word "rich" is vague. How much money does a person have to have before he's rich?

2 WHITE: Every four years the American people elect the president. A member of the Democratic party is the president. Therefore, every four years the American people elect one of the Democrats.

BLACK: You commit the fallacy of equivocation. The phrase "the president" has two meanings: "the president as such" and "the present president".

3 WHITE: If your girl friend is mad, you can't have a pleasant evening with her. And she is mad. So if you want a pleasant evening, don't spend it with her.

BLACK: That's invalid thinking, because the word "mad" can have two meanings, "angry" and "insane".

4 WHITE: You tell me that my money will be safer and will earn a higher return if I invest it in the Lion Mutual Fund rather than in the Prudent Tradesman's Fund. But I conclude that that's not so, for I know that you earn an 8 per cent commission by selling shares in the former but no commission on the latter.

BLACK: My friend, you are accusing me of having a selfish motive. You attack me instead of disproving what I said. You've committed the *ad hominem* fallacy.

5 WHITE: You grant me that no fishes have feathers and that all sharks are fishes. Therefore, you've got to grant that no sharks have feathers.

BLACK: Invalid. You are committing the fallacy of division, by reasoning from whole (fishes) to part (sharks).

6 WHITE: Surely there must be something unsound about the current indeterministic theory of quantum mechanics, for Einstein himself opposed it, saying that he could not believe that God would play dice with the universe.

BLACK: You are appealing to authority. That is the fallacy of the argument *ad verecundiam.*

7 WHITE: I define God as the basic reality of the universe, whatever that may be. The universe exists, and therefore its basic reality, whatever that may be, must exist too. Thus I prove that there is a God.

BLACK: That definition is incorrect. Lots of people don't mean that by the word "God".

6. *Inductive Reasoning*

INDUCTION AND PROBABILITY

If the premises of a valid deductive argument are true, its conclusion must necessarily be true also. By definition, a valid deductive argument has to be conclusive; its conclusion must be 'contained in' its premises. Because of this, its conclusion cannot embody conjectures about the empirical world that go beyond what its premises say; if it did the argument could not be conclusive. On the other hand, an inductive argument, as we define it, has a conclusion embodying empirical conjectures about the world that go beyond what its premises say; in an inductive argument, the conclusion is not 'contained in' the premises. Thus in an inductive argument the truth of the premises cannot absolutely ensure the truth of the conclusion, and the argument cannot be conclusive in the way deduction can be. But if the premises of an inductive argument are true and the reasoning is good, then it is reasonable to believe the conclusion; the conclusion is *probably* true.[1]

[1] In order to emphasize the contrast between induction and deduction, we

Inductive reasoning is of great importance because so many of our beliefs about the world cannot be proved by deduction alone. If they are to be proved at all, the reasoning in support of them must include inductive reasoning; it cannot all be deductive. For example, it is a very ordinary belief that if a person eats bread for lunch it will nourish him, whereas if he eats arsenic it will poison him. What reasoning can we employ in justification of these beliefs? Fundamentally, the belief that bread will nourish and that arsenic will poison is supported by past experience, by our observation of past cases in which these effects occurred. Thus, the direct way of reasoning here is to infer that bread will nourish us if we eat it today, since bread that we know of in the past has usually nourished, and that if we eat arsenic today it will poison us, since arsenic that we know of in the past has usually poisoned. This reasoning is obviously inductive in character.

To be sure, we could reason deductively that, since bread always nourishes, it will nourish us today and that, since arsenic always poisons, it will poison us if we eat it today. But this deductive reasoning depends on major premises that themselves require justification. How do we know that bread always nourishes and that arsenic always poisons (not just in the past, but always)? Here the direct answer would be that we know this, if at all, by induction; in the past this is what happened, and so probably it is what always happens. In justifying beliefs like these about how things happen in the world, we must sooner or later resort to inductive inference; deduction alone would not suffice for complet-

---

shall speak of inductive conclusions as being probable, no matter how well established they are. This is a departure from ordinary usage, for in ordinary discourse a well-established inductive conclusion, e.g., that the sun will rise tomorrow, is called certain rather than highly probable. But for purposes of logic it is convenient to conceive of probability in a broader sense, applying it to the conclusions of all arguments that are not deductive. By using the term in this way, we emphasize the difference between deductive and nondeductive reasoning.

ing a proof. Because our actions are so largely based upon beliefs arrived at by induction, the English philosopher Bishop Butler declared, "Probability is the guide to life".

With inductive arguments, just as with deductive ones, we have to distinguish between the truth of the conclusion and the logical validity of the reasoning. However, in inductive reasoning the situation is more complicated than in deductive reasoning, since we must allow for variations in the degree to which, according to the speaker, the premises supposedly make it reasonable to believe the conclusion. That is, we must allow for variations in the degree of probability the speaker claims that his premises confer on his conclusion.

A speaker claims a high degree of probability for his conclusion if he says "My past experience is such-and-such ; therefore it is practically certain that arsenic is always poisonous". He claims a much lower degree of probability for his conclusion if he says "My past experience is such-and-such, and so it is rather likely that arsenic is always poisonous". An inductive argument that is perfectly legitimate when a moderate degree of probability is claimed for the conclusion (e.g., "He's a Hindu, and so quite likely he's a vegetarian") can become fallacious if an unduly high degree of probability is claimed for the conclusion (e.g., "He's a Hindu, and so he's sure to be a vegetarian").

What then should we mean by calling an inductive argument valid ? An inductive argument is a valid argument if the degree of probability claimed for its conclusion is indeed a reasonable degree of probability to attribute to that conclusion, relative to the given premises. The argument is a *non sequitur* if it claims for its conclusion a degree of probability that it is unreasonable to attribute to the conclusion, relative to the given premises.

Keeping this in mind, we can see that an inductive argument may reach a true conclusion without being a logically valid argument. (In this respect, induction is like deduction.) For instance, suppose a person sees a black cat cross his path and infers that bad luck is surely imminent; soon after, he is struck by lightning. Here his conclusion happens to have been true, but his reasoning may well be invalid all the same, for, relative to what he knew at the time he made the inference, it may not have been very probable that he was going to have bad luck. The conclusion accidentally turned out to be true, but the reasoning was logically bad.

Also, an inductive argument may reach a false conclusion even though the reasoning involved is logically good and starts from true premises. (In this respect, induction is unlike deduction.) For instance, suppose there has been a thunderstorm every afternoon at five o'clock for the past week, and I infer that there will rather likely be one tomorrow too. Here my data are true and my reasoning may well be perfectly valid, yet it is possible that my conclusion is false; perhaps no storm occurs on the morrow. Here it is reasonable for me to make this inference, even though the conclusion may turn out not to be true.

To grasp this character of inductive reasoning, we must understand the notion of probability. When we speak of the degree of probability of a conclusion, we are referring to the degree to which it is reasonable to believe the conclusion; probability here is the same thing as rational credibility. Probabilities in this sense are sometimes, but not always, numerically measurable, as we shall see.

This is not the only sense of the term "probability", to be sure. A quite different sense is involved when a physicist speaks of the probability of decay of a uranium atom; what he means is, roughly, the *relative frequency* with which uranium atoms do, in fact, disintegrate. Probability in that sense is always numerical. Mathematical formulations of the theory of probability often employ the term "probability" in that relative-frequency sense rather than in the sense of rational credibility.

But now, probability when understood as rational credibility is a *relative* matter, in this respect: The degree to which it is reasonable to believe something depends upon how much we know. The very same conjecture takes on different degrees of probability relative to different amounts of evidence. For example, if all we know about Hugo is that he is twenty years old, then, relative to this evidence, the conjecture that he will be alive next year is highly probable and very reasonable to believe (for we know that most twenty-year-olds survive). But if we learn that young Hugo loves fast driving and has already had several accidents, the probability is distinctly diminished. And if we learn in addition that he has just collided with a concrete abutment at 90 miles per hour then, relative to this augmented evidence, the probability of his being alive next year is very much further reduced. Relative to our original information, the conjecture that he will survive was highly probable; relative to our augmented information, it has only a low degree of probability. This illustrates how changes in available evidence can change the degree to which it is reasonable to believe a conclusion. And it illustrates how probability is something quite different from truth, for the conjecture could be highly probable without being true or could be true without being very probable.

Probabilities always are relative to evidence, yet often we speak of *the* probability of something, without specifically stating to what evidence this probability is related. When we speak of *the* probability of a sentence, we mean its probability relative to *all* the information that we possess. If someone asks, "What is the probability that there is life on Mars?", he means "What is the probability, relative to all the evidence now available?". The degree of probability may have been different in times past when there was less evidence, and it will surely be different in the future when more evidence is gathered.

This brings us to another basic difference between deductive and inductive reasoning. Deductive arguments are *self-contained* as regards validity in a way that inductive arguments are not. Thus, the question whether it is deductively valid to argue "No deciduous trees are conifers; all fig trees are deciduous; therefore no fig trees are conifers" is a question whose answer depends solely upon the logical relation of the stated premises to the conclusion. No further information about botany or anything else (excluding logic, of course) is required. Indeed, there exists no other sentence (excluding sentences that express principles of logic) the truth or falsity of which has any decisive bearing upon whether this reasoning is deductively valid.

In general, when we are determining whether a deductive argument is valid, we may limit our attention strictly to the stated premises, except for deductive arguments having suppressed premises (which we shall discuss in Chapter 7); even with them the unstated premises always are limited in number and can, in principle, be stated in full. Notice, however, that we are calling deductive arguments 'self-contained' merely as regards the question of their validity (Do they commit fallacies of *non sequitur?*), not as regards the question of their successfulness in proving their conclusions (Are they sound in every way?).

Inductive arguments are not self-contained in this way. Consider the argument: "Hugo is twenty; most twenty-year-olds survive another year, and so probably Hugo will reach twenty-one". The person who presents this argument is not just claiming that the conclusion *would* be probable *were* the stated premises *all* our relevant evidence; if he were making only that very uninteresting, milksop claim, his remark would be a mere conditional sentence, not an inference at all. The arguer is claiming something more significant: He is claiming that the conclusion *is* reasonable to believe in the light of *all* that we know. He is concerned with the degree of probability of the conclusion relative to all the directly and indirectly relevant evidence that we possess.

How much evidence is this? A great deal—indeed, indefinitely much, for so many of the things we know about the world have at least indirect bearings on the question of Hugo's survival. (Our knowledge of the longevity of other people, of the longevity of other animals, of the general regularity of nature, all is indirectly relevant.) If we tried to list all the empirical sentences we know to be true that are at least indirectly relevant to the question of young Hugo's survival, we would find that we had embarked upon a task that we could not complete or at any rate that we could never be sure that we had completed. There are indefinitely many such sentences, and in trying to list them all we never could be certain that we had not omitted some.

In an inductive argument the explicitly stated premises are only a tiny part, although usually the most noteworthy part, of the indefinitely vast amount of information about the world upon which the conclusion depends. Each bit of this known but unstated information has a bearing upon whether the argument is inductively valid. But where reasoning involves relevant premises so rich that we cannot be sure even of stating them completely, we cannot expect to be able to impute to the premises and conclusion any specific logical form in virtue of which the argument would be valid or invalid. We cannot rely on considerations of logical form for judging the validity of inductive reasoning. Thus inductive arguments are not 'self-contained' in the way that deductive arguments are, which makes their whole logic profoundly different, for it means that formal rules cannot play the central role in inductive logic that they do in deductive logic.

INDUCTIVE GENERALIZATION

Suppose that we have met some swans and have observed each of them to be white. This information is not enough to prove deductively whether all swans are white or even whether the next swan we meet will be so. But here we might construct an inductive argument of the form

INDUCTIVE GENERALIZATION

a, b, c . . . **each has been observed to be** S **and** P.
Nothing has been observed to be S **without being** P.

Therefore, probably, all S **are** P.

Here the conclusion is an "all" sentence and is called a generalization. In terms of our example, $a, b, c,$ . . . would be the individual swans that have been observed; "S" would be interpreted to mean "swans", and "P" would be interpreted to mean "white things". This is the simplest form of inductive generalization.

A kindred but slightly more complicated form of reasoning would start from evidence that a certain percentage of observed S are P, and it would pass to the conclusion (a statistical generalization) that probably approximately the same percentage of all S are P. For example, from the fact that 20 per cent of the birds I have seen today were robins, I might infer that probably about 20 per cent of the birds now in my part of the country are robins.

Some arguments of this type are strong arguments; some are weak arguments. In trying to judge how strong such an argument is (that is, in trying to judge the degree of probability with which the conclusion follows from the evidence), we need to take account of various factors that determine how reasonable it is to suppose that the things observed constitute a 'fair sample' of S in general, with regard to being P. How reasonable is it to suppose that the particular swans that we have observed constitute a 'fair sample' of swans in general, with regard to color? Five factors should be considered.

1. The degree to which $a, b, c,$ etc., have been observed to be alike (besides the mere fact that each is both S and P) is important. This is called the *positive analogy*. For instance, suppose that all the observed swans were female and American.

Then our argument would be relatively weak, for we would not be entitled to feel very confident that our sample is representative of the whole class of swans with regard to color; we have not excluded the real possibility that it is only female swans, or perhaps only American swans, that are white. In general, the greater the positive analogy among the observed instances, the weaker is the argument, other things being equal.

2. Also important is the degree to which *a, b, c,* etc., have been observed to differ one from another. This is called the *negative analogy*. For instance, if we have observed swans in winter and in summer, in the wilds and in captivity, young and fully grown, then our argument is strengthened. We have increased the probability that the sample is representative as regards color, for we have excluded the possibilities that it is only swans in winter, or only wild swans, or only young ones that are white. In general, the greater the negative analogy among the observed instances, the stronger is the argument. (Notice that the extent of the positive analogy and the extent of the negative analogy are two quite independent matters; having much positive analogy need not entail having little negative analogy.)

3. Also we should consider the *character of the conclusion;* we must take account of how much it says. The more sweeping the generalization that we seek to establish, the less is its probability relative to our evidence, and the weaker is our argument. For example, "All swans are white" is a generalization that says more than "All American swans are nonblack". The less specific the subject term and the more specific the predicate term, the more a universal generalization says. Statistical conclusions too can differ in how much they say; that at least 10 per cent of the birds in this wood are robins is a statistical generalization that says less than does the generalization that between 19 and 21 per cent of birds in this state are robins.

In addition to these three factors, there are two others, perhaps less fundamental but also deserving notice.

4. We should consider the *number of observed instances* (*a, b, c,* etc.). An increase in the number of observed instances normally means an increase in the strength of the argument. Here a rather abstract question may be raised: Does an increase in the number of observed instances, just as such, necessarily increase the probability of the generalization? Or does the conclusion become more probable only because additional observed instances ordinarily mean an increase in the extent of the negative analogy among the observed instances? Suppose that the number of observed instances were to be increased without the negative analogy thereby being increased. Would this strengthen the argument, or would this leave the probability of the conclusion unchanged? Philosophers disagree in their views about this abstract question. Fortunately, the matter is very academic, for in actual practice whenever we increase the number of observed instances we usually also increase the extent of the negative analogy among the observed instances.

5. Finally, we should consider the *relevance* of *S* to *P*. How probable is it that there would be a connection between the property of being a swan and the property of being white? Are these properties that may reasonably be expected to be correlated? Here we must rely upon knowledge gained through previous inductions. In our example we might reasonably suppose that being a swan is relevant to being white, since we know (from previous inductions) that birds of the same species usually have the same coloring.

In practice, we should take all five of these factors into account, weighing them together, when we seek to decide whether a specific inductive argument is relatively strong or relatively weak. We need to use common sense as we ask ourselves whether we are entitled to suppose that our observed instances constitute a 'fair sample' of the whole class about which we are generalizing.

As we try to weigh the strength of an inductive argument, three main types of mistake should be avoided. We shall call these the fallacies of forgetful induction, hasty induction, and slothful induction. All three are mistakes that can arise in inductive reasoning of any type, but we shall consider them now just in connection with inductive generalization. First there is the mistake that arises from neglecting some of the relevant empirical information that we possess. This is the fallacy of *forgetful induction*. Where the conclusion is a generalization, we speak of the fallacy of forgetful generalization.

For example, suppose someone wishes to estimate how many polo players there are in a given city. He visits a golf club there and interviews the first 500 people he meets, of whom 10 per cent say that they play polo. He then concludes that it is highly probable that just about 10 per cent of the people in this city are polo players. This is an example of very faulty reasoning. His mistake lies in forgetting that people met in a golf club are usually sportsmen and relatively well-to-do; sportsmen and the well-to-do play polo more than other people do, as polo is a sporty and expensive game. These are facts that we all know, if we only stop to think. Thus there is positive reason to believe that this sample is not representative of the population of the city at large, with respect to polo playing. Under the circumstances, this man's conclusion is not highly probable, as he imagines, but really has a very low degree of probability.

A second type of mistake in inductive reasoning is the fallacy of leaping to a conclusion when the evidence is too slight to make the conclusion very probable. This is the fallacy of *hasty induction*. With regard to inductive generalization, this has traditionally been called the fallacy of hasty generalization. For example, suppose a young man for the first time meets a girl from Martha

Jefferson College; he finds her dumpy and dull, and so the next day he tells his friends that all the girls from Martha Jefferson are 'pigs'. Here his reasoning is illogical, for he has based a sweeping generalization upon very slight evidence; the probability of the conclusion relative to his data really is very low, yet he states his conclusion as though it were highly probable. His mistake is that he leaps to a conclusion on the basis of very little evidence. This is somewhat different from the mistake made by the man who visited the country club; he collected a considerable amount of evidence but, in evaluating it, forgot about relevant information that was available to him.

The third type of mistake is the mistake of treating a conclusion as though it were less probable than it is. If a conclusion is something that, for one reason or another, we would prefer not to believe, all too often we refuse to accept it even after the evidence has piled up strongly; we persist in believing that the conclusion is improbable when it is not. We call this the fallacy of *slothful induction*. When it arises in connection with inductive generalization, it is the fallacy of slothful generalization.

Suppose the question is whether Hugo is a driver who will have relatively few accidents in the long run. In March the Buick he was driving ran into a tree. His father then bought him a Chrysler, but in April it collided with a telephone pole. His indulgent father then bought him a Pontiac, but in May it struck a stone wall. His still indulgent father then bought him a Dodge, but in June it plunged into a river. The father, thinking back over the available evidence, begins to wonder whether it does not perhaps point toward the generalization that, if young Hugo is allowed to continue driving, he will comparatively often have accidents. But Hugo insists that it is just a series of unfortunate coincidences; after all, a person can have some accidents without necessarily having a bad record in the long run. He urges his father to buy him a Cadillac, so that he can show how safe a driver he really is.

Here is an instance of slothful generalization. Hugo is refusing to face the facts, for the evidence is sufficient to make it very probable that he is not a safe driver; the probability, which a prudent father ought to recognize, is that if Hugo is given more cars he will smash them soon.

Exercise 25

Our first rocket ship to Mars has just landed. The astronauts begin to explore and encounter ten Martians, all of whom they observe to be three-legged, insectlike creatures with long antennae who live underwater in the canals. They infer that probably all three-legged insectlike Martians live underwater. Consider whether (and why) this inference would be made stronger or weaker by the following alterations.

1 Suppose that the observed Martians are of various colors: some purple, some pink, some yellow, some green.

2 Suppose that 100 Martians are observed.

3 Suppose that all the observed Martians are blue and live together in a particular spot.

4 Suppose the astronauts infer that all three-legged, insectlike Martians live underwater in canals and not in ponds.

5 Suppose that all the astronauts' observations so far have been made during the morning.

6 Suppose the astronauts infer that all three-legged, insectlike Martians go into the water at least sometimes.

Which of the following generalizations are highly probable, relative to our available evidence?

1 History shows that tyrannical governments do not endure.

2 The more exercise a person gets, the healthier he is.

3 Cows usually lie down when it rains.

4 The more hours per week a child spends in school, the more he will learn.

5 You get what you pay for.

6 The more paying freight you load aboard a cargo plane, the greater the profit earned from the flight will tend to be.

What fallacies, if any, are committed by the following inductive inferences?

1 Oh, the Western United States is all very dull and uninteresting, so different from what it's like here in Boston. I know, because I once spent a weekend with my sister in Minneapolis.

2 In 1936, during the Depression, the *Literary Digest* magazine conducted a preelection poll. They selected names at random from telephone books and then asked these people how they were going to vote. A considerable majority of those questioned said that they were going to vote for Alf M. Landon, the Republican candidate. The *Literary Digest* therefore predicted that Landon would be elected President.

3 People of Italian extraction are especially likely to be criminals. Think of Al Capone and Lucky Luciano.

4 Murders are always discovered, sooner or later. Just think back: When did you ever hear of a murder that hadn't been discovered?

5 I interviewed fifty students in the lounge of the Student Union, asking them whether they preferred to study in a noisy place. Thirty-five of them said, yes, that they disliked quiet and enjoyed studying in noisy, bustling places. I infer that the majority of students do not like to study where it is quiet.

6 One August afternoon I set up in my garden an insect trap having a fan to suck in the insects. After operating the trap for one hour, I emptied out the dead insects, sorted, and counted them. Although there were hundreds of insects, the only large ones were butterflies and grasshoppers. I infer that there probably are no large moths in this region during August.

Describe in some detail methods, which would not be unreasonably expensive or difficult to carry out, by means of which we could get strongly probable answers to these questions:

1 Are people who eat an apple a day significantly healthier on the whole than those who do not?

2 Are athletes who drink liquor able to run significantly less fast and far than athletes who do not drink?

INDUCTIVE ANALOGY

An analogy is a parallel or a resemblance between two different things. Sometimes we use literal language to talk about analogies, and when we use figurative language we nearly always employ analogies. To use language in a *figurative* way is to stretch words beyond the bounds of their normal literal uses. Figurative language often is used for description, though sometimes also as a basis for argument. Simile and metaphor are the two most familiar forms of figurative language.

A *simile* is a statement that one thing is *like* something else of a very different type or that one thing *does* something as if it were something else of a very different type. A metaphor states that one thing *is* something else of a very different type or that it *does* something very different from what it literally does do. In Shakespeare's account of Cleopatra on the Nile we find a combination of forms of description:

The barge she sat in, like a burnished throne,
Burned on the water; the poop was beaten gold.

Here the claim that the barge was like a burnished throne is a simile; to say that it burned on the water is to use a metaphor; and to say that its poop was beaten gold is literal, nonfigurative description. A simile or metaphor says something which, if taken literally, would be false or even absurd; when we understand that it is intended to be figurative, we see that it rests upon an analogy of a kind not ordinarily noticed, an analogy that may be vivid and illuminating.

Often we use analogies in our discourse just for purposes of description, but sometimes we employ them also as a basis for reasoning. In connection with inductive generalization, we have already noted the importance of the positive and negative analogies among the observed instances; but we shall see that there are other inductive inferences in which analogy plays a still more prominent role. This happens when an arguer points out an analogy between two things for the purpose of proving something about one of them.

Suppose that the postman once met a boxer dog and found that it had a bad temper and a tendency to bite; if he now meets another boxer dog, he may reason by analogy that this dog also is likely to have a bad temper and a tendency to bite. Here his reasoning rests upon analogy, for, from the fact that the present dog resembles the past one in breed, he infers that probably it resembles it in temperament as well. Moreover, his reasoning is inductive, since the conclusion (that this new dog has a bad temper and will bite) expresses an empirical conjecture going beyond the evidence then available to the postman.

We can describe this type of reasoning in more general terms if we notice that sometimes there may be more than one past instance upon which the inductive analogy is based. For example, suppose that we have observed a number of swans in the past (call them a, b, c) and have observed each of them to be white; now we learn of another swan (call it d) whose color we have not yet had opportunity to observe. We may reason by analogy that, since this new bird resembles the already observed ones in species, probably it will resemble them in color as well. Here the reasoning rests upon an analogy drawn between the present bird and a number of previously observed ones.

INDUCTIVE ANALOGY

a, b, c each has been observed to be S and P.
d is an S.

Therefore probably d is P.

The form of this reasoning is closely akin to that of inductive generalization, but the difference is that here the conclusion is a singular sentence rather than a universal generalization.

Some philosophers have held that an argument like this, which reaches a singular conclusion, ought to be interpreted as involving two steps: first, the inferring of an inductive generalization ("Since a, b, c each has been observed to be S and P, therefore probably all S are P"); and second, a deductive syllogism ("All S are P; d is an S; therefore d is P"). However, there is no reason why we must interpret the reasoning in this way. Moreover, this interpretation misleadingly suggests that the singular conclusion is no more probable than the inductive generalization, whereas actually the singular conclusion usually would be far more probable than the corresponding generalization.

In judging the strength of an argument of this type, we need to take account of the five factors discussed in connection with inductive generalization and also of one additional factor.

1. We must consider the extent of the positive analogy among the observed instances, a, b, c; that is, the respects (not counting being S and being P) in which the previously observed instances are known to be alike. In the example of the postman, there was only one past instance; there the question of positive analogy among the previously observed instances does not arise.

2. Also we must consider the extent of the negative analogy

among the observed instances, that is, the respects in which they are known to differ from one another. The greater the extent of these differences, the stronger is the argument.

3. We must consider how much the conclusion says. Does it make a very informative claim or is it comparatively vague? The more the conclusion says, the weaker is the argument. For example, the conclusion "This dog will bite" says more than does "This dog will bark or bite".

4. We should consider the number of observed instances, a, b, c, etc.; the more of them there are, the stronger is the argument.

5. We should consider what our past experience tells us about the probable relevance of S to P.

6. The additional very important factor that must be taken into account is the degree of analogy between the new thing d on the one hand and the previously observed instances a, b, c, etc., on the other hand. If it is known that d has properties that none of a, b, c, etc., possesses, or if it is known that all a, b, c, etc., possess properties that d lacks, then the argument is weaker than it would otherwise be. For example, if we know that a, b, c, etc., are all European swans but that d is an Australian swan, then our argument is weakened. But if d, to the best of our knowledge, is very like a, b, c, etc., then the argument may be quite strong.

When an argument by analogy is weak, sometimes a good way of showing that it is weak is to show that the available evidence permits us to construct other arguments by analogy that are no weaker but that reach an opposite conclusion. If I think that the postman is unduly worried about the analogy between the present boxer dog and the one he met in the past, I may try to show him the weakness of his reasoning by constructing an equally strong argument in support of the conclusion that this dog will not bite. I remind the postman that this new boxer belongs to old Mrs. Jones who is well known for her amiable pets; the postman is forgetting that her cats are very friendly, so is her goat, and so is her pet crow. By analogy, since this dog resembles the cats, goat, and crow in being a pet of good old Mrs. Jones, probably it resembles them also in being friendly. Here I am able to use a *counteranalogy* in order to exhibit the weakness of the original argument by analogy.

Exercise 26

> *Hubert has bought a new Torpedo automobile every year for the past ten years, and none of them ever broke down. This year he intends to buy another, for he reasons that it probably will not break down either. Consider whether, and why, his argument would be made stronger or weaker by each of the following alterations.*

1 Suppose that each of his past cars was an eight, while this year's product is a six of radical design.

2 Suppose Hubert had been buying Torpedoes for twenty years.

3 Suppose he learns that the whole engineering staff at Torpedo Motors has just been fired.

4 Suppose his past cars have been various models: sixes, eights, sedans, coupes, etc.

5 Suppose that the new Torpedoes, unlike the old, look like motorboats and are painted in six-tone color schemes.

6 Suppose Hubert has found not merely that his previous Torpedoes did not break down but that they gave superlative performance in every way.

7 Suppose that, instead of predicting that his new car will not break down during the year that he intends to own it, Hubert predicts just that his car will not break down during the first month.

8 Suppose he predicts that none of the new Torpedoes will break down.

In each case state whether the analogy involved is used just for description or whether it is the basis for an argument. If there is an argument, describe its structure and discuss its strength.

1   Mistresses are like books. If you pore upon them too much they doze you and make you unfit for company; but if used discreetly, you are the fitter for conversation by 'em.

WYCHERLEY, The Country Wife

2   Why then should the education of apes be impossible? Why might not the ape, by dint of great pains, at last imitate after the manner of deaf mutes, the motions necessary for pronunciation? I do not dare decide whether the ape's organs of speech, however trained, would be incapable of articulation. But because of the great analogy between ape and man and because there is no known animal whose external and internal organs so strikingly resemble man's, it would surprise me if speech were absolutely impossible to the ape.

LA METTRIE, Man a Machine

3   Every one who really thinks for himself is like a monarch. His position is undelegated and supreme. His judgments, like royal decrees, spring from his own sovereign power and proceed directly from himself. He acknowledges authority as little as a monarch admits a command; he subscribes to nothing but what he has himself authorized. The multitude of common minds, laboring under all sorts of current opinions, authorities, prejudices, is like the people, which silently obeys the law and accepts orders from above.

SCHOPENHAUER, The Art of Literature

4   "Do you think," said Candide, "that men have always massacred each other, as they do today, that they have always been false, cozening, faithless, ungrateful, thieving, weak, inconstant, mean-spirited, envious, greedy, drunken, miserly, ambitious, bloody, slanderous, debauched, fanatic, hypocritical, and stupid?"

"Do you think," said Martin, "that hawks have always eaten pigeons when they could find them?"

"Of course I do," said Candide.

"Well," said Martin, "if hawks have always had the same character, why should you suppose that men have changed theirs?"   VOLTAIRE, *Candide*

5   Words are like leaves; and where they most abound,
Much fruit of sense beneath is rarely found.

           ALEXANDER POPE, "Essay on Criticism"

6   Johnson told me, that he went up thither without mentioning it to his servant, when he wanted to study, secure from interruption; for he would not allow his servant to say he was not at home when he really was. "A servant's strict regard for truth (said he) must be weakened by such a practice. A philosopher may know that it is merely a form of denial; but few servants are such nice distinguishers. If I accustom a servant to tell a lie for *me*, have I not reason to apprehend that he will tell many lies for *himself*."

           BOSWELL, *Life of Johnson*

HYPOTHESES ABOUT CAUSES

Next we shall consider inductive arguments that aim to establish conclusions about relations of cause and effect. Much of our thinking about the world involves questions of causes and effects; we need to know not merely what phenomena take place but also which phenomena cause which others. A sentence saying that one thing is cause of another thing (e.g., "Arsenic causes death") normally has to be an empirical sentence; it must be supported by inductive reasoning based upon observational evidence. Let us consider the sort of evidence and the sort of reasoning that are required. (To be sure, there are necessary sentences about causal relations, e.g., "Fatal poisons cause death". But these are comparatively trivial and uninteresting.)

A fallacy related to causes occurs often in political speeches and in other common kinds of careless thinking. Suppose someone argues, "The Great Depression began in the United States soon after Herbert Hoover took office as President. Therefore Hoover must be to blame for causing the Depression". This is an inductive argument, an argument whose conclusion is a hypothesis about cause and effect (that the Depression was an effect caused by Hoover). But it is a very bad argument. It commits the fallacy of *post hoc, ergo propter hoc* (Latin: "after this, therefore on account of it"). This fallacy is a special case of the general fallacy of hasty induction. Here the speaker has leaped from the evidence that the Depression began soon after Hoover took office to the conclusion that the Depression began because Hoover had taken office. This is too hasty a leap. To be sure, the fact that the Depression began soon after Hoover took office may, if there is no contrary evidence, make it faintly probable that perhaps Hoover was the cause, but this fact is utterly insufficient to make it highly probable that he was the cause. We would need much more evidence before we could reasonably attach any strong probability to the conclusion.

In order to know that one thing is the cause of another, we need to know that the first thing happened or existed earlier than the second, but we need to know a great deal more besides. (In most ordinary cases a cause certainly must precede its effect; whether there are some cases in which a cause may merely be simultaneous with its effect is a point disputed by philosophers, upon which we need not enter.)

What does it mean to say that one thing is a cause of another? What more is involved, beyond the claim that the former thing happened earlier? Let us consider another case: A doctor gives an experimental drug to a patient suffering from a serious disease; next day the patient's symptoms are relieved, and he gradually recovers. Is the doctor entitled to say that the drug caused the cure? In order to discuss this matter we do not necessarily have to worry about the inner biochemical processes taking place in the patient's bloodstream. The Indians knew that quinine causes relief from malaria, although they knew nothing about how it does so. It is possible to know that x causes y without knowing the intervening steps by means of which x causes y. But what does it mean to say that the drug caused the cure? To claim that taking this dose of the drug caused the patient's cure surely is to claim, for one thing, that what has happened here is an instance of a general regularity. This implies that anyone who is sufficiently similar to this patient and who has the same symptoms will be cured of them upon taking the drug. The claim that the drug cured the patient would be refuted if we discovered that other sufficiently similar patients were not cured by it.

For another thing, to claim that this dose cured this patient surely is to claim that, if the patient had not had the drug, he would not have been cured (at least, not when he was). This seems correct. Yet someone might object: What sense does it make to talk about what would have occurred if something that did happen had not happened? We cannot go back and change the past; how could we ever find out whether the patient would have recovered without the drug? We must answer this objection by pointing out that talk about what would have happened to this patient derives its sense from its implicit reference to what does happen to other sufficiently similar patients on other sufficiently similar occasions. When we say that, if this patient had not had the dose, he would not have been cured, we are implicitly claiming that other patients with the same symptoms, whose situation is similar to that of this patient except that they do not get the drug, are not cured.

Putting together these points and generalizing them, we may say that a sentence of the form "x causes y" by its very meaning normally implies not only that x takes place or begins to exist prior to y but also that, in cases of some certain kind, x always is present if and only if y is. This is part, though to be sure not all, of what is meant by speaking of causes.

Someone might object to what has been said, on the ground that it is vague to speak of "cases of some certain kind" or of cases that are "sufficiently similar". Of course it is vague but that is not a ground for objecting; the general notion of causation is a rather vague notion, though not on that account a useless notion.

Another aspect of the notion of cause is that we commonly speak about *the* cause of an event. For instance, a coroner is asked to determine *the* cause of a victim's death. There are innumerable events, each of which in a sense could be said to have caused the death: The victim died because his brain ceased to receive oxygen, because his blood stopped circulating, because his heart stopped beating, because a bullet traveled toward his body, because his enemy pulled the trigger, and so on. Each of these events is such that death in closely similar cases occurs if and only if the given event occurs. But the coroner will report as the cause of death that a bullet passed through the heart. When he calls this *the* cause of death, the coroner is not denying that many other events belonged to the chain of causes and effects that eventuated in death; the coroner is doing his duty by focusing attention upon one especially significant event in the chain. This event, which he calls *the* cause, is especially significant because it is the event upon which we can best focus our attention if we want to assign responsibility for such a death and upon which we can best focus our efforts if we want to prevent or control deaths of this type.

The nineteenth-century English philosopher John Stuart Mill described several fundamental ways of detecting causes. These are known as *Mill's methods*. When properly understood and not overrated, these methods are useful in guiding our thinking about causes. We shall consider three of these methods, discussing them first in connection with a concrete example.

Suppose that some of the students who eat in the Coolidge College cafeteria are taken ill after lunch. We investigate a few of the cases and gather the following data:

Student *a* ate soup, ate fish, ate salad, and got ptomaine.

Student *b* ate soup, ate no fish, ate salad, and got ptomaine.

Student *c* ate no soup, ate fish, ate salad, and got ptomaine.

These data will enable us to reach a conclusion about the cause of the food poisoning, provided that we may make a certain assumption. We must be entitled to assume that one and only one of the factors listed (eating of soup, eating of fish, eating of salad) is the cause of the food poisoning. If we may assume that, we can use what Mill called the *method of agreement:* We reason that the cause must be present in each case where the effect is present. Here eating salad must have been the cause of the ptomaine, since it is the factor with regard to which all the cases agree.

On another occasion, students again are taken ill. This time we collect the following data:

Student *a* ate meat, ate pie, ate ice cream, and got ptomaine.

Student *b* ate no meat, ate pie, ate no ice cream, got no ptomaine.

Student *c* ate meat, ate no pie, ate no ice cream, got no ptomaine.

Again, before we can draw any definite conclusion, we must be entitled to assume that the cause is some one of the factors on the list. But if we may make this assumption, we can use what Mill called the *method of difference:* We reason that any factor present in cases in which the effect is absent cannot be the cause. Thus, by process of elimination, we see that eating ice cream must have been the cause of the food poisoning on this occasion.

On still another occasion we again find students being taken ill after eating in the cafeteria. This time we collect the data:

Student *a* ate one hamburger and got ptomaine with fever of 101°.

Student *b* ate two hamburgers and got ptomaine with fever of 102 °.

Student *c* ate three hamburgers and got ptomaine with fever of 103°.

Here we are concerned not with the simple presence or absence of cause and effect but rather with the degree to which cause and effect are present. When we infer from these data that the hamburgers caused the ptomaine, we are employing what Mill called the *method of concomitant variation.* If a factor is present in all and only those cases in which the effect is present, then the more closely its variations in degree are correlated with the variations in degree of the effect, the greater is the probability that this factor is the cause.

Mill regarded these three[2] methods as useful both as a guide in collecting data and planning new experiments to discover causes and as a guide in reflecting about the strength of arguments that try to prove conclusions about cause and effect. His methods are useful in both these ways: for planning further inquiries and for evaluating results that have been obtained. However, we must not make the mistake of assuming that these simple methods provide an infallible way of detecting causes. Far from it, for in any overall piece of inductive reasoning within which we make use of Mill's methods, we always must evaluate the probability that we have actually included the cause among the factors of which we take account. Unless we are entitled to think it probable that we have done this, use of these methods is not legitimate.

Fallacies involving Mill's methods occur frequently. A crude example is this: Suppose that one day a man eats popcorn while watching television and suffers indigestion; the next day he eats pizza while watching television and suffers indigestion; the next day he eats cheesecake while watching television and suffers indigestion. Using the method of difference, he argues that neither popcorn nor pizza nor cheesecake caused his indigestion, and he concludes that watching television caused it (perhaps because of the electrical radiations). Here the reasoning is absurd, for the list of factors of which he took account omits overeating, which certainly ought to have been considered as a possible cause.

---

[2] In his *System of Logic,* Mill discusses two additional methods, the joint method of agreement and difference and the method of residues. But these are just slightly more complicated ways of using the method of agreement and the method of difference; they do not introduce any new principle.

As another example, suppose it is found that in a certain town those young people who regularly attend church relatively seldom get into trouble with the police, while those who do not attend church relatively more often do get into trouble with the police. Using the method of difference, the local religious leaders point to these facts as proof that religion causes improvement in the moral fiber of the young. Is this a reasonable conclusion? Not if it is assumed that these data by themselves confer any very high degree of probability upon the conclusion. There are certainly other factors that should be taken into account before we could say that any strong proof had been given. Is it not very possible, for instance, that their wholesome family environment causes some young people both to be religious and to be law-abiding, whereas the unwholesome family environment of others causes them to be neither religious nor law-abiding? Here is a really serious possibility that merits investigation.

Exercise 27

In each case, which of Mill's methods is being employed? Discuss the soundness of the reasoning.

1 On the average, children born between May and October seem to get slightly higher scores in intelligence tests than children born from November to April. Is it the season of conception or birth that somehow affects the intelligence of children, in so far as these tests can measure it, or is it the intelligence of the parents that influences the season of conception of the child? The second must surely be the explanation: for example, when one compares the average scores of winter and summer children who are brothers and sisters, the difference between them almost completely disappears.

P. B. MEDAWAR, The Future of Man

2 Does a college graduate earn enough in a lifetime to compensate for the four or more years when he was paying to learn

rather than being paid to work? Some figures recently released by the Bureau of the Census prove that the answer is yes. These figures, based on the year 1958, show that a man who graduated from high school and worked until age sixty-four could expect to earn a total of $231,500 during his working lifetime. A college graduate also working until age sixty-four could expect to earn $383,000. Going to college does pay!

3 A survey conducted at the Warren G. Harding University revealed that 70 per cent of students on the honor roll could type, while only 30 per cent of the students not on the honor roll could do so. The faculty, anxious to improve academic standards, decided that henceforth all freshmen who cannot type must enroll in a compulsory typing course.

4 Psychologists who have tested thousands of people working in American business have discovered that top executives generally have much larger vocabularies than lower-level employees do. Therefore if you want to rise to the top in business, you should work to enlarge your vocabulary.

5 In the city where you live the divorce rate is high: There are two divorces each year for every three marriages. Therefore if you want your marriage to endure, you should move to some other city where your chance of staying married will be greater.

6 A survey of high-school students in Newton, Massachusetts, shows that those who do not smoke have significantly higher IQ's and attain higher academic grades than those who do smoke. It is appalling to realize that smoking can have this sort of effect upon the mental ability of adolescents.

7 Senator Progshire says that history has disproved the theory that large Federal deficits contribute to economic growth. "For the past six years", Progshire says, "Federal deficits have averaged a heavy six billion dollars per year, and yet economic growth has been a slow-moving despair of economists during this very period".

8   Public school students in Springfield, Missouri, were given a physical fitness test. Then students ranking in the top 40 per cent of their classes on the basis of physical performance were compared in other ways with a random cross section of students. Members of the select group were found to have a grade average of 2.48 while the average of the others was 2.19 (2.00 represents a C average). Those in the high-fitness group participated in 50 per cent more extracurricular activities and had an absentee record 30 per cent lower than the cross-section group. The select group, in the opinion of their deans and counselors, displayed a far more positive and enthusiastic attitude toward school. Here is proof at last that vigorous physical activity is of all-round benefit to young people.

9   The unconscious . . . has . . . ways . . . of informing us of things which by all logic we could not possibly know. . . . I recall one time during World War II when I was returning home from Bollingen. . . . The moment the train started to move I was overpowered by the image of someone drowning. This was a memory of an accident that had happened while I was on military service. . . . I got out at Erlenbach and walked home. . . . Adrian, then the youngest of the boys, had fallen into the water at the boathouse. It is quite deep there, and since he could not really swim he had almost drowned. . . . This had taken place at exactly the time I had been assailed by that memory in the train. The unconscious had given me a hint.   CARL G. JUNG, *Memories, Dreams, Reflections*

NUMERICAL PROBABILITIES

We have been using the word "probability" in the sense that has to do with inductive arguments, identifying the degree of probability with the degree to which it is reasonable to believe the conclusion on the basis of the evidence. Probability is always a relative matter, in that it makes sense to call a conjecture probable only relative to some evidence, never just in and of itself; a conjecture, whether true or false, may have a high degree of probability relative to one body of evidence and a low degree of probability relative to some other body of evidence.

Various symbols can be used to represent probability, but we shall employ a pair of slanting strokes: $/\!/$. We shall use strokes between two sentences to form an expression that names the probability of the first sentence relative to the second. Thus, if we let "H" be one sentence and "E" another, we write "$H/\!/E$" as a name for the probability of the former relative to the latter, that is, the degree to which it would be reasonable to believe the former if the latter were the evidence one had. According to this conception, if there were cases in which completely reasonable men could differ in their judgments about the credibility of a conclusion on the basis of given evidence, in those cases we could not speak of *the* probability. For simple normal cases, however, it seems safe to assume that men could not disagree without being unreasonable.

In the expression "$H/\!/E$", "H" is the hypothesis (the conclusion) whose probability we are weighing, and "E" is the evidence (the premise, or conjunction of premises) upon which the probability is based. If we let "H" represent the sentence "All swans are white", "H'" represent "The next swan we meet will be white", and "E" symbolize our evidence regarding swans that we have observed to be white, then we can write

$$H'/\!/E > H/\!/E$$

That is, the probability that the next swan will be white is greater than is the probability that all swans are white, relative to our evidence. Here we make a comparison between two degrees of probability, although we have not assigned a definite numerical value to either.

One small reservation is necessary. We shall speak of the

probability of a hypothesis sentence relative to the evidence sentence only where the evidence sentence is not a contradiction. Where "E" represents a contradiction, other sentences cannot have any sort of probability, high or low, relative to it, as we are interested in considering the probabilities of hypotheses relative only to evidence that might possibly be true. To put it another way, when an inductive argument is found to have inconsistent premises, we must reject the argument completely; there is no point in thinking that the conclusion possesses any sort of probability, high or low, relative to inconsistent premises.

There is a maximum possible degree of probability. Knowing that a sentence is true occasionally puts one in a position of being so certain of another sentence that no new observations could increase one's certainty. Then the probability of the second sentence relative to the first has the maximum possible value. This happens when (and only when) the first sentence deductively implies the second. For instance, the probability of "Some white things are swans" relative to the evidence "Some swans are white" has this maximum value. It is conventional to correlate the number 1 with this maximum degree of probability. Writing "W" for the first sentence and "S" for the second, we have

$$W /\!/ S = 1$$

There is also a minimum possible degree of probability. Knowing that "Some swans are white" is true, one is in a position to assign the minimum degree of belief to the sentence "All swans are black" ("B" for short); that is, no additional evidence should further diminish one's belief in hypothesis "B", for the degree to which it is reasonable to believe "B" has hit rock bottom. It is conventional to correlate the number zero with this minimum degree of probability. Thus we say

$$B /\!/ S = 0$$

This minimum degree of probability arises when (and only when) the hypothesis is contradicted by the evidence.

All other degrees of probability fall between these two extremes. Degrees of probability falling between these extremes sometimes are comparable with one another and sometimes are not. We can say that, relative to the historical evidence we now possess, it is more probable that there was such a man as Plato than that there was such a man as Homer, and it is more probable that there was such a man as George Washington than that there was such a man as Plato. But it does not make sense to ask for an exact measure of how much more probable one of these hypotheses is than another. Moreover, suppose someone asks whether, relative to present evidence, the hypothesis that there was such a man as Homer is more or less probable than is the hypothesis that there is no life on Mars. We cannot answer, because there is no answer. The two hypotheses are very different, and there is no basis upon which to compare their degrees of probability.

If there is no reason for calling one probability greater than another, we cannot maintain that they must be equal, for that view would lead to absurdities. For instance, it would lead us to say that the probability that there was such a man as Homer is equal to the probability that there is no life on Mars (since we have no reason for calling one probability greater than the other); it would also lead us to say that the probability that there was such a man as George Washington is equal to the probability that there is no life on Mars (since again we have no reason for calling one probability greater than the other). This would imply that the probability that Homer existed equals the probability that Washington existed; yet these probabilities are not equal. Thus we must conclude that it is sometimes, but not always, possible to compare degrees of probability of this kind.

In certain special but important kinds of cases, however, we not only can compare probabilities; we can compare them so fully that numbers between 0 and 1 can be assigned to represent their degrees. Use of numbers means that every numerical probability is comparable with every other (either greater, smaller, or equal). Also, we can go further and introduce arithmetical operations such as addition and subtraction. In what sort of situation may numbers be used to measure probabilities? The most straightforward kind of cases in which this is possible are ones like those involved in some gambling games, where the events in which we are interested can be analyzed into certain fundamental possibilities that are equally reasonable to expect.

Consider the rolling of dice. If someone shows us a pair of dice and we have no positive reason for thinking them irregular, the reasonable thing to suppose is that these dice, when rolled, will behave generally as do most other dice. That is, we believe that the various faces of each die will come up just about equally often in the long run, although their sequence will be unpredictable, and that there will be no detectable correlation, in the long run, between the sequence in which faces come up on one die and on the other.

Granting this, what is reasonable to expect regarding the outcome of the next roll of these two dice? It is certain that on the next roll each die must show one and only one of its six faces. (Otherwise a genuine roll would not have been achieved.) We have for each die six mutually exclusive and exhaustive alternatives, which are equally reasonable to expect; therefore, each of these outcomes must be assigned a probability of $\frac{1}{6}$. Then what is the probability of getting, say, a total of seven with the two dice? Here we must reason as follows: With two dice, each of which can land in just one of six equally probable ways, there are thirty-six equally probable outcomes. We write "1–1" to represent the first die landing with one dot up and the second die landing with one dot up, etc. Of these outcomes there are six (underlined in the list) that yield the result in which we are interested, that is, showing a total of seven dots.

1–1	1–2	1–3	1–4	1–5	1–6
2–1	2–2	2–3	2–4	2–5	2–6
3–1	3–2	3–3	3–4	3–5	3–6
4–1	4–2	4–3	4–4	4–5	4–6
5–1	5–2	5–3	5–4	5–5	5–6
6–1	6–2	6–3	6–4	6–5	6–6

Thus the probability of rolling seven equals 6 divided by 36, or $\frac{1}{6}$. Here we are following the general principle that the numerical probability of a result is equal to the number of outcomes favorable to that result divided by the total number of possible outcomes. This principle makes sense only when we use an exhaustive list of mutually exclusive and equally probable outcomes, but it is one way in which we can assign numerical values to some probabilities.

Once we have obtained some numerical probabilities, we can make use of certain elementary laws for deriving further numerical probabilities from ones already known. First there is the law relating the probability of a sentence to the probability of its negation.

LAW OF NEGATION

$$-p /\!/ q = 1 - p /\!/ q$$

The probability of the negation of a sentence, relative to given evidence, is equal to 1 minus the probability of the sentence itself relative to that same evidence. Notice here that the short dash symbolizes negation—only a sentence can have a negation, a number cannot—while the long dash is the subtraction sign—only numbers can be subtracted from one another, not sentences. The strokes are our probability sign, which must not be confused with a division sign, for only sentences are probable relative to one another, and only numbers can be divided by one another.

Let us apply this law of negation to the case of rolling dice. What is the probability of not rolling seven on the next roll of the two dice? This must be 1 minus $\frac{1}{6}$ (the probability of rolling seven), that is, $\frac{5}{6}$. We can see the correctness of this answer if we look at the list and count the number of ways in which the two dice could fall so as to yield a total different from seven. There are 30 out of 36, and so the probability is indeed $\frac{5}{6}$.

Another law is designed for calculating the probability of a conjunction.

LAW OF CONJUNCTION

$p \& q /\!/ r = p /\!/ r \times q /\!/ r \& p$

This law tells us that the probability relative to given evidence that two things both will come true equals the probability of the first multiplied by the probability of the second when we assume that the first is true. What is the probability that on the next roll of the dice we will obtain a total greater than four and less than seven? Using the law of conjunction, we reason as follows: The probability of getting a total greater than four and less than seven equals the probability of getting a total greater than four (30 divided by 36, since 30 possible outcomes are favorable out of the total of 36) multiplied by the probability of getting a total less than seven, on the assumption that our total is greater than four (9 divided by 30, since there are 30 possibilities where the total is greater than four; of these, 9 are favorable to its being less than seven). Thus we have $\frac{30}{36} \times \frac{9}{30} = \frac{9}{36} = \frac{1}{4}$. If we look at the total list of possible outcomes (Table 1), we see that the law of conjunction has given us the correct result. Table 1 is drawn up to indicate how the law of conjunction has led us to the proper answer in this case.

We can apply the law of conjunction in a simpler way in cases where the happenings that concern us are *independent;* that is, where the probability of q is unaltered by the assumption that p is true. Suppose we want to calculate the probability of getting heads on the first toss of a coin and getting heads also on the second toss. Here we must multiply the probability of getting heads on the first toss (which is ½, when there is no reason to think the coin abnormal) times the probability of getting heads on the second toss (which is again ½). The probability is simply ½ times ½, or ¼, because here the two events are independent in the sense that what happens on the first toss does not alter the probability of getting

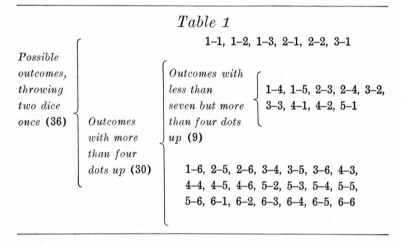

Table 1

Possible outcomes, throwing two dice once **(36)**

1–1, 1–2, 1–3, 2–1, 2–2, 3–1

Outcomes with more than four dots up **(30)**

Outcomes with less than seven but more than four dots up **(9)**

1–4, 1–5, 2–3, 2–4, 3–2, 3–3, 4–1, 4–2, 5–1

1–6, 2–5, 2–6, 3–4, 3–5, 3–6, 4–3, 4–4, 4–5, 4–6, 5–2, 5–3, 5–4, 5–5, 5–6, 6–1, 6–2, 6–3, 6–4, 6–5, 6–6

heads on the second toss. Where the happenings are independent in this way, we can use the law of conjunction in the simple form

$$p\&q/\!/r \;=\; p/\!/r \times q/\!/r$$

We also have a law designed for calculating the probability of a disjunction; that is, the probability that at least one of two things will come true.

LAW OF DISJUNCTION

$$p \vee q/\!/r \;=\; p/\!/r + q/\!/r - p\&q/\!/r$$

This law tells us that the probability of a (nonexclusive) disjunction equals the sum of the separate probabilities of its components, minus the probability of their conjunction. For instance, with two dice, what is the probability that either both dice will read alike or that the total will be less than six? The law tells us that this must equal the probability that both dice will read alike (6 divided by 36), plus the probability that their total will be less than six (10 divided by 36), minus the probability that both dice will read alike and have a total less than six (2 divided by 36). Thus the probability equals $\frac{7}{18}$. We can confirm the correctness of this result by looking again at the complete list of outcomes (Table 2).

Table 2

Possible outcomes, throwing two dice once (36)	Outcomes when both dice read alike (6)	3–3, 4–4, 5–5, 6–6
		1–1, 2–2
	Outcomes with less than six dots up (10)	1–2, 1–3, 1–4, 2–1, 2–3, 3–1, 3–2, 4–1
		1–5, 1–6, 2–4, 2–5, 2–6, 3–4, 3–5, 3–6, 4–2, 4–3, 4–5, 4–6, 5–1, 5–2, 5–3, 5–4, 5–6, 6–1, 6–2, 6–3, 6–4, 6–5

We can calculate the probability of a disjunction in a simpler way if the components cannot both be true. What is the probability that a single die will land with five dots up or with six dots up on a single throw? Here the probability is $\frac{1}{6}$ plus $\frac{1}{6}$ minus zero. We subtract nothing, since the die cannot show two different faces on a single throw. Thus, in cases where the outcomes are mutually exclusive, we merely add the separate probabilities in order to get the probability of the disjunction.

One of the practical uses of these rules for calculating probabilities is deciding whether a gamble is a reasonable one.

Suppose that someone invites you to draw two cards from a well-shuffled bridge deck, the first card to be returned and the deck reshuffled before the second card is drawn. He bets you even money that you will not get a spade on either drawing. Would it be reasonable to accept such a bet?

In order to answer, we must calculate your probability of winning. To win, you must draw a spade either on the first trial or on the second trial. There are thirteen spades in the deck of fifty-two cards, and so your probability of succeeding on the first draw is $13/52$, or $1/4$; your probability of succeeding on the second draw is the same. But to obtain the probability of your succeeding the first time or the second time, we cannot simply add these two fractions and call that the answer. (According to that fallacious procedure of reckoning, it would be absolutely certain that you would succeed at least once in four drawings—an absurd result.) By the law of alternation, we must add the two probabilities and then subtract the probability of succeeding both times, which, according to the law of conjunction, is $13/52 \times 13/52$, or $1/16$. Thus the probability of winning the bet is $1/4$ plus $1/4$ minus $1/16$, or $7/16$. Your opponent's probability of winning, according to the law of negation, is 1 minus $7/16$, or $9/16$. He has a greater probability of winning than you have, and if the odds are even money it would normally be foolish to accept such a bet.

If your opponent offers better odds in your favor, it may no longer be unreasonable to accept the bet. If he wagers $9 to your $7, your probability of winning ($7/16$) multiplied by the amount you stand to win ($9) equals your probability of losing ($9/16$) multiplied by the amount you stand to lose ($7). The result of multiplying a probability by an amount of gain or loss is called a *mathematical expectation*.[3] We say that a bet is a *fair bet* when

[3] Gain and loss should perhaps be measured in terms of utility (amount of benefit or harm), not just in terms of money. If winning $9 would merely make one a little less poor, while losing $7 would drive one into bankruptcy, then the expectation of loss on the bet is really greater than the expectation of gain, though not in dollar terms.

the mathematical expectation of gain is equal to the mathematical expectation of loss for each gambler. For it to be reasonable to accept a bet, the mathematical expectation of gain should be at least as great as the mathematical expectation of loss.

Now, to say, for instance, that the probability is $\frac{1}{6}$ that a pair of dice will land with a total of seven spots up does not mean that we can definitely expect this outcome to occur once in every six rolls of the dice. Far from it; there is only a moderate probability that this will occur exactly once in a given sequence of six throws. And the probability is very low indeed that in a long series of throws every sixth one will yield this particular outcome. What we can say, however, is that it is highly probable that in the long run just about one-sixth of the outcomes will yield a total of seven spots up. The larger the number of throws, the higher is the probability that the fraction of them yielding the outcome seven will differ from $\frac{1}{6}$ by less than any specified percentage. The longer the run, the more probable it is that the relative frequency with which an outcome occurs will closely approximate the probability of that outcome. This principle, which is sometimes referred to as the *law of large numbers*, or the *law of averages*, is fundamental to statistical inference.

The mathematical notion of limit is needed for a more exact formulation of this principle. Let x be the probability of a certain outcome (such as getting a total of seven in rolling two dice). Let y be the number of trials (the number of times the dice are rolled). Let z be the fraction of these trials in which that certain outcome occurs. And let w be an arbitrarily chosen percentage (such as 1 per cent, 0.01 per cent, etc.). Then the principle is that, for each choice of w, the probability that the absolute value of the difference between z and x will be less than w increases toward 1 as its limit, as y increases without bound.

Misunderstanding of this principle leads to a common and insidious fallacy, the *Monte Carlo fallacy*. Suppose that a man is playing roulette, and he notices that a certain number has not come up for a long time. He reasons that, because this number has not come up for a long time, there is an increased probability that it will come up on the next spin of the wheel. Or a man is rolling dice, and he notices that seven has not been thrown as often lately as was to have been expected; he therefore decides to accept at odds of less than 5 to 1 a bet that seven will be thrown on the next roll of the two dice. In both these cases a fallacy is being committed. Both these men are confused in their thinking and are laying their bets foolishly. The law of large numbers does not tell us anything about the probability of what will happen on the next throw; it tells us only about a long-run probability.

It is a complete mistake to think that in this kind of case the relative infrequency of an outcome in the past makes it more probable that it will occur in the future. This kind of thinking runs directly contrary to the whole basic idea of inductive reasoning: the idea that we should expect for the future the *same* sort of thing that we have observed in the past. Those who commit the Monte Carlo fallacy make the mistake of expecting for the future the opposite of what they have observed in the past, because of their misunderstanding of the meaning of the principle about long-run probabilities.

The Monte Carlo fallacy perhaps is best classified as a fallacy of ambiguity. The arguer assumes that "It is improbable that a certain number will fail to come up in n trials" means "Relative to the evidence that the wheel has spun $n-1$ times, without stopping on that number, it is probable that it will stop there the nth time". Whereas in fact what the sentence means is "Relative to our general evidence about roulette wheels, it is improbable that a wheel will spin n times without ever stopping on that number". Confusion between these two meanings engenders the fallacy.

Exercise 28

Use the laws of probability to solve the following problems.

1   On the basis of his past performance, the odds are 2 to 1 (that is, 2 out of 3) that Clovis will pass mathematics, 3 to 2 that he will not pass physics, but 3 to 2 that he will pass physics if he passes mathematics. What is the probability that he will pass both courses?

2   A coin is to be tossed twice. What is the probability of getting tails on both tosses?

3   A coin is to be tossed three times. What is the probability of getting heads on all three tosses? At what odds would it be reasonable to bet on this?

4   Three cards are to be drawn in succession from an ordinary bridge deck; a card will not be returned to the deck before the drawing of the next card. What is the probability that all three cards drawn will be hearts?

5   Suppose someone offers you 12 to 1 odds that you cannot get a six at least once in two throws of a die. Is it reasonable to accept this bet?

6   Clovis and Hugo are aboard a sinking ship; there is only one place left in the last lifeboat. Clovis happens to have a single die with him, and he makes this proposal: Hugo shall roll the die three times, and if he gets six at least once then the place in the lifeboat is his; otherwise it is Clovis's. Is this fair?

7   On earth there are two sexes, male and female, which are equally numerous. On Mars there are three sexes, alpha, beta, and gamma, which are equally numerous. Which is more probable: that an earth parent who is going to have two children will have at least one male child or that a Martian parent who is going to have three children will have at least one alpha child?

Evaluate the following arguments.

1 So far as we know, there are just two possibilities: Either a Republican will win the next election or he will not. Therefore, relative to the information we possess, the probability of a Republican winning equals $\frac{1}{2}$.

2 The Smiths are going to have a child, and the probability is $\frac{1}{2}$ that it will be a boy and $\frac{1}{2}$ that it will be a girl. Therefore, the probability that the Smith's next child will be both a boy and a girl is $\frac{1}{2}$ times $\frac{1}{2}$, or $\frac{1}{4}$.

3 Yesterday this slot machine paid off one time out of twenty, on an average. Since today I've played it nineteen times without winning, I can be pretty confident of winning if I play just once more.

4 The O'Briens have fifteen children, all of them girls. By the law of averages, this cannot go on. Therefore it is very probable that their next will be a boy.

5 The ABC airline has an outstanding safety record. They have not had a crash in four years of busy operations. But by the law of averages it is very unlikely that this can go on, and so they are probably due for some bad crashes soon. You had better not fly with them.

EXPLANATORY HYPOTHESES

So far, we have considered some special types of inductive arguments and the special considerations that bear upon their strength. But there is also a more general way of looking at inductive reasoning, a point of view that is often appropriate when we are evaluating the strength of inductive arguments of various types. We may think of the conclusion of an inductive argument as a hypothesis, a conjecture about the empirical world, and we may think of the premises as data presented in support of that hypothesis. From this point of view, it is possible for us to ask, Is this hypothesis a plausible *explanation* of the data? Asking this question can often help when we are trying to form a clear view of the strength of the inductive argument itself. An inductive argument establishes a high probability for its conclusion provided it is possible to regard the conclusion as a hypothesis supplying a reasonable explanation of the data contained in the premises.

To go back to the example used in discussing inductive generalization, let us suppose that we have observed many white swans and never have observed a swan that is not white. How strongly does this evidence support the conclusion that all swans are white? Here it is helpful to adopt this new viewpoint and ask, How well does the hypothesis that all swans are white explain the fact that we have obtained these observations? Our data make the generalization highly probable only if the generalization itself helps to provide the most probable explanation of why these were the data that we obtained. Are there other equally reasonable ways of explaining why it has happened that all the swans we have seen have been white? Is it perhaps that we have looked only at American swans and have missed nonwhite swans in other countries? Is it perhaps that we have looked at swans only in summertime and have missed nonwhite swans in other seasons? In any such case, the inductive argument is weak; if not, it is stronger. Asking ourselves whether the generalization provides the most reasonable explanation of the data is a good way of helping to evaluate the degree of probability that the data confer on the generalization. This general point of view can be helpful in connection with most types of inductive inference.

When we adopt this point of view and ask about the reasonableness of some explanatory hypothesis, we should bear in mind that for any set of data there always are many incompatible ways in which the data might conceivably be explained. Sometimes one line of explanation is definitely very much better than all other conflicting lines of explanation. If the silver spoons are missing from their rack on the dining-room wall; if the maid, who had left hastily, is arrested and found to have the spoons concealed in her car; and if she confesses to having stolen them, then, in the light of these data, by far the most reasonable explanation is that the maid stole the spoons, just as she says. We might well say, "That's the only possible explanation", by which we would mean that this is the most probable explanation.

Yet even here it is perfectly conceivable that the true explanation could be something different. Conceivably, there may have been an open window through which a crow, attracted by the glitter of the spoons, carried them off one by one and concealed them in the maid's car; she, having been disappointed in love, was in such a low state of mind when apprehended by the police that she readily confessed to the action of which they accused her. This is a conceivable hypothesis, though a very improbable one. The point is that always, if we use imagination, we can think of alternative explanations. We never are absolutely limited to a single hypothesis, since there always are alternative conceivable explanations. We always are faced with choice, and we need to choose the most reasonable hypothesis.

Various factors combine to make one explanatory hypothesis more probable than another. These are not describable in any sharp, precise way, but we can say something about them.

We are likely to think that the extent to which it 'fits the facts' contributes greatly to determining the probability of an explanatory hypothesis. If one hypothesis succeeds in explaining more of the data than another does, this increases the probability of the former. Suppose that only the solid-silver spoons and none of the plated spoons are missing. The hypothesis that the maid stole the spoons explains this, for the maid would know that the plated spoons were of less value, whereas the hypothesis that an unknown crow stole the spoons does not explain this. However, whether a hypothesis 'fits the facts' is not a simple yes-or-no matter. Although the crow hypothesis does not *easily* fit the fact that only the solid-silver spoons are gone, still we could think of some auxiliary hypothesis which, when combined with the crow hypothesis, would provide a conceivable explanation of this troublesome fact. Perhaps there were two crows, both attracted by the shininess of the spoons; the larger crow carried off all the spoons, and then the smaller crow, out of spite, brought back as many spoons as it could but was not strong enough to lift the heavier solid-silver spoons and so returned only the plated ones. This is a far-fetched yet not a totally impossible line of explanation.

There is no limit to the lengths to which we can go in making any hypothesis 'fit the facts', if we are imaginative enough in thinking of auxiliary hypotheses. In the end, perhaps the best way of looking at the matter is this: We should not think that we have to choose between one single hypothesis and another (e.g., the hypothesis that the maid stole the spoons versus the hypothesis that a crow did). Instead we should think of the choice as lying between whole *sets* of hypotheses (the hypotheses that the maid stole the spoons just as she said and that crows had nothing to do with it versus the hypotheses that one crow stole the spoons and another brought back some of them, and the maid had a lover who disappointed her, etc.). As we think over the total body of known data, we ask ourselves, Which *set* of hypotheses best explains these data? If one set of hypotheses stands out as giving a much more reasonable line of explanation than does any other set, then all the hypotheses of that set are probably true.

When we compare sets of hypotheses with one another, it is helpful to invoke the notion of *simplicity*. Other things being equal, the simpler a set of hypotheses, the more probable it is as an explanation of the data. Although we cannot define this notion of simplicity in any rigorous manner, it can assist us in our reflections. When we supplement the crow hypothesis with auxiliary hypotheses so as to provide a consistent explanation of all the observed data, what makes this line of explanation less reasonable than the line of explanation employing the maid hypothesis? The decisive factor is that the maid hypothesis provides a simpler line of explanation.

In various ways it is a simpler explanation. The explanation that makes the maid guilty is simpler because it does not require us to postulate the existence of any entities that have not been observed, whereas the line of explanation making the crow guilty requires us to postulate the existence of two crows and a lover, none of which we have observed. A set of hypotheses is simpler the fewer the entities, and also the fewer the kinds of entities, in which it requires us to believe. Moreover, a set of hypotheses is simpler and more probable if it attributes usual and direct operations to phenomena, rather than elaborate and unusual ones. In this respect too, the crow hypotheses are poor, for they require us to suppose that these crows have carried out a very elaborate operation, which would be very unusual indeed in terms of what we know of crows from our past experience with them and with similar birds.

Occasionally *inconsistency* creeps into an explanation. If there is an inconsistency in the way it treats the facts, an explanation cannot have much probability. To take another example, some people have been puzzled at the paintings of El Greco: the human figures he painted seem strangely distorted, unnaturally tall and thin. Suppose that someone tries to explain this peculiarity of his painting by means of the hypothesis that El Greco suffered from astigmatism, which made him see things in this strangely distorted manner; and as he saw them, so he painted them.

This explanation may sound plausible at first; yet it is wholly unacceptable as it stands, for it deals inconsistently with the facts. If El Greco had bad eyes that made him see everything in a distorted manner, this defect would have been operative not merely when he looked at his models but also when he looked at his canvases. Thus a distorted figure drawn on his canvas cannot have looked the same to him as did his model. This attempted explanation fails to explain; the hypothesis that El Greco had bad eyes could conceivably be true, but it is not supported by the mere fact that he painted in this distorted way. (One could supplement it with the auxiliary hypothesis that he wore corrective glasses when and only when he looked at his canvases; but then we do not have a simple set of explanatory hypotheses.)

A still more extreme inconsistency occurs if the explanatory hypothesis employs a self-contradictory notion. The spoons having disappeared, suppose someone suggests the hypothesis that pixies have carried them off. We point out that no one has seen any pixies, or heard them, or felt or smelled or tasted them. No one has experienced pixies in any way, even though sometimes people have looked for them rather diligently. This person replies, "Well, I think it was invisible pixies that carried away the spoons. These pixies cannot ever be heard or touched or smelled or tasted; not with the unaided senses, nor with scientific instruments either. But I believe they're there, all the same, even though we cannot detect them. Science never will be able to demonstrate their presence, but it cannot prove that they aren't there".

This hypothesis is a queer one. It is advanced as though it were a hypothesis that made sense, that is true rather than false but that never could conceivably be verified or refuted. The difficulty here is that we are invited to suppose that there are little manlike creatures which are invisible, intangible, and in every way absolutely undetectable. This hypothesis employs a self-contradictory notion. To say that something is really there is to say that it could conceivably be detected. The notion of a pixie which is there but absolutely undetectable is inconsistent. The hypothesis that there are absolutely undetectable pixies is necessarily false, as much so as is the hypothesis that there are married bachelors.

We have mentioned some of the factors that determine the degree of probability of an explanatory hypothesis. However, when we ask how *good* an explanation is, this comprehends more than just its probability. Probability is one component that helps to make an explanation good, but it is not the only one. Another component is the power of the explanation to illuminate the phenomena for which it aims to account. We commonly seek an explanation for a phenomenon because the phenomenon is strange, out of the ordinary, different from what was to have been expected or, at any rate, isolated, its connections with other phenomena unknown. We ask "Why are the silver spoons missing?", for this is unexpected when in the past they have always been in their rack. We ask "Why does soda fizz?" because this seems strange when most liquids do not, and soda does so only when the bottle is opened. We ask "Why do the planets move in elliptical orbits?" because this fact seems anomalous and isolated, when we do not grasp its relation to other facts.

In answering this sort of question, the explanation tries to remove the strangeness, the anomaly, the puzzle by showing how the thing being explained harmonizes with other known and conjectured facts. We explain the action of soda water by pointing out that it contains carbon dioxide under pressure, which must escape when the bottle is opened. (This explanation gives the cause.) Newton explained why the orbits of the planets are elliptical by showing how this is a special case of the inertial and gravitational way in which all bodies everywhere in the universe move. (This is not a causal explanation but is none the worse for that.) The point here is that a good explanation not only must be probable, in the light of the data; it also must account for the data in an illuminating way that helps us to grasp their connection with other facts. We can see that there is a difference between probability and explanatory force if we remember the old example (from Molière) of someone asking "Why does opium cause sleep?" and receiving the answer "Because of its soporific power". Here the explanation merely redescribes the data in a totally unilluminating manner. It is certain that opium possesses 'soporific power', but that does not provide a good explanation.

With regard to Newton and gravitation, sometimes we speak of gravitation as 'causing' objects to fall, and so on. But gravitation is not the cause of falling in the sense in which, say, germs are the cause of malaria. The germs are entities distinct from the pathological results they produce; it would not be senseless to speak of germs without malaria or of malaria without germs. But gravitation is not some additional entity, over and above moving bodies; to talk about gravitation is to talk about how bodies move.

Thinking of work like Newton's, people sometimes say, "Science doesn't tell us why things happen, only how they happen; it doesn't really explain, it only describes". This remark reflects a misunderstanding of the nature of explanation, for describing and explaining are not entirely distinct activities.

Exercise 29

In each of the following cases, what is the phenomenon being explained and what is the explanation given of it? If you think an explanatory hypothesis false, indicate what evidence you possess that counts against it. Was it improbable at the time it was offered?

1   Boy! Lucius! Fast asleep? it is no matter;
    Enjoy the heavy honey-dew of slumber:
    Thou hast no figures nor no fantasies
    Which busy care draws in the brains of men;
    Therefore thou sleep'st so sound.   SHAKESPEARE, *Julius Caesar*

2   Among the noteworthy actions of Hannibal is numbered this, that although he had an enormous army, composed of men of all nations and fighting in foreign countries, there never arose any dissension either among them or against the prince, either

in good fortune or in bad. This could not be due to anything but his inhuman cruelty, which together with his infinite other virtues, made him always venerated and terrible in the sight of his soldiers, and without it his other virtues would not have sufficed to produce that effect.

MACHIAVELLI, *The Prince*

3 Soon as the untroubled sleep of death has gotten hold of a man and the nature of the mind and soul has withdrawn, you can perceive then no diminution of the entire body either in appearance or weight. . . . Therefore the whole soul must consist of very small seeds and be inwoven through the veins and flesh and sinews; inasmuch as, after it has all withdrawn from the body, the exterior contour of the limbs preserves itself entire and not a tittle of the weight is lost. Just in the same way when the flavor of wine is gone or when the delicious aroma of a perfume has been dispersed into the air or when the savor has left some body, yet the thing itself does not therefore look smaller to the eye, nor does aught seem to have been taken from the weight, because sure enough many minute seeds make up the savors. . . . LUCRETIUS, *On the Nature of Things*

4 An ordinary scientific law explains only some kinds of phenomena (the laws of physics explain some physical events, the laws of psychology explain some psychological events, etc.). But here is a law which is much better and which is of more profound significance, because it explains everything that happens. The law is: Everything always acts in such a way as to realize its potentialities. Thus, stones fall because this realizes their potentiality for falling; fish swim because of their potentiality for swimming; and so on. This law gives the ultimate explanation which explains everything that happens.

5 The love of the man sinks perceptibly from the moment it has obtained satisfaction; almost every other woman charms him more than the one he already possesses; he longs for variety. The love of the woman, on the other hand, increases just from that moment. This is a consequence of the aim of

nature which is directed to the maintenance, and therefore to the greatest possible increase, of the species. The man can easily beget over a hundred children a year; the woman, on the contrary, with however many men, can yet only bring one child a year into the world (leaving twin births out of account). Therefore, the man always looks about after other women; the woman, again, sticks firmly to the one man; for nature moves her, instinctively and without reflection, to retain the nourisher and protector of the future offspring.

SCHOPENHAUER, *The World as Will and Idea*

6 When we see that the three classes of modern society, the feudal aristocracy, the bourgeoisie and the proletariat, each have their special morality, we can only draw one conclusion, that men consciously or unconsciously, derive their moral ideas in the last resort from the practical relations on which their class position is based—from the economic relations in which they carry on production and exchange.

ENGELS, *Anti-Dühring*

7 As eminently religious men have in all ages been among the most cruel and oppressive . . . so eminently philanthropic men . . . are apt to be . . . the most unsound in their views and the most reckless in their action. The explanation in each case is the same . . . both feeling themselves to be *well-mounted*—having a good aim in view and an unexceptionable steed beneath them—conceive that they have nothing to do but to throw the reins upon the neck of the animal, shut their eyes and ride as hard as they can;—satisfied that the inherent excellence of the hobby they bestride will carry them over all obstacles . . . an opposing principle is only a five-barred gate to be overleapt; an inconvenient fact is a thing to be shied at and rapidly passed by on the other side; antagonistic rights are only hedges to be scrambled through, or foot passengers to be ridden down. . . . Persuaded of the goodness of their cause and the benevolence of their feelings, they care little how bad are their arguments or how doubtful are their facts.

The Economist, 1862

8 Twenty million Americans smoke Wheeze, the cigarette whose popularity is fastest growing. There must be a reason. It must be because Wheeze cigarettes are so good for your throat.

AN EXAMPLE: SMOKING AND LUNG CANCER

During recent years public health authorities in Western countries have noticed a great increase in the rate of deaths from lung cancer. At the beginning of the present century, only a tiny fraction of all deaths were caused by lung cancer; by the mid-1960s (in the United States and some other Western countries for which records are available), a much larger percentage of deaths had been attributed to this disease.[4] How can we explain the change? What cause has been operating?

The cause must be some factor, or factors, more strongly present now than in the past. (Here we think in terms of the method of concomitant variations.) Smoking of cigarettes has increased a great deal during the last few decades, but so have air pollution, nervous tension, the use of automobiles, and many other factors. So far as we can tell by a crude use of the method of concomitant variations, any one or any combination of these factors might perhaps be responsible for the increase in deaths from lung cancer. Many hypotheses seem possible: Perhaps the increased use of autos keeps people from walking and so weakens their lungs through lack of exercise; or perhaps air pollution harms the lungs of city dwellers by poisoning their air; and so on. But the hypothesis that smoking is a major factor in the increase in deaths from lung cancer begins to seem more probable than some of the other hypotheses when we remember that cigarettes are known to contain nicotine, which is a poison. If the nicotine in

[4] For instance, in 1930 in the United States the death rate from lung cancer was 3 per 100,000 persons per year. In 1955 it was about 25 per 100,000 persons per year. The rise in this death rate has been rapid and steady, year by year.

two packs of cigarettes were chemically purified and injected into the bloodstream, the dose would be lethal. Perhaps lung cancer is some subtle form of nicotine poisoning. It seems plausible that a substance that can kill quickly when a large amount of it enters the bloodstream might also kill slowly when small amounts are steadily inhaled into the lungs. This is an argument by analogy, and it is far from conclusive; it merely adds a little to the probability of the hypothesis that the increase in smoking has caused the increase in deaths due to lung cancer.

Another argument by analogy which supports this same conclusion is based on the observed fact that, when tar extracted from cigarette smoke is smeared on the skins of mice, the mice contract skin cancer. This argument too is far from conclusive, for the skin of a mouse is rather different from the lungs of a man; still, the analogy adds more to the probability of the hypothesis. A further piece of reasoning by analogy is based on the fact that prolonged exposure to some kinds of irritants is known to be capable of producing cancer in men; for instance, it was established in England in the eighteenth century that chimney sweeps, who used to have to crawl through the soot of narrow chimneys, got one kind of cancer much more often than other people did. If exposure to chimney soot can result in human cancer, then by analogy we may suspect that cigarette smoke can produce the same result.

These arguments support the hypothesis that smoking is the main factor in lung cancer, but they are not sufficient to prove this; it is proper to speak of a proof when and only when the inductive probability becomes so strong that there is no longer room for reasonable doubt about the truth of the hypothesis. (There always remains room for conceivable doubt about it, but conceivable doubt is not always reasonable doubt.)

Realizing that much more evidence was needed regarding the possible connection between smoking and lung cancer, medical scientists in recent years have carried out dozens of studies. One of the most important of these was a study conducted by Dr. E. Cuyler Hammond, working under the auspices of the American Cancer Society.[5] Dr. Hammond and his associates began by interviewing American men between fifty and sixty-nine years of age, none of whom then had any serious illness, so far as was known. They found out where these men lived and what the smoking habits of each man were. Over a period of forty-four months they kept track of 187,783 men, of whom 11,870 died during that time. The cause of death was determined as accurately as possible in each case. Of the deaths, 2,249 were due to cancer, and in these cases an especial effort was made to determine precisely what type of cancer caused the death. After collecting all these statistics, Dr. Hammond analyzed them and found some striking facts. Some of his findings are shown in the accompanying table.

Amount of smoking	*Number of men*	*Number who died of lung cancer*	*Age-standardized lung-cancer death rate per 100,000 men per year*
Never smoked	32,392	4	3.4
Less than one-half pack of cigarettes per day	7,647	13	51.4
One-half to one pack of cigarettes daily	26,370	50	59.3
One to two packs of cigarettes daily	14,292	60	143.9
More than two packs of cigarettes daily	3,100	22	217.3

[5] E. C. Hammond and D. Horn, "Smoking and Death Rates," *Journal of the American Medical Association*, 166: 1159–1172, Mar. 8, 1958, and 166: 1294–1308, Mar. 15, 1958.

This table does not list men who smoked cigars or pipes or nonsmokers who formerly had smoked cigarettes regularly, and it lists only those deaths which were very definitely diagnosed as caused by bronchogenic carcinoma, the principal type of lung cancer. The right-hand column in the table is calculated from the earlier ones but includes a correction to allow for the fact that the men of the different groups did not have quite the same average ages (and younger men normally have a lower death rate from lung cancer).

This table shows that, for the group of men studied by Dr. Hammond, there was a very strong correlation, or concomitant variation, between the amount of cigarette smoking and the frequency of death from lung cancer. Do these observations entitle us to make an inductive generalization about the population at large? Or is it likely that these figures are unrepresentative and just reflect some accidental coincidence limited to this observed group of individuals?

For example, is it possible that Dr. Hammond's smokers lived in the cities, where they were subject to air pollution, while his nonsmokers lived in the country, where the air is clean? If this were so, it might be that the real correlation is between air pollution and cancer, rather than between smoking and cancer. But Dr. Hammond looked into this and found that for those of his men who lived in cities the death rate from lung cancer was just about the same as for those of them living in the country. (In another study, it was found that inhabitants of the Channel Islands, where the air is unpolluted, suffered lung cancer just as city dwellers do and that, of those who smoked more, more died of the disease.) Here, because the number of men who were observed was so large and because Dr. Hammond's method of investigation was careful, there is an absolutely overwhelming probability that these figures were not produced by some accidental coincidence.

We definitely are entitled to make the inductive generalization

that probably, for the population at large, there is a strong correlation between smoking and lung cancer. If we seek to explain
why Dr. Hammond got these results, by far the most probable
hypothesis is that these results were representative of the population at large. This conclusion is strengthened still further when
we notice that other large-scale studies made by other medical
scientists all give results closely similar to Dr. Hammond's. Dr.
Hammond also found very ominous correlations between smoking
and rates of death from other diseases, especially heart disease;
but we shall confine our discussion to lung cancer.

Let us return to the question whether the increase in cigarette
smoking *caused* the increase in deaths from lung cancer. On the
basis of data available in the mid-1960s, we know that cigarette
smoking has been greatly on the increase during the last few
decades, and we have strong evidence for the generalization that
the more people smoke, the more they die from lung cancer. But
we must not make the mistake of supposing that the presence of a
correlation is sufficient to prove that there is a cause-and-effect
connection. So far, there are three possibilities which seem to
remain open: (1) Perhaps the increase in smoking was the cause
of the increase in lung cancer, either because smoking directly
causes lung cancer or because smoking weakens people in some
way so that they more easily fall prey to cancer; or (2) perhaps
the increase in lung cancer in some way caused the increase in
smoking, possibly because having cancer creates a craving for
tobacco; or (3) perhaps there was some third factor, such as
nervous tension, which tended to cause some people both to smoke
and to contract lung cancer. We must weigh the plausibility of
these three competing hypotheses.

Hypothesis 2 can be dismissed almost at once, for we know
that most smokers who died of lung cancer had smoked steadily for
many years; their smoking habits became fixed long before they
contracted the disease. There is no evidence that people who

contracted the disease increased their smoking thereafter. Thus it is very improbable that the disease caused the smoking.

Hypothesis 3 deserves careful consideration. Nervous tension seems to be a very plausible 'third factor'. One piece of evidence against this hypothesis is derived from study of what happened in Norway during 1940 to 1945. During those years the rate of death from lung cancer there showed a sharp reduction; previously it had been rising, and after 1945 it rose again. During those wartime years of 1940 to 1945 Norway was suffering under Nazi occupation; there must have been far more nervous tension than usual for the Norwegians. Cigarettes, however, were scarce. Here, by the method of difference, we argue against hypothesis 3 and in favor of 1. Thus it seems quite improbable that hypothesis 3, with nervous tension as the 'third factor', can be correct.

Might there be some as yet wholly unknown 'third factor' which was responsible? Does some obscure hereditary tendency predispose some people both to smoke and to suffer lung cancer? Certainly this is logically possible, and at present there is no direct evidence against it. But there is no positive evidence whatsoever in its favor. It would be unreasonable to regard such a hypothesis as probable if a simpler and more direct explanation is available.

Hypothesis 1 provides the simplest and most direct explanation. Hypothesis 1 also is supported by various kinds of further evidence in addition to the arguments by analogy already mentioned. For one thing, it is known that pipe smokers sometimes get cancer of the lip, tongue, or mouth; and it is likely that in these cases the smoking is the cause of the cancer, for the disease affects those very parts that are exposed to the hot smoke. (Pipe smokers, like cigar smokers, do not suffer lung cancer nearly as often as cigarette smokers do; this is easily explained by the fact that they do not inhale, whereas most cigarette smokers do so.) If pipe smoke causes cancer of the mouth, it is reasonable to suppose that cigarette smoke can cause cancer of the lungs.

Another kind of evidence is derived from microscopic examinations of tissues from the lungs of persons who died from causes other than cancer. A great many such examinations have been made, and they reveal that in the lungs of heavy smokers there is general widespread scarring and thickening of the tissue, with the formation of spots in which the cells have begun to grow in the distorted manner characteristic of incipient cancer. The tissue of the lungs of persons who have been heavy smokers exhibits these modifications, which are not found in the lung tissue of nonsmokers. The amount of scarring and thickening of tissue seems to be roughly proportional to the amount of smoking that the person has done. These observations strongly suggest that regular exposure to tobacco smoke produces a gradual cumulative deterioration of the lung tissue; in the lungs of some smokers this deterioration goes so far that it becomes lung cancer, but the deterioration is slow enough so that the majority of smokers die of other causes before this can kill them. It seems to be possible for an occasional nonsmoker to suffer lung cancer, perhaps caused by air pollution; but it certainly looks as though smoking is overwhelmingly the most important factor in the incidence of the disease.

It is all too easy for us unconsciously to allow our wishes and personal preferences to influence our thinking about inductive problems. People who enjoy smoking and who are not accustomed to disciplined thought find it easy to talk themselves out of accepting the unpleasant conclusion that smoking is the main factor causing lung cancer. They say that we should wait for further evidence before forming an opinion, that we must not be hasty, that it is too early yet to tell, etc.

But imagine that the hypothesis that houseflies produce cancer were to have gained anywhere near as much evidence in its favor as there now is in favor of the hypothesis that smoking does so. If that were to happen, these same people would be as enthusiastic about accepting the housefly hypothesis as they now are reluctant to accept the smoking hypothesis. They would demand an immediate government crusade to exterminate the fly. The difference is that everyone dislikes the housefly anyway and is glad to believe the worst about that insect, whereas people enjoy smoking and want to believe the best about it. One of the most important kinds of intellectual maturity is to have learned to rise above these emotional prejudices so that one can view evidence impartially, regardless of whether the conclusions toward which it points are pleasing or depressing.

The hypothesis that cigarette smoking is the principal factor in causing lung cancer is now very highly probable in light of the evidence. It has been highly probable ever since the late 1950s. It still is logically possible that some surprising new information might come to light to show that cigarettes are not to blame after all; that is *logically possible*, but present evidence makes any such development *highly improbable*. We must always be prepared open-mindedly to welcome any new developments that may overturn established hypotheses, for that is the scientific attitude; yet we must not be reluctant to accord due weight to the evidence we now possess, for it is folly to refuse to draw a conclusion when strong evidence already is at hand. Has it been 'proved' that cigarettes are the main cause of lung cancer? The evidence is so strong that it constitutes a proof in the sense that there remains no room for reasonable doubt. But the evidence still falls far short of providing us with as complete a proof as we hope to get later, after more research has been done. There remains much still to be learned, especially about the biochemical processes by means of which the cause produces its effect.[6]

[6] For fuller accounts of evidence bearing on this problem, see the following:
E. Cuyler Hammond, "Smoking and Death Rates: A Riddle in Cause and Effect," *The American Scientist*, 46 (4): December, 1958.
Smoking and Health, Report of the Royal College of Physicians, Pitman Publishing Corp., New York, 1962.

Exercise 30

Analyze the value of each of the following comments.

1 The weakness of all these studies is that they consider only samples out of the population. What are a mere 187,000 men, compared with the hundreds of millions of men in the Western world ?

2 There is nothing alarming about these statistics concerning increased deaths from lung cancer. You must expect more people to die of lung cancer nowadays, for the population is considerably larger than it used to be.

3 Dr. Hammond did not include any women in his figures. His sample is not representative of the population at large as regards sex, so why should we expect it to be representative in any way ?

4 Some of the other diseases, like cholera and typhoid, are under control now, and so people do not die of them. Obviously, we have to expect relatively more people to die of lung cancer. Therefore we need not accuse smoking of doing harm.

5 Air pollution is much worse now than it used to be. In some cities like Los Angeles and London there are days when anyone breathing the air can taste how bitter it is from chemical pollution. And the pollutants are dangerous too; we know that smog wilts vegetables and in strong concentrations causes deaths. Air pollution, rather than smoking, may well be the cause of the increased deaths from lung cancer.

6 No one has proved that there could not be some as yet unknown 'third factor' which causes people to smoke more and also causes them to suffer more lung cancer. This would mean that

---

E. Cuyler Hammond, "The Effects of Smoking," *Scientific American*, 207: July, 1962.

Smoking and Health, Report of the Advisory Committee to the Surgeon General, U. S. Public Health Service, 1964.

smoking and cancer are not cause and effect but are both effects of some unknown cause. It might be some hidden genetic factor. Here at the Tobacco Industry Research Institute, we hold the view that something like this must be the explanation.

7 Even if it is something about cigarettes that does cause lung cancer, I don't believe it's the tobacco that is to blame. The smoke from the cigarette paper may well be the cause.

8 We should set up a committee of impartial scientists who would study all these data and come to a careful, scientific conclusion about whether cigarettes are harmful. Unfortunately, it is very hard now to find scientists who would be fit to serve on such a committee, because so many of them have already made up their minds one way or the other. We could not appoint anyone from the American Cancer Society or from the Surgeon General's Advisory Committee, because both those groups are no longer impartial; they already have officially declared that they regard cigarettes as the principal cause of lung cancer.

7. *Applications*

CHOOSING THE RIGHT DEDUCTIVE TECHNIQUE

In our study of deductive reasoning we became acquainted with several methods for testing deductive arguments. There were Venn diagrams, the rules of the syllogism, truth tables, the method of quantificational deduction, and so on. If we are to make successful use of these methods in dealing with actual examples, it is important that we take care always to choose a suitable method for the problem at hand. If we are unwise in our choice of method, we may easily arrive at a misleading answer regarding the validity even of an argument correctly symbolized. Unwise choice of method would not lead us to regard an invalid argument as valid, but it might lead us to regard a valid argument as invalid.

Each method is concerned with a *sufficient* condition for deductive validity. Being valid according to a correctly constructed Venn diagram is sufficient to ensure that an argument is valid; being valid according to a correctly constructed truth table is sufficient to ensure that an argument is valid; and so on. But no one test gives a *necessary* condition. That it cannot be shown to be valid by a Venn diagram does not guarantee an argument to be invalid, since it may be valid for some quite different reason. That it cannot be shown valid by a truth table does not guarantee an argument to be invalid, since it may be valid for some quite different reason; and so on. But of course, if an argument has no reason for being valid other than its syllogistic form, then, if it cannot be shown to be valid by a Venn diagram, it is invalid. If an argument has no reason for being valid other than its truth-functional form, then, if it cannot be shown to be valid by a truth table, it is invalid, and so on.

The method of quantificational deduction studied in Chapter 4, including as it does the laws of truth-functional deduction, is a method powerful enough to show the validity of all valid deductive arguments of all the main types that we have studied (except the identity arguments mentioned in the section on fallacies of ambiguity in Chapter 5). However, it generally is wisest on each occasion to employ the most elementary method that will apply efficiently to the example. By so doing, we usually reduce the work for ourselves and thereby minimize the chance of error. Moreover, unlike the method of quantificational deduction, the more elementary methods of Venn diagrams, the rules of the syllogism, and truth tables, where they are applicable, can provide negative demonstrations of the invalidity of invalid arguments. Thus, whenever a more elementary method such as that of Venn diagrams can conveniently be applied, it is usually wise to employ it rather than the more complicated method of quantificational deduction.

In the same spirit, when symbolizing an argument, it generally is wise to employ the fewest letters that can suffice to exhibit the relevant logical structure of the reasoning. It is not advisable to use more letters than are absolutely needed, for that again increases both the amount of work involved and the risk of error.

Exercise 31

Choose the wisest method to show whether each of the following deductive arguments is valid.

1 Everyone who knows Belinda worships her. Some people do not worship Belinda. Therefore, some people do not know her.

2 If I study hard, I shall earn a college degree. Either I get encouragement from my parents or I won't get a college degree. Therefore, if I don't get encouragement from my parents, I won't study hard.

3 Clovis dislikes anyone who likes Hugo. Everyone who likes Hugo likes Mavis. Hence Clovis dislikes everyone who likes Mavis.

4 If we are not short of drinks, we shall have a party. We are not short both of food and drinks; in fact, we are short of food. Therefore, we shall have a party.

5 There is an animal that eats every kind of food any bird eats. All vultures are birds. Hence there is an animal that eats every food any vulture eats.

6 Anything you can do I can do better. You can do cartwheels. Therefore, I can do cartwheels better than you can.

7 If the examination is hard and Clovis is sleepy, then he will not pass. But he is going to pass, and he is not sleepy. Therefore the examination will not be hard.

8 Anyone who flies to Mars will have to have a safe spaceship. Therefore, unless there are safe spaceships, no one will fly to Mars.

9 Either all farm commodities should be subsidized or else none of them should be. Not all of them should be. Therefore, none of them should be.

10   If all citizens can vote, then some imprisoned criminals can
vote. But no imprisoned criminals can vote. Therefore,
some citizens cannot vote.

THE ENTHYMEME

In ordinary discourse a person often presents a deductive argument without bothering to make explicit what all his premises are.
Sometimes he has a premise fairly definitely in mind but does not
bother to state it because it is common knowledge, too obvious to be
worth mentioning. An argument is called an *enthymeme* if one
or more of its premises are unstated. Originally the term "enthymeme" was restricted to syllogisms. Nowadays the term is
extended to deductive arguments of any type having unstated
premises. We might also call a deductive argument an enthymeme
when its conclusion is clearly indicated but without being put into
words. There is little point in extending the term "enthymeme"
still further to cover inductive arguments, since if we did so (in
light of the first section of Chapter 6) we would never have any
inductive arguments that we could be sure were not enthymemes.

When we meet a deductive argument whose conclusion does
not validly follow from the stated premises alone, we must consider
whether there is some unstated premise that is being taken for
granted by the arguer. If so, we should try to state this premise
explicitly so that we can see in full the logical structure of the
argument, to tell whether it is valid. Naturally, it is not easy to be
certain what unstated premises a person may have in the back of
his mind, but we simply do our best to judge what the arguer is
thinking. For instance, if someone says, "Robinson must be a
lawyer, for he belongs to the Bar Association", his argument is an
enthymeme. We should not reject his argument as bad reasoning
just because the premise "Robinson belongs to the Bar Association"
does not by itself logically imply the conclusion "Robinson is a

lawyer". Instead, we should realize that there is an unstated premise, "All persons who belong to the Bar Association are lawyers"; this is a piece of common knowledge and does not need to be stated outright. When we notice the unstated premise, we see that the reasoning is logical.

However, not all seemingly invalid deductive arguments deserve to be regarded as enthymemes. For example, suppose that in a political controversy we encounter the argument "All Marxists are socialists, and so all socialists must be Marxists". It would be foolish to regard this argument as an enthymeme having the unstated premise "If all Marxists are socialists, then all socialists are Marxists". To regard the argument in that way would be to think of it as committing a fallacy of begging the question, since in an actual political controversy the conclusion of the argument could not be less doubtful than is this conditional sentence. But the original argument does not really beg the question; it is a *non sequitur* instead. The speaker's real mistake is thinking that an **A** can be converted. It is fairer to say that the original argument is invalid on account of its form, rather than to say that it is valid but has a question-begging unstated premise.

Ordinarily, an arguer leaves unstated only such premises as he thinks are perfectly obvious to his hearers. We cannot blame someone who constructs an argument for leaving unstated some of his premises; if the unstated premises are obvious pieces of common knowledge, he is perfectly justified in doing so. He is to blame, however, if the unstated premises upon which his argument depends are dubious and questionable. Still worse is the mistake of careless thinkers who regard as common knowledge things that not only are not known to be true by most people but are not true at all. It is the duty of a really conscientious arguer to make explicit all premises that critical listeners are likely to want to challenge. If he fails to do this, he is not presenting his argument perfectly candidly.

What is 'common knowledge'? By saying that an arguer is entitled to leave unstated such premises as belong to common knowledge, we mean that these unstated premises should be truths known to practically all persons of the type for whom the argument is intended. Naturally, the standards are different for arguments directed to different groups of hearers; some things that could reasonably be left unstated in an argument addressed to scientists would need to be stated explicitly in an argument addressed to laymen; some things that one would reasonably leave unstated in an argument addressed to adults would need to be given explicitly in an argument addressed to children; and so on.

Exercise 32

Which of the following arguments are enthymemes? (Example 5 is not itself an argument, but it describes one.) What are the suppressed premises in each case? Are they premises that it is reasonable to leave unstated?

1 Accustom thyself to believe that death is nothing to us, for good and evil imply sentience, and death is the privation of all sentience.   EPICURUS

2 Death is nothing terrible, else it would have appeared so to Socrates.   EPICTETUS

3 We reject all merely probable knowledge and make it a rule to trust only what is completely known and incapable of being doubted. . . . But if we adhere closely to this rule we shall find left but few objects of legitimate study. For there is scarce any question occurring in the sciences about which talented men have not disagreed.

DESCARTES, *Rules for the Direction of the Mind*

4 It seems a proposition, which will not admit of much dispute, that all our ideas are nothing but copies of our impressions, or, in other words, that it is impossible for us to *think* of

any thing which we have not antecedently *felt*, either by our
external or internal senses. . . . To be fully acquainted, therefore, with the idea of power or necessary connexion, let us
examine its impression.

HUME, *Enquiry Concerning Human Understanding*

5 The God of Israel was impiously represented by the Gnostics
as a being liable to passion and to error, capricious in his
favour, implacable in his resentment, meanly jealous of his
superstitious worship, and confining his partial providence to
a single people and to this transitory life. In such a character
they could discover none of the features of the wise and om-
nipotent Father of the universe.

GIBBON, *Decline and Fall of the Roman Empire*

6 If you begin to teach the opinions of other people before
you teach how to judge of their worth, of one thing you may
be sure, your pupil will adopt those opinions whatever you
may do, and you will not succeed in uprooting them. I am
therefore convinced that to make a young man judge rightly,
you must form his judgment rather than teach him your own.

ROUSSEAU, *Emile*

7 No child under the age of fifteen should receive instruction
in subjects which may possibly be the vehicle of serious error,
such as philosophy, religion, or any other branch of knowledge
where it is necessary to take large views; because wrong
notions imbibed early can seldom be rooted out, and of all the
intellectual faculties, judgment is the last to arrive at maturity.

SCHOPENHAUER, "On Education"

8 "For my faith," he continued, "I will not change it. Your
own God, as you say, was put to death by the very men whom
he created. But mine," he concluded, pointing to his Deity—
then alas! sinking in glory behind the mountains—"my God
still lives in the heavens and looks down on his children."

PRESCOTT, *The Conquest of Peru*

NONINDUCTIVE REASONING BY ANALOGY

In Chapter 6 we considered inductive arguments by analogy. One of our examples was the reasoning of a postman, who, on the basis of his past experience with boxer dogs that bit, reasons that probably the new boxer looming in his path will bite also if approached. This is an argument by analogy; it is definitely inductive in nature, for the conclusion (that this dog will bite if approached) embodies conjectures regarding what future sense experience can reveal, conjectures that go beyond the present evidence. However, not all reasoning by analogy is inductive in this sense, leading to conclusions embodying empirical conjectures that go beyond the data.

Let us consider an example of an argument by analogy which is not inductive. At a certain university a rigorous honor code specifically lists lying and cheating as offenses punishable by expulsion. Suppose it is discovered that a student has written a bad check and used it to purchase merchandise. The question now arises whether this student has violated the honor code; is writing a bad check a violation of the rule against lying and cheating? (We shall suppose that whoever first wrote the code never considered this question and that there are no known precedents about it.) Someone might try to dismiss this question by saying, "Well, it's all a matter of definition. If by 'lying' you mean something that includes writing bad checks, then he's guilty; and if you don't mean that by the word 'lying', then he's innocent. It's just a matter of what you choose to mean by a word. Just decide how you want to define your terms, that's all".

This comment suggests that the question about the interpretation of the honor code is just a trivial verbal question. As we remember from our discussion of definitions (Chapter 5), a verbal dispute is one that has no true or false solution and that arises solely because people choose to use words differently, not because they differ in their beliefs. For example, one person may insist that the fox's posterior appendage is the brush and not the tail; someone else may claim that of course it is the tail, for whoever heard of a brush growing on an animal? Here the issue is purely verbal, for the two parties to the dispute do not disagree about what the fox's appendage is like; they disagree only about what word should be applied to it.

But is the question about the honor code a trivial verbal question, in the way the question about the fox's appendage is? Surely not. The question whether a violation of the honor code has been committed is a serious and substantial question. It cannot be settled by making an arbitrary decision about how to use a word; that would not be fair to the accused student. The decision reached will affect our action toward the accused student, and our actions ought not to be arbitrary. We have to engage in some careful thinking, if we are to reach a fair decision; we have to weigh the arguments pro and con.

Deductive arguments are likely not to be of much use in this problem. Suppose someone tries to settle the problem deductively by arguing: "All cases of cheating violate the honor code; all cases of writing bad checks are cases of cheating; therefore, all cases of writing bad checks violate the honor code". Although this argument is valid, it does not succeed in proving its conclusion, for if we were dubious about whether the conclusion is true, then we are pretty sure to be at least equally dubious about the minor premise. Here the deduction commits the fallacy of *petitio principii*. No purely deductive line of reasoning is likely to be of much help in settling this problem.

Nor are inductive arguments likely to help much. Whichever conclusion we want to establish here (that writing a bad check is, or is not, a violation of the honor code), in either case the conclusion does not embody any predictive conjecture about future experience going beyond what is already known. No purely inductive line of reasoning would be helpful here, for the conclusion is not of the inductive sort.

What sort of reasoning would be appropriate to this problem? Someone would be making a helpful and relevant contribution to the discussion if he were to reason as follows: "Lying and cheating are indisputably offenses against the honor code; now, writing a bad check is very like lying, because signing your name to a bad check is like falsely stating that you have money in the bank. Also, writing a bad check is very like cheating, for you persuade the merchant to accept the check in exchange for merchandise by deceiving him into thinking the check good. Since writing a bad check is so like lying and cheating in these respects, it therefore resembles them also in being a violation of the honor code". At the heart of this reasoning are the analogies between writing a bad check, on the one hand, and lying and cheating on the other hand. The whole argument essentially depends upon these analogies; the argument as a whole is a good argument if and only if these are good analogies.

Here it is worthwhile to notice the distinctive character of this sort of reasoning. This is reasoning by analogy. Hence, unlike deductive reasoning, it does not claim to be absolutely conclusive; at best, it gives us good reason for accepting the conclusion. On the other hand, this sort of reasoning by analogy differs also from inductive reasoning. For inductive arguments by analogy lead to conclusions embodying predictive conjectures about what the future course of experience will bring to light, whereas the sort of reasoning by analogy that we now are considering does not lead to that sort of conclusion. (Reaching the conclusion that the student is guilty certainly is not the same as predicting that he will be treated as guilty; nor is it the same as predicting that his conduct will have observable consequences different from those it would have had, had he been innocent.)

Someone may object that this sort of argument ought to be interpreted as an enthymeme having an unstated premise. The idea would be that, if an appropriate additional premise were supplied, the argument would become definitely deductive. But there are two difficulties with this idea. First, in this sort of case it is hard to state another premise which is both known to us and sufficient to render the argument deductively valid. Second, even if we could state such a premise, adding it to the argument would surely make the argument into a *petitio principii*. For instance, the auxiliary premise "Whatever is like lying and cheating ought to count as an honor offense", even if we did not know it to be false, would be more dubious than the conclusion that we are trying to establish. It would seem that someone who insists upon regarding this argument as a deductive enthymeme must say either that the argument is a *non sequitur* or that it depends upon false premises or that it begs the question; in any of these three cases, he will have to say that the argument is of no value for proving its conclusion. But this argument and others like it are not worthless for proving conclusions. They sometimes are very good arguments, whose premises provide real reason for believing their conclusions.

This sort of noninductive reasoning by analogy is a valuable and fundamental type of reasoning, to which we often resort in cases where other types of reasoning are unsuccessful. Although there are no formal rules about when arguments of this sort are good and when they are bad, we can say that the reasoning is good when the analogies are good and that it is bad when the analogies are bad. If one thinks that an argument by analogy employs a bad analogy and reaches a wrong conclusion, one way of attacking it is to point out weaknesses in the analogy.

For example, someone might attack the argument about the honor code, claiming that the analogy upon which it rests is not a good analogy. He might argue that lying and cheating are not that much like writing bad checks; sometimes a person writes bad checks unintentionally, just because he is mistaken about his bank balance, and this is unlike lying, which always is intentional. And even when bad checks are intentionally written, the people who write them often are not intending to defraud their creditors permanently; they just intend to delay the payment for a while. The original argument drew a parallel between bad-check writing on the one hand and lying and cheating on the other; this counterargument claims that the cases are not sufficiently parallel to justify the conclusion that was drawn. We could not decide which viewpoint is more correct until we had reflected very fully about the likenesses and differences between these actions.

A more vivid way of attacking an argument that seems to employ a weak analogy and reach a wrong conclusion is to think of a counteranalogy pointing in an opposite direction. Thus, if someone says, "Maybe this boy did write bad checks, but emotionally he is just a child, and so we should make allowances for him, as we would for a child", someone else might reply, "Well, just because he is childlike, he needs to be dealt with severely, for children who are not sharply corrected persist in their delinquent habits". Here the original analogy is met by a counteranalogy; the weakness of the original argument is brought out by showing that, by reasoning which is no worse, one can reach just the opposite conclusion.

Exercise 33

In each of the following arguments, what is the conclusion being argued for? What analogy is being employed to support the conclusion? To what extent is the argument successful in establishing its conclusion?

1 The man who eats in idleness what he has not himself earned, is a thief, and in my eyes, the man who lives on an income paid him by the state for doing nothing, differs little from a highwayman who lives on those who travel his way.

ROUSSEAU, *Emile*

2 It would not seem open to a man to disown his father (though a father may disown his son) ; being in debt, he should repay, but there is nothing by doing which a son will have done the equivalent of what he has received, so that he is always in debt. But creditors can remit a debt; and a father can therefore do so too.   ARISTOTLE, *Nichomachean Ethics*

3 "Then you should say what you mean," the March Hare went on.

"I do," Alice hastily replied; "at least—at least I mean what I say—that's the same thing, you know."

"Not the same thing a bit!" said the Hatter. "Why, you might as well say that 'I see what I eat' is the same thing as 'I eat what I see'!"

"You might just as well say," added the March Hare, "that 'I like what I get' is the same thing as 'I get what I like'!"

LEWIS CARROLL, *Alice in Wonderland*

4 But me—look at the growth of hair in front,
It hangs before me ; down my back it tumbles,
Good, rich, coarse hair all up and down my body.
Don't tell me man-grown hair is out of fashion ;
A tree's not beautiful when grey and bare,
A horse without his mane's not fit to look at ;
Feathers become a bird as wool does sheep,
So a deep-matted run of hair looks handsome
On any man who has the luck to wear it.
It's true I seem to have a single eye,
One eye that blazes bravely in my forehead.
Big as a shield. Sometimes it rolls. Why not ?
The sun looks down from where he rides the heavens,
Sees everything and with a single eye.   OVID, *Metamorphoses*

5 That the aggressor, who puts himself into the state of war with another, and unjustly invades another man's right, can, by such an unjust war, never come to have a right over the conquered, will be easily agreed by all men, who will not think

that robbers and pirates have a right of empire over whomso-
ever they have force enough to master, or that men are bound
by promises which unlawful force extorts from them. Should
a robber break into my house, and, with a dagger at my throat,
make me seal deed to convey my estate to him, would this give
him any title? Just such a title by his sword has an unjust
conqueror who forces me into submission.

LOCKE, Of Civil Government

6 A foolish consistency is the hobgoblin of little minds, adored
by little statesmen and philosophers and divines. With consistency a great soul has simply nothing to do. He may as
well concern himself with his shadow on the wall.

EMERSON, "Self-Reliance"

7 A majority taken collectively is only an individual, whose
opinions, and frequently whose interests, are opposed to those
of another individual, who is styled a minority. If it be
admitted that a man possessing absolute power may misuse
that power by wronging his adversaries, why should not a
majority be liable to the same reproach? Men do not change
their characters by uniting with each other; nor does their
patience in the presence of obstacles increase with their
strength. For my own part, I cannot believe it; the power to
do everything, which I should refuse to one of my equals, I will
never grant to any number of them.

DE TOCQUEVILLE, Democracy in America

8 If the mystical truth that comes to a man proves to be a force
that he can live by, what mandate have we of the majority
to order him to live in another way? . . . It mocks our utmost
efforts, as a matter of fact, and in point of logic it absolutely
escapes our jurisdiction. Our own more 'rational' beliefs are
based on evidence exactly similar in nature to that which
mystics quote for theirs. Our senses, namely, have assured us
of certain states of fact; but mystical experiences are as direct

perceptions of fact for those who have them as any sensations
ever were for us.

WILLIAM JAMES, *The Varieties of Religious Experience*

LOGIC IN USE

It is one thing to be acquainted with the general principles of
logic; it is another to be able to apply them intelligently when
analyzing and criticizing actual arguments. We derive relatively
little practical intellectual benefit from an acquaintance with
logical principles unless we become able to apply them. To do this
effectively takes practice, common sense, general knowledge, and
mastery of language.

When we meet a piece of argumentative discourse that we
wish to analyze in a systematic manner, a proper first step is to
unravel the structure of the reasoning, noting what the conclusions
and what the premises are. The next step is to classify each bit of
reasoning: Is it deductive, inductive, or what? Then we can ask
what is its specific type (syllogism? inductive generalization?).
Next we can evaluate the validity of each bit of reasoning in
terms of the considerations relevant to its type. This should tell us
whether the overall reasoning is valid. The final step is to consider
whether the reasoning succeeds in proving its conclusion. Is there
any fallacy of inconsistency or of begging the question? Are the
premises reasonable to believe? Here we must draw upon our
general knowledge.

In criticizing reasoning, our task is twofold. We aim to avoid
being deceived by unsound reasoning, and we aim to recognize
sound reasoning as sound. People with a glib half knowledge of
logic sometimes understand the former aim without comprehend-
ing the latter. Having learned the names of a few fallacies, for
instance, they conclude that whenever they meet someone else's
reasoning the proper procedure is to cry out indiscriminately the

name of some fallacy. They think that logical criticism is all negative criticism, always finding fault, always accusing others of having made mistakes. But this attitude is shallow and harmful. A person who develops it is worse off intellectually than he would have been had he never studied any logic or learned the names of any fallacies; what little he has learned he uses so crudely that it does more harm than good.

Even more debased than this are the regrettable intellectual habits of those who, perhaps through experience in debating, learn enough about rhetorical techniques to realize that a vigorous case can be made on either side of almost any issue. They have the idea that the whole point of logic is always to score debating victories over one's opponent. Focusing all their attention on the superficial persuasiveness of arguments, they lose sight of validity and soundness. Sometimes they remain perfectly content with whatever thoughtless opinions they themselves happen to have acquired, and they use all their argumentative talents for the purpose of persuading others that these opinions are right.

Reasoning at its best is not a competitive but a cooperative enterprise. A balanced attitude must involve a willingness on our part to recognize and to accept good reasoning whenever an opponent is able to present it to us, in addition to a willingness to recognize fallacies whenever they occur and not just when they are committed by others. The ideal is that we should be dispassionate and objective as we distinguish between good and bad arguments and as we evaluate the degrees and respects in which arguments that are neither wholly good nor wholly bad are good and bad.

Exercise 34

The following discussion[1] *deals with the question, Should we eat people? Discuss the soundness of each bit of reasoning.*

[1] Suggested by "The Reluctant Cannibal," from *At the Drop of a Hat* by Michael Flanders and Donald Swan.

FATHER: Have some meat, boy. It's prime Baptist missionary.

SON: No, thank you, sir. I don't eat people.

FATHER: What's this? What nonsense have you picked up at the university?

SON: I don't eat people.

FATHER: This will never do.

SON: I won't eat people. Eating people is wrong.

FATHER: All right, son, all right. I see that I'll have to reason with you. I know that you've been studying logic, so if you'll kindly pay a little attention, I'll just prove to you that eating people isn't wrong.

1 First of all, people always have eaten people, and they always will eat people. You can't deny that. Eating people must be right.

2 All our kind of people agree that eating people is the thing to do. How could they all be wrong?

3 Anyway, it's obvious why you say "Don't eat people". It's because you're a coward, afraid of ending up in the stew yourself. So we needn't take your view seriously.

4 Now, people around here don't like people who don't eat people; and people they don't like, they're likely to eat. I wonder if you realize how dangerously unreasonable your position is.

5 It must be some of those foreign-born professors up at the university who gave you this idea. But they're all pale-faced, and not one of them ever met a payroll; they're effeminate and impractical. You shouldn't listen to them.

6 Besides, it's Communists who don't believe in eating people. I never thought a son of mine would go away to the university and come back a Red.

7 And now for one moment please just pay attention and think. What one food is the best possible food for us? What one

food contains all the substances our bodies need? The answer is, people. And you can't deny that we ought to eat what's best for us. It follows logically that we ought to eat people.

8 And if you don't believe in eating people, son, my business associates and my customers will hear about you, they'll be shocked, they'll blame me, I'll be forced out of business, I won't be able to earn anything, and your poor mother and I will go hungry. Don't do that to us, boy. You can see that eating people is right.

9 If you say "Don't eat people", you might as well say "Don't beat people". Your logic is laughable.

10 It was our system of free-eating enterprise that made this country what it is. Obviously, you're a person who wants to destroy our prosperity and freedom.

11 Our entire internal economy is based on people-eating. If we stopped eating people, hungry hordes of the unemployed uneaten would crowd our streets, while other hordes of unfed eaters would starve. But it is right to prevent starvation and unemployment, and since eating people does this it is not wrong but right.

12 If your demand that we stop eating people were granted, why, next someone would demand that we stop eating animals, then vegetables, then minerals. We'd end with nothing to eat at all.

13 You say "Don't eat people". But I hold in my hand a photo taken only ten years ago which clearly shows you dining on a large people-steak.

14 Why is it that you are so insincere and deceitful? What foreign power are you in the pay of?

15 You say that eating people is wrong. But I put it to you: Would you want your sister to marry a vegetarian?

16 In your tone of assumed moral superiority, you say that it's wrong to eat people. But last night you ate with gusto a large chunk of rare cow's flesh. That cow's name was Billy, he was a good and kind cow with large brown eyes that looked at us very trustingly. You ate my saintly Billy, yet you have the nerve to say that it's wrong to eat people.

17 Dr. E. T. M. Young, writing in a recent issue of *The American Anthropophagist*, declares: "Next to marshmallow whip, cannibalism is the noblest gastronomical achievement of mankind". That should settle the matter.

18 The Bible itself endorses the eating of people for dinner. It is written: "Blessed are those servants whom the Lord when he cometh shall find watching: verily I say unto you, that he shall . . . make them meat, and will come forth and serve them". (Luke 12:37)

The following discussion is concerned with the question whether drinking water should be fluoridated. Discuss the convincingness of each piece of reasoning.

1 MR. PRO: Fluoridation of drinking water has been tested successfully both in Newburg, New York, and in Grand Rapids, Michigan. After the children of these cities had been using the fluoridated drinking water for only five years, they already had 60 per cent fewer new dental cavities per 1,000 children per year. In a nearby town that had been used as a control group and had not been receiving the fluoridated water there was little change. Often, just by looking in a child's mouth, a dentist can tell whether the child comes from a place with fluoridated water—there's so much difference in the incidence of dental cavities.

2 MR. CON: Your statistics don't prove that fluoridation deserves the credit. What about other factors, such as better medical care, that helped to improve the teeth of these children?

3 Anyway, your statistics concern only children. They don't show anything about what happens to adults' teeth.

4 My figures show that, after several years of fluoridation, Newburg, New York, had a total of almost 50 per cent more cases of tooth decay among school children, as well as over 50 per cent more heart disease and kidney trouble among adults, than had the 'control' city, whose water was unfluoridated.

5 We all know that tooth decay is caused by improper diet and poor dental hygiene. So it would be better to eliminate these *causes* than merely to treat the *effect* of them, which is tooth decay. Fluoridation is the wrong approach to the problem.

6 Moreover, fluorine is the most dangerous toxic chemical on earth; it is so powerful in its corrosive effect that it is used to etch glass. The idea of putting that sort of chemical into our drinking water is just insane. Fluoridation is a menace to health.

7 Careful control of the size of the dose of any medicine administered is essential; that's the benchmark of medical science. But when this fluoride chemical is put into the water reservoirs, there is no way of being absolutely sure that it will be evenly distributed, so that no one gets a dangerous overdose.

8 Fluoridation may have harmful consequences which far outweigh a cavity, and its effects may not be successfully determined for years to come. It is unwise to proceed with fluoridation at the present time.

9 MR. PRO: Drinking water has been artificially fluoridated in many cities for quite a few years now, and scientists who have studied the health records have never found any evidence that fluoridation harms anyone. And some other places have always had water containing natural fluorides; people there are as healthy as anywhere else.

10 If you lived in a place where the water had natural fluorides in it, would you try to take them out? Of course not. So why object if fluorides are put in?

11 Both the American Medical Association and the American Dental Association have formally endorsed fluoridation. Surely they are trustworthy authorities.

12 MR. CON: Many medical associations are opposed to fluoridation. For instance, the Texas Medical Association declined to recommend it. And the Association of American Physicians and Surgeons declared, "We condemn the addition of any substance to public water supplies for the purpose of affecting the bodies or the bodily or mental functions of the consumers".

13 The people don't want it either. Out of 56 cities where really fair elections on the matter were held, 42 turned it down.

14 It's not hard to explain why some doctors favor fluoridation. For instance, one of its leading advocates has been Dr. Speare, dean and research professor of nutrition at the Harding University Medical School. Dr. Speare received in the past six years over $360,000 from the food processors, the refined sugar interests, the soft-drink people, and the chemical and drug interests; half of this was marked for Dr. Speare's personal direction (according to the *Congressional Record*). Every true nutritionist knows that it is refined sweets, soft drinks, and refined flour that are the basic causes of defective teeth. Is it any wonder that the processors of these foods are so active in helping the chemical interests to cover up for them? Is it any wonder that Dr. Speare, and the others like him, are so fiercely loyal to certain commercial interests?

15 MR. PRO: In most towns nowadays the water supply already contains various artificial elements, such as chlorine, alum, and copper sulfate. These chemicals are needed to ensure that our water is safe. We have to prevent outbreaks of typhoid fever, for instance. Nobody objects to these chemicals nowadays, so why object to fluoridation?

16 MR. CON: Perhaps it is all right to put chlorine in the water in order to prevent typhoid. But tooth decay is not a dangerous communicable disease. Tooth decay is far from being one of our most pressing problems. No one has died of it yet! Fluorine is a different matter from chlorine.

17 The primary freedom that our Western civilization offers is the right of the individual to make his own choice and decision in a personal matter. Every citizen has the right to take only those medicines that he chooses to take. But fluoridation of the water supply is a form of compulsory mass medication. It infringes the inherent right of the citizen. Why needlessly destroy that right?

18 If an individual wants fluoridated water, he should buy the fluoride for himself and add it to his own water.

19 MR. PRO: It would be more expensive and also a great nuisance for individuals to add fluoride to their personal water. It is far more efficient to have this done by the city.

20 The city compels children to attend school; it compels drivers to obey traffic regulations; and it compels property owners to obey zoning laws. If it is all right for the city to do these things, why shouldn't it improve our water supply too?

21 MR. CON: The fluoridators are at work to brainwash the nation so that we will meekly accept and be forced to partake of this vicious cumulative poison with our water, our coffee, our vegetables, all our cooking, and through our pores every time we bathe.

22 MR. PRO: Fluoridation is opposed by a crackpot, antiscientific minority. I do not believe that a minority ever has the right to keep the majority from getting what they want. In any city where a majority of us want fluoridation, we should have it; that is the democratic way.

8. *The Philosophy of Logic*

THE STATUS OF LOGICAL LAWS

We have now spent a good deal of time discussing laws of logic, both deductive and inductive. But what is the nature of these laws? What are they about? What makes them true? Philosophers have long been interested in trying to account for the essential nature of the laws of logic; this philosophical problem deserves our attention. In Chapter 1 some preliminary suggestions were made about the nature of logical laws; now let us try to discuss the matter more fully, considering alternative views. The reader must bear in mind that the issues to be discussed are controversial. Philosophers do not agree about them, and many philosophers would disagree with the things that this chapter will say.

When we speak of laws of logic, we are referring to principles such as these, for example:[1]

---

[1] Some writers use the phrase "laws of logic" to refer only to sentences that are logically true on account of their form, like "Snow is white or it is not" rather than to sentences that mention other sentences, as our examples do. According to that more pedantic usage, our examples would have to be referred to as "laws of metalogic".

Every sentence of the form "p and not p" is false.
Every E sentence is equivalent to its own converse.
No valid syllogism can have an undistributed middle term.

What kind of sentences are these laws? How do we know them to be true? How is it that they can be of use to us? Let us consider in turn four different philosophical views as to the nature of these laws. It will suffice if we focus our attention upon quite elementary laws of logic, since the status and character of more intricate laws can be expected to agree with that of the elementary laws.

Are Logical Laws Inductive Generalizations?

First let us consider the suggestion that the laws of logic are inductive generalizations, empirical truths about how things in the world behave, like the laws of physical science, though more general. This view has not been very widely held by philosophers, but it deserves our attention. According to this view, we can confirm these laws of logic by making observations of how things happen in the world. This would mean, for example, that past experience is the real basis of our confidence that all sentences of the form "p and not p" are false. According to this view, just as having observed many ravens that are black and none that is not entitles us to believe that all ravens are black, similarly our having observed many sentences of the form "p and not p" that are false and none that is true justifies our belief that all such sentences are false. We have met the sentences "Today is Tuesday and it is not", "Snow is white and it is not", and so on; in each case, investigation of the calendar or of snow, or of whatever is the subject of the sentence, has revealed that the sentence is false. Hence we may properly infer by induction that the world probably is so constructed that every sentence of this form is true.

Is this a satisfactory view about the nature of the laws of logic? Like many another view in philosophy, this view offers us a comparison of one thing with another, a comparison partly misleading and partly illuminating.

If we have observed many ravens, all of which were black, we would believe the inductive generalization that all ravens are black, and we would not expect it to be refuted by further observations. However, we still would understand quite clearly what it would be like for the generalization to be refuted by the discovery of some kind of nonblack raven; if we were to read a report of such a discovery, it would be surprising but not unintelligible. Our past experience of black ravens is needed to support the generalization precisely because the generalization says something that could conceivably be refuted by experience. A universal sentence saying nothing that experience could conceivably refute (e.g., "All bachelors are unmarried") would not need to be supported inductively by evidence drawn from past experience. Thus, it is a general characteristic of inductive generalizations that we always can understand fairly clearly the possibility of observations that would refute them.

Are elementary laws of logic like this? Can we describe what it would be like for observations to refute the logical law that all sentences of the form *"p* or not *p"* (when understood in the normal way) are false? Suppose we met a creature that claimed to be both a man and not a man, or an object which somebody said was both a tree and not a tree. Suppose, moreover, that the creature insists that it is not merely in some ways like a man and in some ways not like a man; it claims more than that and insists that it both is and is not a man. The person, similarly, insists that the object is not merely in some ways like a tree and in some ways unlike but that the object both is a tree and is not a tree. These claims are unintelligible. They fail to make sense and are quite unlike the case of the nonblack raven. No matter what we might observe of the creature or the object, nothing about it could prove to us that it both has and lacks the very same property. No matter what we might observe, it could not refute our conviction that all sentences of the form "p and not p" are false.

Thus it is misleading to say that the laws of logic are inductive generalizations. They are unlike inductive generalizations in that they could not be refuted by any describable observations. If they could not be refuted by any describable observations, they cannot need to be supported by evidence drawn from past observation. The view that our knowledge of logical laws rests upon past experience cannot be right. These laws must be known by us in some other way. So much for the misleading aspect of the view that laws of logic are like inductive generalizations.

However, there is also an illuminating aspect to this comparison of the elementary laws of logic with inductive generalizations. Although these laws do not need evidence from experience to show that they hold true, such evidence serves to show their utility. These laws are of use because the world happens to be the kind of world that it is. This is a generalization based upon experience and could be refuted by experience. Suppose, for instance, that the universe were under the governance of a powerful and malicious demon of superhuman intelligence who disliked anybody who reasoned in accordance with logical laws. The demon might see to it that any such person was supplied with misleading evidence—evidence which, when logically interpreted, led to false conclusions. For instance, if there were both white and black swans in the world, the demon would arrange that logical thinkers observed only the white ones; logical thinkers would then infer the false conclusion that all swans are white. The demon might also arrange that illogical thinkers were supplied with evidence of kinds such that from it, with habitual illogic, those thinkers would infer true conclusions.

If the demon were clever enough and powerful enough, he

could cause logical people to reach relatively few true conclusions and illogical people to reach relatively many true conclusions. Under these circumstances, logic would lose its utility, and illogical thinking would be more profitable than logical thinking; this is not to say, however, that the principles of logic would be untrue in such a world. Thus, although our knowledge that these elementary laws of logic are true does not rest upon observation, our knowledge of their utility does, for it is through observations and past experience that we know our world not to be like the far-fetched world just described.

Are Logical Laws A Priori Insights into Reality?

There are some philosophers who have agreed that the elementary laws of logic are necessary rather than empirical sentences, but who still have held that these laws express very general facts about the nature of the universe—facts that cannot be known merely through understanding the meanings of logical words (like "and" and "not") but that must be apprehended in some other way, though not through inductive inference based on sense experience. How can general facts about the universe be known, if not by induction, though?

The answer of these philosophers has been that somehow through the faculty of reason—through the mind's power of rational insight into the nature of things—we can know these laws to be true. According to this view, the logical law that no sentence of the form "*p* and not *p*" is true is not primarily a law about sentences, about language, but rather a law about things. Roughly speaking, it would be a law to the effect that no thing in the universe can have a property and at the same time lack that property. We would grasp this general fact about the universe not on the basis of sense experience but rather through the mind's power of rational insight.

This view also embodies a comparison. Knowledge of logical

laws is compared to a sort of vision, a nonsensory vision. This comparison, like the preceding one, has both an illuminating and a misleading aspect. Its illuminating aspect is that it emphasizes the difference between logical laws and empirical generalizations, by insisting that knowledge of logical laws is a priori rather than empirical. By speaking of rational insight, this view rightly suggests that we can grasp the truth of elementary logical laws by 'seeing' that they hold, that is, just by thinking about them.

But there is a definitely misleading aspect to this view also. Speaking of insight into the nature of reality suggests that the process by which we come to know logical laws is a kind of seeing with the eye of reason—seeing into the inner essence of things, seeing general facts essentially embedded in the nature of the world. The view suggests that by a kind of penetrating and occult clairvoyance we succeed in gazing into the abstract innards of the universe. This is misleading, for it makes the whole matter seem far more mysterious, far more occult, than need be. It conveys a wrong impression of the reflective thinking that is involved in grasping logical laws. The view seems to suggest that by staring very intently with the mind's eye we come to understand that sentences of the form "*p* and not *p*" are false. That is not so, however. We come to understand this through remembering how the words "and" and "not" are used in normal cases and through fitting together what we remember of this. Someone who accepted the doctrine of rational insight might be inclined to sit blinking his mind's eye and waiting for his rational vision to clear, when what he should be doing is to marshal what he knows about how he uses certain words when he speaks his own language. The view we are discussing misleadingly suggests that someone might fully understand the uses of the words "and" and "not" and yet, if his rational insight were clouded, might remain ignorant of the law that sentences of the form "*p* and not *p*" are false. But this could not happen, for if anyone doubts whether sentences of the form "*p* and not p" (when normally understood) are false, his doubt by itself is sufficient to prove that he does not understand the uses of these words.

Do Logical Laws Describe Operations of the Mind?

Quite a few philosophers have held a third view about the nature of logical laws. They have believed that these laws describe how the human mind works, that they are generalizations about how people think. The real meaning of the logical law that all sentences of the form "p and not p" are false would be that the human mind cannot think a contradiction; the human mind lacks the power to believe a sentence of the form "p and not p", for it is under a compulsion to reject all inconsistency. According to this view, in studying logic we are studying the capacity of the human mind to maintain certain types of beliefs and the compulsions to which the mind is subject that prevent it from maintaining certain other beliefs. Most of those who hold this view would not seek any explanation of why the human mind is subject to such compulsions, except perhaps that God benevolently made it so or that there is evolutionary survival value in having these compulsions.

This view embodies a comparison between logical laws and laws of psychology. Again, there is an illuminating aspect to the comparison, although also there is a misleading aspect. The value of the comparison lies in the fact that logical laws are related to what the mind can believe. For example, it is rather as though the human mind were subject to a compulsion not to believe contradictions, for truly a person cannot believe a contradiction if he fully comprehends that it is a contradiction. People often hold contradictory beliefs, but only when they do not fully recognize them as such.

However, this view that logical laws describe how the mind works is misleading insofar as it tends to suggest that logic is a branch of empirical psychology, which is not the case. The principle that people cannot full knowingly believe contradictions really is not an inductive generalization belonging to psychology. Instead, it is a necessary truth reflecting something about what it means to understand a contradiction; part of what it means to say that someone fully understands a contradiction is that he does not believe it. Logic, indeed, has very little to do with empirical facts about human minds. (Empirical facts about human psychology enter into logic, if at all, only in connection with the discussion of logical fallacies.) When logic tells us that no sentence of the form "*p* and not *p*" is true, this is best regarded as a remark about sentences, not as a remark about minds. Mental phenomena are not the subject matter of logic; its subject matter consists of sentences and arguments, which may be about anything whatever. Logic is not a branch of psychology, for psychology is an empirical, inductive study of how people and animals think and behave, whereas logic is a nonempirical, noninductive study of such matters as the validity of arguments.

Are Logical Laws Verbal Conventions?

Some recent philosophers have advocated still another view about the status of the laws of logic, the view that these are verbal conventions. The logical law that all sentences of the form "*p* and not *p*" are false is compared to a stipulative definition. According to this view, the meaning of the law is that we have arbitrarily decided always to apply the word "false" to that sort of sentences containing "and" and "not". We maintain this stipulation because it proves to be a convenient way of speaking but not for any other reason.

According to this view, the logical law cannot be regarded as a necessary truth; it really is neither true nor necessary, for all it does is to express an arbitrary verbal convention, which we could alter if we decided that it would be convenient to do so. Perhaps it would never prove convenient to alter this particular verbal convention, but some thinkers have actually urged that we alter the corresponding law stating that all sentences of the form "*p* or not *p*" are true. They have suggested that it would be more convenient to do without the principle of excluded middle. According to this view, such a proposal is perfectly legitimate, and a logic that regards some sentences as neither true nor false might be more convenient for some purposes than is our standard logic.

This view compares logical laws to stipulative definitions and, like the earlier views, has both illuminating and misleading aspects. The view rightly calls to our attention that the elementary laws of logic are embedded in our language and that it is the character of language, more than the character of the world, that is revealed by logical laws. To have learned to use the words "not" and "and" in their standard sense is to have learned that sentences of the form "*p* and not *p*" are false. Somebody who thinks that a sentence of this form might be true thereby shows that he does not understand the standard meaning of the words "and" and "not". Furthermore, how words are used is a matter of arbitrary convention. It is a matter of historical accident that we use the word "and" to express conjunction and the word "not" to express negation. These conventions certainly could be changed legitimately, if we decided to do so.

There is a misleading element in this view, however. For this view holds that logical laws are arbitrary in nature and that the laws themselves might perfectly well have been otherwise if we had chosen to have them otherwise. But what would it be like for our present logical laws to be untrue? What would it be like for the world to contain, say, things that both were and were not trees—in the standard senses of "and" and "not"? This does not make sense. The law that all sentences of the form "*p* and not *p*" are false, when understood in the normal way, is a law that cannot be false. Since it cannot be false, we certainly could not *make* it false.

Confusion arises here because of an ambiguity. The proponent of this view neglects the difference between a logical law considered merely as dealing with sentences of the form *"p* and not *p"* and a logical law considered as dealing with these sentences *understood in the standard manner.* If a logical law dealt merely with marks and sounds, the law could arbitrarily be changed merely by changing the meanings we attach to the marks and to the sounds. For instance, we could decide to let "and" express disjunction; that would certainly change the law. But when the logical law is understood as dealing with sentences understood in a particular way, the law cannot be changed by any human power, or by any power at all, for it is necessarily true.

Looking back over these four views, we see that each contributes something to our understanding of the matter, yet none is adequate. It is not good enough to describe the laws of logic as inductive generalizations about how things in the world behave; it is not good enough to call them rational insights into the nature of the universe; it is not good enough to call them generalizations about how human minds work; nor is it good enough to call them arbitrary verbal conventions. This may encourage us to return to the account suggested in the final section of Chapter 1. Putting it in a more positive way, we may say that the laws of logic are necessary truths about sentences and arguments, which hold true in virtue of the ways words are used and which we grasp through mastering our language.

DOES ALL DEDUCTIVE REASONING BEG THE QUESTION?

We turn now to another and more specific problem in the philosophy of logic. The distinctive feature of deductive arguments is that they are, or claim to be, conclusive; that is, a deductive argument makes the claim that, since the premises all are true, the conclusion must necessarily be true also. Put another way, the de-

ductive argument claims that there would be an outright contradiction involved if any person were to assert the premises but deny the
conclusion. If the conclusion said anything wholly new and independent of the premises, there could not then be any contradiction involved in asserting the premises but denying the conclusion;
the argument could not then have the conclusive character of a
valid deductive argument. Thus we see that, if an argument is to
be both deductive and valid, its conclusion cannot say something
new or independent of its premises. In this sense, the conclusion
of a valid deductive argument cannot go beyond the content of
its premises; it can only bring out what is already contained in the
premises. But this fact gives rise to a philosophical puzzle.

Mill's Criticism of Deduction

This puzzle has troubled philosophers since the time of Plato,
but the classic statement of the puzzle was offered by John Stuart
Mill.[2] Mill was particularly concerned with the categorical syllogism, because in traditional logic the syllogism was regarded as the
fundamental kind of deductive argument. Mill considered the
syllogism, noted that its conclusion must always be contained in
the premises if the argument is to be valid, and concluded that this
makes the syllogism a worthless style of reasoning.

Consider the syllogism "All teetotalers are avaricious; Calvin
is a teetotaler; therefore Calvin is avaricious". Mill charged that
an argument like this is worthless because it must beg the question.
How could you really know that all teetotalers are avaricious,
unless you had already observed each and every teetotaler and
found him to be avaricious? But in doing this, you would have
had to observe Calvin himself and note that he is avaricious. Thus
you would have had to learn that the conclusion is true *before* you
could have learned that the major premise is true. This makes the
syllogism worthless as a means of proving the conclusion. The

[2] J. S. Mill, *A System of Logic,* Book II, chap. III.

syllogism is a *petitio principii*, for anyone who was in doubt about the conclusion should be at least equally in doubt about the premises.

Not all syllogisms are quite like this example. We might have a syllogism that involved no circularity of reasoning with respect to its major premise, for instance, "All bachelors are unmarried; Calvin is a bachelor, and so he is unmarried". This syllogism has a necessary major premise, and we do not have to observe all bachelors including Calvin before we can know that all of them are unmarried; we know this in virtue of the meanings of the words involved. Even in this example, however, there still remains a circularity in the reasoning. For how could we know that Calvin is a bachelor unless we first had found out that he is unmarried? If we did not know that he was unmarried, we could not possibly know that he was a bachelor. Thus again we have to know the conclusion *before* we can know a premise. Here the circularity arises with respect to the minor premise rather than the major; but the reasoning again is a begging of the question.

Mill considered that all deductive reasoning suffered from this sort of circularity. No deductive argument could ever be used really to prove anything, for always one would have to know the truth of the conclusion before one could know the truth of all the premises; always the premises would be at least as dubious as the conclusion itself. Because all deductive reasoning seemed to him to be useless, Mill came to the conclusion that all genuine reasoning that proves anything is what we would call inductive in nature.

If I am trying to prove that Calvin is avaricious, the evidence from which I really reason is that Wilbur, whom I've met, is an avaricious teetotaler; that Hubert, whom I've met, is an avaricious teetotaler; and so on. The actual evidence that I have is about other particular individuals. This is the evidence that I must use if I am to make a useful inference about whether Calvin is avaricious. An argument of this type, in which one reasons from evidence about some individual cases to a conclusion about another individual case, is what we have called an inductive argument by analogy. Mill contended that this was the fundamental type of argument that we use in our thinking whenever we are employing reasoning that can really prove anything.

Is Mill right about this? Can it be true that deductive reasoning, which we have spent so much time studying, always is basically worthless and never can prove anything? The idea that deductive reasoning always commits the fallacy of begging the question sounds very paradoxical and puzzling; yet can we maintain that deduction is of any use, when we admit that the conclusion of a valid deductive argument has to be contained in its premises?

The Value of Deduction

Mill surely was right in insisting that inductive reasoning is extremely important in our thinking and that our empirical beliefs about the phenomena of nature, about past history, and about future predictions ultimately involve inductive reasoning and not deduction alone. How do we know that the sun will rise tomorrow? Our knowledge of this is based upon our observations of the regular behavior of the sun and other heavenly bodies in the past. How do we know that the Washington Monument is still there on the Mall and has not vanished into thin air overnight? It is because of our past observations of the durability of buildings. As we go speeding down the highway, what right do we have to assume that the pavement continues out of sight around the bend rather than plunging into a fiery pit? It is because of our past experience with the reliability of United States highways.

No doubt we can justify some of the facts that we know about the world by deducing them from other more general facts that we know about the world. But, in the end, those more general facts must themselves be established inductively, if we are to know them.

Mill is surely right that induction (as we call it; he used the word somewhat differently) is very important and that merely deductive proofs of empirical conclusions would never be complete. He rightly emphasizes the importance of induction and the limitations of deduction in our reasoning about empirical matters.

However, Mill surely puts his point too strongly. It is a serious exaggeration to say that, whenever we have an argument whose conclusion is deductively contained in its premises, there we always have a fallacy of begging the question. It is true that whenever we have the fallacy of begging the question, there we have an argument whose conclusion is contained in its premises; but the converse does not hold true. Sometimes we can have arguments that are deductively valid, whose conclusions are indeed contained in their premises, yet which are of real value as proofs.

Suppose that a man lives in the suburbs but works in the city; he commutes every day. He knows perfectly well that it takes him ten minutes to get from his house to the station, thirty-five minutes by train into the city, ten minutes by subway, and then five minutes to walk to his office, and the same on the way back. And he knows perfectly well that ten plus thirty-five plus ten plus five equals sixty, and that there are sixty minutes in an hour. He knows these separate facts very well indeed. But it may come as a surprise to him, and perhaps a shock, if someone now points out that he is spending two full hours every working day of his life just traveling back and forth. This conclusion follows deductively from the premises; the man knew perfectly well that the premises of the argument are true; but he had never before noticed the conclusion contained in the premises.

An argument begs the question if its conclusion is contained in its premises in such a way that a person would not know the premises to be true without having noticed that the conclusion is true too. The example just given is a simple deduction that does not beg the question. Its conclusion is indeed contained in its premises, but it takes some thinking to detect that the conclusion is there, and so the argument succeeds in showing us something important that we had not noticed before. This is the kind of case in which deduction has its value. The point of deductive reasoning is that it helps us to grasp consequences that we had not noticed but that are contained in what we already believe. And naturally in more complicated cases the conclusion might be far more deeply hidden. This happens often in mathematical reasoning, where very elaborate deductive arguments sometimes are employed in order to bring out the consequences of sets of premises.

IS ALL INDUCTIVE REASONING INVALID?

Mill believed that he had discovered a fatal weakness in deductive reasoning, and so he put his faith in inductive reasoning instead. But is inductive reasoning really legitimate? Here too a philosophical puzzle arises.

Hume's Criticism of Induction

The Scottish philosopher David Hume in the eighteenth century had already raised a serious question about induction.[3] What right do we have to trust inductive reasoning?, Hume asked. In any inductive argument the conclusion goes beyond what the premises say and makes some kind of prediction or conjecture which further observations may or may not support. There never is any logical contradiction involved in asserting the premises of an inductive argument but denying the conclusion. This means that there never is any logical certainty that the conclusion must be true, just because the premises are. If this is so, how can an inductive argument have any logical force at all? If the truth of the premises does not guarantee the truth of the con-

[3] David Hume, *Enquiry Concerning Human Understanding*, Sec. IV.

clusion, why should we trust or rely upon inductive reasoning? Consider examples. In our past experience we have always found that bread is nourishing to eat and arsenic is poisonous. We have observed many occasions when people have eaten bread and stayed healthy, and we have observed some occasions when people ate arsenic and died. But have we any logical right to believe that this must continue to be so in the future? It is perfectly conceivable that from tomorrow onward people who eat arsenic will be nourished by it whereas those who eat bread will be poisoned by it. If this is so, how can we claim that what we have observed in the past gives us any real reason for making inferences about what must happen in the future? How can we claim really to know anything about what will poison us and what will not?

Hume came to the conclusion that we do not have any reason for trusting inductive arguments. Inductive reasoning is invalid and never really enables us to know anything, he felt. Thus Hume was led to a sceptical point of view, doubting that we ever can know anything about as yet unobserved phenomena. Hume recognized that people constantly indulge in inductive thinking, and he developed a theory to explain why people do this. He theorized that human minds are constructed in such a way that they have a certain built-in tendency to expect for the future the same sort of thing they have experienced in the past. Whenever a person has observed something happening often in the past, he expects to find that same thing happening in the future; the more frequent the past experience has been, the stronger is the expectation for the future. But this is an irrational tendency in human nature, Hume thought; our minds work this way, but there is no logical justification for it.

Some philosophers, seeking to escape Hume's sceptical conclusion, have thought that we may justify inductive reasoning by noticing how successful it has been in the past. Looking at our past experience, we see that inductive thinking has frequently led us to true conclusions. Is this not a good reason for trusting induction for the future too? This sort of argument is unsatisfactory as a reply to Hume's scepticism; it offers an inductive argument in favor of the reliability of induction, and that begs the question, so far as the sceptic is concerned. Since he is dubious of the legitimacy of induction, he will be at least equally dubious regarding this particular piece of inductive reasoning. Here is a subtler kind of *petitio principii,* in which it is the form of reasoning itself that is question-begging.

Other philosophers have thought that we may justify inductive reasoning by introducing the assumption that nature is uniform and regular and that the kind of things that have happened in the past will continue to happen in the future. If we take it as an additional premise in our reasoning that things in nature happen uniformly, this supposedly gives us reason for believing, say, that arsenic which has always poisoned in the past will continue to do so in the future. The idea is that, if we assume the 'uniformity of nature', we can infer that what has happened in the past will continue to happen in the future. However, there are two difficulties about this theory.

First, it is very hard to see how we could formulate a sentence that would adequately perform the role required of this proposed additional premise. (What kind of uniformity would it be, and how much?) Second, even if we were able to word such a sentence satisfactorily, we would have no way of knowing it to be true, except by induction. There is nothing else we know from which we could deduce such a sentence. Our thinking would be circular if we used inductive reasoning to justify the sentence that itself is introduced for the purpose of justifying inductive reasoning. Thus it seems that we have no way of justifying induction.

The conclusion that we have no real reason for believing that bread is not going to poison us or that arsenic is going to do so is paradoxical and puzzling. We use inductive thinking all the time; can it really be an illogical process without any justification?

The Validity of Inductive Reasoning

Hume's criticism of induction was a valuable contribution to philosophy, for Hume made it because he had recognized that inductive arguments are not conclusive and that one always can consistently deny the conclusion without contradicting the premises. Earlier philosophers had not clearly understood this and had not fully grasped the difference between induction and deduction.

Hume was surely not correct, however, in believing that this fact means that inductive thinking is not good reasoning at all, that it has no logical force whatever. The difficulty is that Hume thought deductive reasoning to be the only legitimate type of reasoning; when he found that inductive arguments are not deductive in nature, he rejected them as illegitimate. But deduction and induction are two different yet equally important types of reasoning, neither of which can be reduced to the other. It is a misunderstanding to criticize induction just because it is not deductive. We have no more right to do that than we would have to criticize deduction for not being inductive.

The misleading aspect of Hume's sceptical viewpoint becomes clear if we notice what it implies. Hume says that we have no real reason for accepting inductive conclusions; this would imply that someone who chooses to eat arsenic in preference to bread is just as reasonable as someone who elects the opposite menu. Hume thinks we have no rational basis for predicting the future; this implies that one kind of thinking is no more logical than any other kind of thinking for making predictions about the future. It implies that the careful scientist who makes predictions is thinking in no more rational a way than the careless person who relies on 'intuitions' or superstitions. They are all in the same category, all completely irrational in their reasoning, if induction really is illogical.

This viewpoint, however, embodies a misuse of the words "rational" and "logical" (and the whole family of words associated with them). For if we use these words in their normal sense, we have to say that the scientist is more rational and logical in his thinking than is a superstitious person. That is part of what it means to be rational and logical: that one uses carefully scientific inductive methods of thinking rather than carelessly superstitious ones. There is no confusion or mistake involved in this normal use of these terms. The mistake arises only in the minds of people who misunderstand their normal use.

The great merit of Hume's ideas about induction is that Hume succeeded in distinguishing, much more clearly than had earlier philosophers, between induction and deduction. He discovered how our thinking involves two quite different types of reasoning. But he himself, like many a discoverer, was misled by what he found. Because he thought that deduction was the only genuine reasoning, he was led to the conclusion that, since induction differs from deduction, it cannot be good reasoning. What we should try to recognize is that, though they differ, they are both genuine types of what is meant by reasoning.

Glossary of Terms

abusive ad hominem argument: Any *ad hominem* argument that tries to refute a view by attacking the character, qualifications, or motives of the person who advocates the view, rather than by offering direct reasons why the view is false.

ad baculum argument (appeal to force): Strictly speaking, an *ad baculum* argument is any argument that fallaciously employs a threat as though it were a logical reason for believing a conclusion. In a looser sense, when someone stops offering arguments and resorts to force, he may be said to be resorting to the *ad baculum* 'argument'.

addition: A form of deductive argument in which from a premise a conclusion is derived that is a disjunction having one component that is just the same as the premise. This is schematically represented as $p; \therefore p \lor q$.

ad hominem argument: Any argument whose premises, rather than containing evidence having a direct bearing on the conclusion, are related instead to the person who refuses to agree to the conclusion. Such arguments are often, though not always, fallacious.

adjunction: A form of deductive argument where from two premises a conclusion that is their conjunction is derived. This is schematically represented as $p, q; \therefore p \& q$.

ad misericordiam argument (appeal to pity): Any argument whose premises, rather than containing evidence having a direct bearing on the conclusion, instead give reasons why acceptance of the conclusion would prevent someone's misery.

ad verecundiam argument (appeal to authority): Any argument whose premises, rather than containing evidence having a direct bearing on the conclusion, instead give evidence that some supposed authority advocates the conclusion. Such arguments are often, but not always, fallacious.

affirmative sentence: Any categorical sentence is affirmative if it is in **A** or **I** form.

affirming the consequent: A form of reasoning in which one premise is a conditional and the other premise is the same as the consequent of that conditional. This is schematically represented as $p \supset q, q; \therefore p$. This form of reasoning is not deductively valid.

alternation: Disjunction.

ambiguity: To say that an expression is ambiguous is to say that it is unclear which of two or more quite different meanings the expression has.

ambiguity, fallacy of: Any *non sequitur* in which some ambiguity in the argument leads people to misunderstand the logical form of the argument, thus making them regard the argument as valid when it is not.

analogy: A similarity between different things. Sometimes analogies are used for purposes of description, sometimes for purposes of reasoning.

analytical definition: Any definition that aims to describe the accepted meaning of a word or symbol.

antecedent: In a conditional sentence, the component governed by the word "if".

a posteriori sentence: Empirical sentence.

appeal to authority: *Ad verecundiam* argument.

appeal to force: *Ad baculum* argument.

appeal to pity: *Ad misericordiam* argument.

a priori knowledge: Knowledge that we can possess without possessing supporting evidence drawn from sense experience.

a priori sentence: Any sentence that can be known to be true or known to be false a priori.

argument: A formulation in words of one or more premises and of a conclusion that the speaker infers from them.

association: Principles to the effect that in a conjunction of more than two components, or in a disjunction of more than two components, grouping does not matter. Schematically represented, "$(p \& q) \& r$" is equivalent to "$p \& (q \& r)$", and "$(p \lor q) \lor r$" is equivalent to "$p \lor (q \lor r)$".

atomic sentence: Any sentence not containing any other shorter sentence as a component of itself.

begging the question: *Petitio principii.*

biconditional sentence: Any sentence of the form "p if and only if q".

black-and-white thinking: Thinking in extremes; because a sentence is false, it is inferred that some very contrary sentence must be true.

bound variable: To say that a variable in a quantificational formula is bound is to say that the variable there is governed by a quantifier.

broad: To say that an analytical definition is too broad is to say that the definiens applies to some things to which the definiendum does not apply.

categorical sentence: Any sentence in **A, E, I,** or **O** form.

chain argument (hypothetical syllogism): An argument consisting of three or more conditionals. This is represented schematically by $p \supset q, q \supset r; \therefore p \supset r$.

circumstantial ad hominem argument: Any *ad hominem* argument that offers reasons why the opponent would want to accept the conclusion, rather than reasons why the conclusion is true.

collectively: To speak of the members of a group collectively is to speak about the whole group considered as one unit. What is said may not be true of the members of the group considered individually.

commutation: Principles to the effect that in a conjunction and in a disjunction the order of the components does not matter. Represented schematically, "$p \& q$" is equivalent to "$q \& p$", and "$p \lor q$" is equivalent to "$q \lor p$".

complex question: Any question worded so as to contain a concealed questionable assumption.

complex question, fallacy of: Any fallacy caused by the presence of an unjustified assumption concealed in a question.

component: The simpler sentences that together make up a compound sentence are called its components.

composition, fallacy of: The fallacy of inferring a conclusion that speaks of a group collectively from a premise that speaks of the group distributively, when such a conclusion does not follow.

compound sentence: Any sentence containing one or more shorter sentences as parts of itself.

conclusion: In an inference, that which is inferred from the premises.

conditional (hypothetical) sentence: Any "if-then" sentence.

conjunction: Any "and" sentence.

conjunction, law of: Law for calculating the probability of a conjunction. The probability of one event *and* another equals the probability of the first, times the probability of the second on the assumption that the first is true.

conjunctive argument: Any of various forms of argument that depend upon conjunction; as represented schematically, especially, $-(p \& q),\ p;\ \therefore -q$.

consequent: In a conditional sentence, the component not governed by "if".

consistency: A group of sentences is consistent if and only if it is not necessarily impossible that all of them may be true.

contingent sentence: Empirical sentence.

contradiction: Any sentence that is necessarily false. A truth-functional contradiction is a sentence that is necessarily false on account of its truth-functional form.

contradictory sentences: Two sentences are contradictories (or negations) of each other if and only if they are necessarily opposite as regards truth and falsity.

contradictory terms: Two terms are contradictories (or negations) of each other if and only if it is impossible that there could be anything to which both terms apply, yet one or the other must apply to each thing.

contraposition: The contrapositive of a categorical sentence is got by making subject and predicate trade places and negating each. The contrapositive of a conditional is obtained by making the antecedent and consequent trade places and negating each.

contrary sentences: Two sentences are contraries of each other if and only if they cannot both be true but might both be false.

contrary terms: Two terms are contraries of each other if and only if it is impossible that there could be anything to which both apply but possible that there may be things to which neither applies.

conversion, by limitation: The converse by limitation of a universal categorical sentence is got by making subject and predicate trade places and changing the quantity to particular.

conversion, simple: The simple converse of a categorical sentence is got by making subject and predicate trade places. The converse of a conditional is got by making antecedent and consequent trade places.

copula: In categorical sentences, the words "are" and "are not", serving to link subject with predicate.

counteranalogy: An argument by analogy constructed for the purpose of countering or opposing some other argument by analogy.

deduction: Inference in which the conclusion follows necessarily from the premises, or at any rate in which the speaker claims that it does so. Also, an argument is called a deduction in a narrower and more special sense if it is formally arranged in a series of lines so that each line either is a premise or is inferred from earlier lines by means of some principle of inference.

definiendum: In a definition, the word or symbol being defined.

definiens: That part of a definition which gives the meaning of the word or symbol being defined.

definition: A verbal formulation of the meaning of a word or symbol; a rule or recipe for translating sentences in which a word or symbol occurs into equivalent sentences that do not contain it.

definition in context: A definition that shows how to translate sentences containing the definiendum into sentences that do not contain it but that does not provide any one fixed combination of words or symbols that can always be substituted for the definiendum.

De Morgan's laws: Laws that the negation of a conjunction is equivalent to a disjunction of negations and that the negation of a disjunction is equivalent to a conjunction of negations. Schematically represented, "$-(p \& q)$" is equivalent to "$-p \lor -q$", and "$-(p \lor q)$" is equivalent to "$-p \& -q$".

denying the antecedent: Form of argument in which one premise is a conditional and the other is the same as the negation of its antecedent. This is represented schematically by $p \supset q, -p; \therefore -q$. This is not deductively valid.

dilemma: Form of argument having three premises, two of which are conditionals and the other a disjunction. A simple dilemma contains three distinct basic components; a complex dilemma contains four. In a constructive dilemma the components of the disjunctive premise are the same as the antecedents of the conditional premises; in a destructive dilemma the components of the disjunctive premise are negations of the consequents of the conditionals.

disjunction (alternation): Any "or" sentence.

disjunction, law of: Law for calculating the probability of a disjunction. The probability of one event *or* another equals the probability of the first plus the probability of the second minus the probability that both will occur.

disjunctive argument: Any of various arguments that depend on disjunction; represented schematically, especially $p \vee q$, $-p$; $\therefore q$.

distribution, law of: Principle that a conjunction one of whose components is a disjunction is equivalent to a disjunction both of whose components are conjunctions and that a disjunction one of whose components is a conjunction is equivalent to a conjunction both of whose components are disjunctions. Represented schematically, "$p \& (q \vee r)$" is equivalent to "$(p \& q) \vee (p \& r)$", and "$p \vee (q \& r)$" is equivalent to "$(p \vee q) \& (p \vee r)$".

distribution of terms: The subject, S, of a categorical sentence is distributed in that sentence if and only if the sentence says something about every kind of S; the predicate, P, of a categorical sentence is distributed in that sentence if and only if the sentence says something about every kind of P.

distributively: To speak of the members of a group distributively is to say something that applies to each member of the group considered singly. What is said need not be true of the group considered as one unit.

division, fallacy of: Fallacy of inferring a conclusion that speaks of a group distributively from a premise that speaks of the group collectively, when such a conclusion does not follow.

double negation: Principle that the negation of the negation of a sentence is equivalent to the sentence itself; represented schematically, "$-(-p)$" is equivalent to "p". Also, the principle that the negation of the negation of a term means the same as the term itself; e.g., "non-non$S$" means "S".

empirical knowledge: Knowledge that no one can possess unless he has evidence drawn from sense experience to support it.

empirical sentence: Any sentence that can be known to be true or known to be false only on the basis of evidence drawn from sense experience.

enthymeme: Any argument one or more of whose premises is unstated.

equivalence: Two sentences are equivalent if and only if they must necessarily be alike as regards truth or falsity. When two sentences are equivalent because of their truth-functional form, they are said to be truth-functionally equivalent; when two sentences are equivalent because of their quantificational form, they are said to be quantificationally equivalent.

equivocation, fallacy of: Any fallacy of ambiguity in which the ambiguity of some particular word or phrase causes the fallacy.

exclusive disjunction: Any "or" sentence whose meaning is such that the sentence is false if both components are true.

existential instantiation (E.I.): Rule of inference according to which we may infer from an existential quantification any instance of it, with the restriction that the name in the instance must be new to the deduction.

existential quantification: Any symbolized sentence that starts with an existential quantifier whose scope is all the rest of the sentence.

existential quantifier: The expression "$(\exists\ \ )$", where any variable may be put in the gap. "$(\exists x)$" means "At least one thing x is such that".

existential viewpoint: In discussing the interrelations of categorical sentences, the viewpoint from which one takes for granted the existence of things of the kind under discussion.

explanation: Any way of fitting some strange or puzzling phenomenon into the fabric of one's knowledge, by pointing out its cause or by showing that it is a special case of some more general phenomenon. Explanation differs from proof at least in this respect, that one asks for an explanation of a phenomenon only when one is ready to grant that it does occur; one asks for a proof of a phenomenon only when one is not ready to take for granted that it occurs.

explicit definition: Any definition giving as the definiens a single word or phrase that can be substituted for the definiendum.

exportation: A principle of equivalence involving conditionals. Represented schematically, "$p \supset (q \supset r)$" is equivalent to "$(p \& q) \supset r$".

expression: Any word or symbol, or combination of words or symbols.

extension of a general term: All those things to which the term applies.

fair bet: A bet is fair when every party to the bet has the same mathematical expectation of gain and the same mathematical expectation of loss.

fallacy: Any logically defective argument that is capable of misleading people into thinking that it is logically correct.

figure: In a categorical syllogism, the pattern of arrangement of the terms.

forgetful induction: Invalid deductive reasoning in which the mistake is that some of the relevant available data have not been taken into account.

formal fallacy: Any fallacy in deductive reasoning in which the mistake arises because of pure misunderstanding of logical principles.

formula: Any sentence written with logical symbols; also any expression containing logical symbols which, though not itself a sentence, displays some logical structure that a sentence could have.

free variable: In a symbolized quantificational formula, a variable not governed by any quantifier.

general term: Any word or phrase that would make sense if used as subject or predicate in categorical sentences.

hasty induction: In inductive reasoning, the fallacy of overconfidently inferring a sweeping conclusion from weak evidence.

hypothetical sentence: Any conditional sentence.

hypothetical syllogism: Chain argument.

hypothetical viewpoint: In discussing the interrelations of categorical sentences, the viewpoint from which one leaves it an open question whether there exist things of the kinds under discussion.

identity: To say that x and y are identical is to say that they are one and the same thing. The verb "is", in one of its senses, expresses identity.

ignoratio elenchi: Fallacy of irrelevance.

illicit obversion: Fallacious obversion, in which the mistake arises because the term that ought to be replaced by its contradictory is replaced instead by a contrary term.

illicit process: In categorical syllogisms, the fallacy of allowing a term to be distributed in the conclusion when it is not distributed in a premise.

immediate inference: Deductive inference in which a categorical conclusion is inferred from a single categorical premise.

implication: To say that one sentence, or group of sentences, implies another sentence is to say that if the former be true then the latter must necessarily be true too. Where the implication results from the truth-functional forms of the sentences, it is called truth-functional implication; where it results from their quantificational forms, it is called quantificational implication.

inconsistency, fallacy of: The fallacy of reasoning from premises that are inconsistent with one another.

inconsistent sentences: A group of sentences are inconsistent with one another if and only if it is necessarily impossible for them all to be true.

induction: Nondeductive inference in which the conclusion expresses an empirical conjecture that goes beyond what the premises say; that is, the conclusion implies something, not implied by the premises, that can be confirmed or refuted only on the basis of evidence drawn from sense experience.

inductive analogy: Inductive reasoning that reaches a conclusion about a single case on the basis of a similarity between that case and other previously observed cases.

inductive generalization: Inductive reasoning that passes from evidence about some observed members of a class to a conclusion about the whole class.

inference: The deriving of a conclusion from premises.

instance: In the logic of quantification, an instance of a quantification is a sentence exactly like the quantification except that the quantifier has been removed and a name has been substituted for the variable of quantification. In inductive reasoning, individual cases to which a generalization applies or which bear out an analogy are called instances of that generalization or instances of that analogy.

intension of a general term: All those characteristics that a thing must necessarily possess in order that the term correctly apply to it.

invalidity: To say that an argument is invalid is to say that the conclusion does not follow from the premises, or, at any rate, that it does not follow with the degree of probability that the speaker claims for it.

irrelevance, fallacy of: Any *non sequitur* that is neither a pure fallacy nor a fallacy of ambiguity. A fallacy of this sort is misleading when something about the premises distracts attention from the fact that they have no logical bearing upon the conclusion.

large numbers, law of: Statistical principle to the effect that if, for example, a coin is to be tossed (where the probability of getting heads in a single toss is ½) then the greater the number of tosses, the higher is the probability that the fraction of them yielding heads will closely approximate the probability of the single case (i.e., ½).

logical analogy: Reasoning by analogy which aims to show that an argument is invalid (or that it is valid) by pointing out that other similar arguments are invalid (or valid).

logical form: In a sentence or an argument, the logical structure obtained if all nonlogical words are removed, leaving only such logical words as "all", "some", "not", "and", "or", etc.

logical laws: Principles about what kinds of sentences are true because of their logical form; principles about what sentences may be inferred from others; and so on. Also, in another sense, a sentence that is necessarily true because of its logical form may be called a law of logic.

major premise: In a categorical syllogism, the premise containing the major term.

major term: In a categorical syllogism, the term that is the predicate of the conclusion.

mathematical expectation: In a gambling situation, the amount the gambler stands to gain (or lose) multiplied by the probability that he will gain (or by the probability that he will lose).

method of agreement: A method of reasoning about causes, using the principle that the cause of a phenomenon must be a factor that is present in every case in which the phenomenon occurs.

method of concomitant variations: A method of reasoning about causes, using the principle that the cause of a phenomenon must be present to the same degree as is the phenomenon.

method of difference: A method of reasoning about causes, using the principle that any factor present when the phenomenon does not occur cannot be the cause of it.

middle term: In a categorical syllogism, the term that occurs in both premises but not in the conclusion.

Mill's methods: Ways of finding the causes of phenomena, based on the general principle that the cause of a phenomenon must be present when and only when the phenomenon occurs.

minor premise: In a categorical syllogism, the premise containing the minor term.

minor term: In a categorical syllogism, the term that occurs as subject of the conclusion.

modus ponens: A form of conditional argument. It is represented schematically by $p \supset q, p; \therefore q$.

modus tollens: A form of conditional argument. It is represented schematically by $p \supset q, -q; \therefore -p$.

Monte Carlo fallacy: In inductive reasoning, the fallacy of inferring that, because an event has occurred less often in the recent past than was to have been expected, therefore there is an increased probability of its occurring in the near future.

mood: In categorical syllogisms, the forms of the sentences in the syllogism; thus, a syllogism is in the mood **EAE**, for instance, if its major premise is an **E** sentence, its minor an **A**, and its conclusion an **E**.

narrow: An analytical definition is too narrow if the definiendum applies to some things to which the definiens does not apply.

necessary condition: If all cases of A are cases of B, then B is said to be a necessary condition of A. For example, having a middle term that is distributed is a necessary condition of being a valid syllogism. The fact that A is a necessary condition of B may itself be a necessary truth, or it may be an empirical truth.

necessary sentence: Any sentence whose truth or falsity can be known a priori.

negating a sentence: Replacing the sentence by its contradictory.

negating a term: Replacing the term by its contradictory.

negation: Any "not" sentence.

negation, law of: Law for calculating the probability of a negation; the probability that something is *not* so equals 1 minus the probability that it is so.

negation of a sentence: Two sentences are said to be negations of each other when and only when they are contradictories.

negation of a term: Two terms are said to be negations of each other when and only when they are contradictories.

negative analogy: In inductive reasoning by generalization or analogy, the extent of the observed differences among the previously observed cases.

negative sentences: Categorical sentences are said to be negative if and only if they are in **E** or **O** form.

nonexclusive disjunction: Any "or" sentence that counts as true if both components are true.

noninductive reasoning by analogy: Reasoning by analogy in which the conclusion does not express any empirical conjecture going beyond the statements of the premises.

non sequitur: Any invalid argument.

obversion: A categorical sentence is obverted by changing its quality and negating its predicate.

particular sentence: Any categorical sentence that is in **I** or **O** form.

petitio principii (begging the question): Fallacy of using a premise (or a form of inference) whose acceptability is bound to be at least as doubtful as is that of the conclusion supposedly being proved.

positive analogy: In inductive reasoning by generalization or analogy, the extent of the observed similarities among the already observed instances.

post hoc, ergo propter hoc: In inductive reasoning about causes, the fallacy of inferring that, just because one thing happened after another, the later was caused by the earlier.

predicate: In a categorical sentence, the term after the copula.

premise: In an inference, an assumption upon which the conclusion depends.

probability: In inductive reasoning, the degree of confidence that it is reasonable to accord to the conclusion, relative to the available evidence.

proof: Any argument that succeeds in establishing its conclusion.

pure fallacy: Any *non sequitur* that arises purely from misunderstanding of logical principles and not from ambiguities of language or irrelevant distractions.

quality: To specify the quality of a categorical sentence is to state whether the sentence is affirmative or negative.

quantifier: A word or symbol that indicates how many things a sentence is talking about; the words "all", "no", and "some" and the symbols "(x)" and "$(\exists x)$" are quantifiers.

quantity: To specify the quantity of a categorical sentence is to state whether the sentence is universal or particular.

real definition: Many traditional philosophers believed that there is one and only one correct way of describing the nature of each natural being; such description they called a real definition.

reasoning: Thinking that includes the making of inferences.

reductio ad absurdum: Deductive reasoning in which a conclusion is established by showing that its negation leads to something necessarily false. Schematically, one form is $p \supset (q \& -q);\ \therefore -p$.

relevance: In inductive reasoning by generalization or analogy, the extent to which one's background knowledge makes it reasonable to expect that one thing will be associated with another.

revelatory definition: Any description that, by means of a metaphor or in some other way, attempts to point out something fundamental about the nature of the thing being described.

scope of a quantifier: In a symbolized sentence containing a quantifier, that portion of the sentence governed by the quantifier.

self-contained argument: Any argument whose premises can be stated completely so that, in determining whether the conclusion validly follows from them, one need take no account of the truth or falsity of any other sentences (except for sentences expressing logical laws).

sentence: Any combination of words that can serve as a complete utterance, according to the rules of language. In logic the concern is with sentences that are used to make true or false statements.

simplification: Conjunctive argument whose single premise is a conjunction and whose conclusion is the same as one component of that conjunction. This is represented schematically by $p \& q;\ \therefore p$.

singular sentence: A sentence containing at least one singular term. An example is "Socrates is mortal"; this example can be symbolized "All S are M" (if "S" is taken to mean "persons identical with Socrates") or it can be symbolized as "Ma" (if "a" stands for Socrates).

singular term: A word or phrase that purports to apply to exactly one thing. Proper names are one kind of singular terms.

slothful induction: In inductive reasoning, the mistake of underrating the degree of probability with which a conclusion follows from evidence.

square of opposition: A traditional diagram for illustrating the logical interrelations of the different forms of categorical sentence, when all have the same subject and all have the same predicate.

statement: An assertion. To make a statement is to utter (or write) a sentence in such a way as to say something true or false. Strictly speaking, the same sentence might be used on different occasions to make different statements. (By uttering the sentence "You're stupid" while addressing Smith one may make a true statement, yet by uttering that same sentence while addressing Jones one perhaps makes a false statement.) In logic a sentence is called true when the statement that the sentence would most commonly be used to make is a true statement.

stipulative definition: A definition that arbitrarily assigns a new meaning to the word or symbol being defined.

subcontraries: To call two sentences subcontraries is to say that they cannot both be false but may both be true.

subject: In a categorical sentence, the term between the quantifier and the copula.

sufficient condition: To say that A is a sufficient condition of B is to say that all cases of A are cases of B. Having an undistributed middle term is a sufficient condition for being an invalid categorical syllogism.

syllogism: A categorical syllogism is any deductive argument consisting of three categorical sentences that contain three different terms, each term occurring twice, in two different sentences.

symmetry of a relation: To say that a relation is symmetrical is to say that, whenever it holds between a first thing and a second, then it holds also between the second and the first. This is represented schematically by $(x)(y)(Rxy \supset Ryx)$.

tautology: Any sentence that is necessarily true in virtue of its truth-functional form.

term: In categorical sentences, the words or phrases occurring as subjects and predicates are called terms. More generally, any word or phrase that it could make sense to apply to a thing is called a term. (But not all words are terms; the word "not" is not a term, for it makes no sense to say "This thing is a not".)

transitivity of a relation: To say that a relation is transitive is to say that, whenever it holds between a first thing and a second and between the second and a third, then it holds also between the first and the third. This is represented schematically by $(x)(y)(z)[(Rxy \& Ryz) \supset Rxz]$.

truth function: To say that a compound sentence is a truth function of its component sentences is to say that the compound depends entirely upon (is a function of) its components, as regards truth and falsity. That is, knowing about the truth or falsity of each component is sufficient to enable one to determine whether the compound sentence is true.

truth table: Table that shows whether a compound sentence is true or whether it is false, for each possible combination of truth and falsity of its components.

undistributed middle, fallacy of: For a categorical syllogism to commit this fallacy is for its middle term to be distributed neither in the major nor in the minor premise.

universal instantiation: In deductive reasoning, the principle that allows one to infer from a universal quantification any instance of it.

universal quantification: A symbolized sentence that starts with a universal quantifier whose scope is all the rest of the sentence.

universal quantifier: The expression "$(\ )$", where any variable may be put in the gap. "(x)" means "Each thing x is such that".

universal sentence: To call a categorical sentence universal is to say that it is in **A** or **E** form.

vagueness: To say that a word is vague is to say that there is no way of telling where the correct application of it is supposed to stop, as things vary in degree.

validity: To say that an argument is valid is to say that its conclusion logically follows from its premises, as the argument claims. A deductive argument is valid if and only if it would be necessarily impossible for the conclusion to be false if the premises all are true. A deductive argument valid on account of its truth-functional form is called truth-functionally valid; if valid on account of its quantificational form, it is called quantificationally valid. An inductive argument is valid if and only if the degree of support which it claims that its premises provide for the conclusion is indeed the degree of support that the premises do provide for the conclusion.

variable: Any of the letters "x", "y", "z", etc., as used in quantificational symbolism.

variable of quantification: In a universal quantification or an existential quantification, the variable whose occurrences are governed by the quantifier that comes at the beginning.

verbal dispute: A disagreement caused not by any difference of opinion concerning anything true or false but merely by a difference in verbal usage; one speaker prefers to use a word in one way, while his opponent prefers to use the word in another way.

Glossary of Symbols

LETTERS

A, E, I, O: These four boldface capital letters refer to the four forms of categorical sentence.

A, B, C, etc.: Italic capital letters are used in several ways. In Chapter 2 they are used as abbreviations for terms; thus "All *S* are *P*" can symbolize "All Slavs are prudes". In Chapter 3 they are used as abbreviations for whole sentences; thus "*S* ⊃ *P*" can symbolize "If Socrates was wise, then Plato was wise". In Chapter 4 they are used in quantified sentences to express properties and relations; thus "*Sx*" can symbolize "*x* is a Slav" and "*Pxy*" can symbolize "*x* precedes *y*".

a, b, c, etc.: Small italic letters from the beginning of the alphabet are used in Chapter 4 as names of particular objects; they function as proper names do.

p, q, r, etc.: Small italic letters starting with "*p*" are used in Chapter 3 to display the logical skeletons of compound sentences; they function as ellipses do: "*p* ∨ *q*" is like ". . . or ///".

x, y, z, etc.: Small italic letters from the end of the alphabet are used in Chapter 4 as variables; they function as pronouns do.

TRUTH-FUNCTIONAL SYMBOLS

— : The dash expresses negation. "$-p$" is read "not p", or "it is not the case that p".

& : The ampersand expresses conjunction. "$p \& q$" is read "p and q".

v : The wedge expresses disjunction, in the nonexclusive sense. "$p \lor q$" is read "p or q".

⊃ : The horseshoe expresses the conditional, in its truth-functional sense. "$p \supset q$" is read "if p then q", or "p only if q".

≡ : The three lines express the biconditional. "$p \equiv q$" is read "p if and only if q".

QUANTIFICATIONAL SYMBOLS

(x) : Any variable inclosed within parentheses is a universal quantifier. "(x)" may be read "each thing x is such that".

$(\exists x)$: Any variable preceded by a backwards "E" and inclosed within parentheses is an existential quantifier. "$(\exists x)$" may be read "at least one thing x is such that".

PROBABILITY SYMBOL

$/\!/$: The double stroke is used to express probability. These two strokes appear between one sentence and another to form an overall expression that refers to the probability of the first sentence relative to the second. "$p /\!/ q$" may be read "the probability of p, given q".

Index